POSTWAR
LEICESTER
BEN BEAZLEY

SUTTON PUBLISHING

Sutton Publishing Limited
Phoenix Mill · Thrupp · Stroud
Gloucestershire · GL5 2BU

First published 2006

British Library Cataloguing in Publication Data
A catalogue record for this book is available from the British Library.

ISBN 0-7509-4068-9

The biting winters and heavy snowfalls of the years immediately after the war were enjoyed only by children, such
as these seen here leaving Imperial Avenue Infant School. *(Courtesy: M. Ford)*

Typeset in 11/12.5pt Sabon.
Typesetting and origination by
Sutton Publishing Limited.
Printed and bound in England by
J.H. Haynes & Co. Ltd, Sparkford.

Contents

Acknowledgements

Without the assistance of almost an army of people who were so generous with their time, materials and knowledge, I would not have been able to complete this book and I would like to express my gratitude to them all.

In particular I would like to thank Carl Bedford for his insights into the early days of the NHS; Margaret Bonney and all of the staff at the Record Office for Leicestershire, Leicester and Rutland for their help and patience in tracing archival material; Angela Cutting for her assistance in sourcing photographs; John Florance, Stephen Butt and Tony Wadsworth for allowing me access to the Radio Leicester archives and to their own personal material; Tony Green for information on the development of Welford Place; Stuart McGlone for assistance in relation to the early days of BT; Sheila Mileham for her guidance on local authority matters; Sherry Nesbitt for her help on Portal housing; Lionel Roberts for his assistance on civil engineering; Derek Seaton for his encyclopedic knowledge of civic affairs; David Simpson for resolving my queries on military matters; Michael Ward for his accountancy skills; Malcolm Tovey and John Warden for answering my queries on Leicester City Fire Brigade; George Wilson for giving me access to the Leicester City Urban Development Group photograph library, and for his help in understanding planning and development issues.

For allowing me such free access to their personal photograph collections, special thanks must go to Michael Brucciani, Stephen Butt, Colin Chesterman, Geoff Fenn, Margrid Ford, Janice Gunby, Diane James, George Jordan, Inga and Hendrik Raak, Eric Selvidge, E.R. Welford, Margaret and Jan Zientek.

To all of these people, and to any others whom I may have inadvertently missed, I extend my most grateful thanks.

All other pictures are from my own collection.

Ben Beazley

Foreword

Postwar Leicester – what picture do these words conjure up in the minds of residents? Austerity, rationing, utility furniture – a city in monochrome? For those who had come through the Second World War, times continued to be hard in the 1950s, with shortages of food, housing, and jobs, as the traditional industries of the city continued to decline. Even the weather conspired against them, with the harsh winter of 1947/8 still living on in the memory. Yet it was also a time of dramatic change in Leicester, as the city fathers struggled to restore services while beginning reconstruction work. Town planners such as John Beckett in the 1950s and Konrad Smigielski in the 1960s had visionary, if controversial, plans for the city, including some out-of-town estates and remorseless road building which cut a swathe through what had been essentially a medieval town plan. The skyline of Leicester was never to be the same again, as high-rise blocks of flats challenged the dominance of factory chimneys.

But it wasn't just the appearance of the city that was changing. Leicester's people became more diverse with immigration into the city on a much larger scale than ever before. During the 1950s, workers from the West Indies came looking for employment, followed by Indians and Pakistanis in particular during the 1960s, then East African Asians in the 1970s, political refugees from the harsh regimes of dictators such as Idi Amin. The complexity of such a diverse population has changed the face of the city, not least in its number of temples and mosques, but also in the vast range of multicultural goods and services which Leicester offers today.

Ben Beazley tackles the fascinating subject of postwar Leicester in this, his latest work. Taking some of the crucial themes of the period, he uses the rich archive of the Leicester Record Office to tell the story of the city during thirty years of rapid change. No one who reads this book could be left in any doubt about the importance of this vital period in Leicester's history.

Dr Margaret Bonney
Assistant Keeper of Archives, Record Office
for Leicestershire, Leicester and Rutland

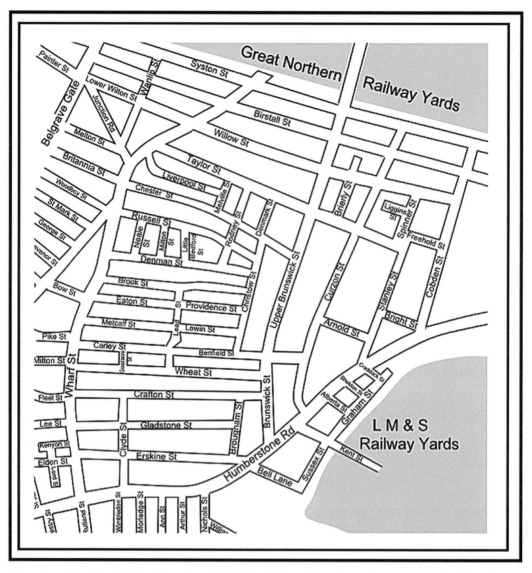

Plan of the Wharf Street District (based on OS: 1930) which was the subject of the Leicester City Council's first major postwar slum clearance scheme.

CHAPTER ONE

Post-1945

When the Second World War finally ended in September 1945 with the surrender of the Japanese forces, Britain began the long climb back to the rebuilding of its war-damaged economy. In this rehabilitation process, Leicester was, to a degree, one of the more fortunate cities. While enduring the same wartime conditions and shortages as everyone else who had been involved in maintaining the Home Front during the previous six years, crucially, Leicester emerged from the conflict with the greater part of its manufacturing capability virtually intact.

Although the city was subjected to eight air raids during the period of the blitz between 1940 and 1941, only one raid – on the night of 19/20 November 1940 – caused extensive damage. This was to be a significant factor for both Leicester's immediate postwar recovery and the town's subsequent industrial potential.

As early as 1944 a Leicester Reconstruction Committee was formed under the chairmanship of Charles Keene – an indefatigable member of the City Council who, having played a key role in the organisation of the city's war effort, was the ideal person to initiate the local authority's postwar redevelopment plans. Central to postwar development was the 'Fifty Year Plan' developed by the City Surveyor, John Leslie Beckett, which included new housing estates and the restructuring of the city's main roads. The old-fashioned tramcar system was to be replaced at an early stage by motorised buses, and ten months after the end of the war, in July 1946, sixty-two new double-decker buses costing £3,400 each were ordered by the City Transport Department. Five months later, in December 1946, came the first tram route closure, that of the Aylestone section, in favour of a dedicated bus service.

In January 1946 the Chief Constable, Oswald Cole, set out on a three-month tour of the Middle and Far East as part of a delegation sent by the government to recruit for Britain's police forces from among the ranks of servicemen awaiting demobilisation. The mission ran into difficulties in the early stages when Cole's companions (two other chief constables) succumbed to illness and had to return home, leaving Cole to complete the greater part of the trip alone. After interviewing over 1,200 servicemen in locations as far apart as Karachi, Batavia and Singapore he returned home on 13 May, having recruited just over 500 men for police forces (including Leicester City) across the country.

On a broader level, Clement Attlee's newly elected Labour government was determined to create improved living conditions for the average citizen.

As soon as possible, the school leaving age was to go up from 14 to 15, with the intention that it would eventually be 16. The Beveridge Report, published in November 1942, outlined the government's vision of a new Welfare State in which everyone, from richest to poorest, would be treated equally. As early as May 1943 the City Council, anticipating the implementation of the Report, adopted some of its provisions, one being that for the first time certain Council employees would be

The city centre was badly damaged by German bombers on the night of 19/20 November 1940. In postwar years, while awaiting reconstruction, many of the sites were used as car parks. Seen here on a rainy day (the police officers are being marched out to their beats from Charles Street Police Station) it presents a gloomy aspect and shows the scale of the work needing to be done. *(Courtesy: Leicestershire Constabulary)*

Although less well known than Konrad Smigielski, John Leslie Beckett, Leicester city's Engineer and Surveyor (1941–64), was responsible for preparing a 'Fifty Year Plan' at the end of the war for the reshaping of Leicester. Beckett began his working life with Liverpool Corporation in 1918. In 1927 he moved for a short time to be Surveyor and Water Engineer at Runcorn, until in 1930 he became Borough Engineer and Planning Officer of Tynemouth in Northumbria. From 1936 until he came to Leicester in 1941, he worked as the Borough Engineer and Planning Officer at Burnley. John Beckett retired in 1964. *(Courtesy: The Municipal Journal)*

During the war the ranks of services such as the fire brigades and police were depleted by men and women going into the armed forces. In order to address this, in January 1946 the Chief Constable of Leicester City Police, Oswald John Buxton Cole, went as part of a government initiative on a three-month recruiting tour to the Middle and Far East. Having interviewed over 1,200 servicemen, he succeeded in recruiting 500 for the various United Kingdom police forces including Leicester City Police. *(Courtesy: Leicestershire Constabulary)*

In the immediate postwar years many firms such as Gimson's, the town's leading timber merchants, were still using a combination of motorised and horse-drawn transport. (The tri-wheeled vehicles are Scammells.) *(Courtesy: G. Fenn)*

entitled to receive up to four weeks' sickness benefit during any twelve-month period. Not all of the councillors were in agreement with this concession. Speaking against it, Councillor Percy Russell made the point that, 'if a man was going to get the same money when he was away sick as when he was well, there would be a great temptation to malinger'. The intention of the government was clear, however – to create a healthier, wealthier and better educated nation.

Four months after the war ended, enrolling fifty-four women students on a two-year course, the first new teacher training college in the country opened in the old Civil Defence Depot at Humberstone. In the same month the management committee of the Leicester Royal Infirmary purchased Brookfield, London Road, from the Leicester Diocese (it had been the residence of the Bishop of Leicester from 1927 to 1940, when it was taken over and used by the British Red Cross as a packaging centre for parcels being sent to British POWs) and it became the Charles Frears School of Nursing.

In preparation for the increased demands of the new Education Act (a higher school-leaving age meant that there would be an increase in pupil numbers) the now redundant Civil Defence depots at Humberstone, Western Park and Wigston Lane were transferred to the Education Committee. It was also decided that supplementary prefabricated buildings should be erected at Harrison Road, Bridge Road, Moat Road and Melbourne Road schools. The changes in the education system played havoc with the Leicester Education Committee's 1945–6 budget, resulting in an application for an increase of £76,528 over the previous year,

In the post-1945 era one of the highlights of the working year for those employed by a company was the 'annual outing'. Seen here on what was probably the first such trip after the end of the war is the workforce of Gimson's on a day trip to Skegness. *(Courtesy: G. Fenn)*

bringing it up to £656,913. Of this increase, 80 per cent was directly attributable to the new Act. Additionally, the Education Committee was obliged to ask for a further £141,515 that year to cover an increase in teachers' pay scales – a sum that, the Committee were at pains to point out, only covered the pay of teachers presently employed by the authority, and not the staffing increases that would result from the increased school-leaving age.

Despite the war having ended, foodstuffs and raw materials were still in extremely short supply, and were to remain so for some years to come. Paradoxically, the cost to Britain of winning the war was almost as great as that to Germany of losing it. The Lend-Lease Act which, since 1941, had allowed America to supply material to Britain and 'other countries upon which the United States' own defence was thought to depend', was officially due to come to an end in August 1945. Out of a total of $51 billion worth of aid given by America to its allies, Britain owed a staggering $31 billion. In view of the state of the British economy it was agreed that this should be reduced to an eventual repayment of $650 million. In February 1946 the Minister of Food, Sir Ben Smith, issued a stark warning that when the remaining supplies under the Lend-Lease Act came to an end, food, including dried eggs (which in 1946 alone cost £25 million) and cereals, would have to be imported from the US, and other countries.

In an effort to offset shortages, foodstuffs from the Commonwealth countries began to appear in Leicester shops. At the beginning of March 1946 the first consignment of bananas seen in the city for six years arrived at Leicester market from Jamaica; by the middle of the summer England had received from Canada and Australia 140 million bushels of wheat and flour, 22.5 million pounds of bacon, and over half a million pounds of lamb and mutton; additionally 15 million tins of kippered herrings arrived from Norway. A 'Leicester League of Housewives', formed in February, sent letters of protest to the Ministry of Food questioning the need for continued rationing. Their efforts, not unexpectedly, were of little avail, and the league was short-lived. Ironically, a new difficulty presented itself at this stage. While countries such as Canada and Australia were in a position to alleviate Britain's food shortages, there was not the shipping, storage and distribution infrastructure to deal with the goods. The British government was obliged to decline an offer of 7,500 tons of meat from Australia because, 'it could not be handled under the present meat ration system', and 2 million cases of apples were similarly refused because of the lack of refrigerated storage. A million cases of fresh eggs and quantities of butter, margarine and tinned goods could not be imported because there were no ships to freight them.

Rationing and shortages were to continue until 1954. In 1946 a tin of dried eggs cost 1s 6d; milk was rationed to 3 pints per person a week, and adults were allowed 9oz of bread a day (manual workers 15oz).

One area in which it was possible to ease the restrictions early on was clothing and shoes. From the middle of March 1946 constraints on clothing styles were lifted. Dresses with pleats, pockets and velvet trimmings were once more available in Lewiss's and other department stores. The number of coupons required for clothing purchases was reduced by a third and men's, boys' and women's raincoats could once more be double-breasted, with pockets, buttons and shoulder straps. In a city where one of the main industries was the manufacture of shoes, after April the lifting of the ban on high heels, sandals, brogues and sports shoes resulted in a boom in footwear sales.

In the early summer of 1946 the Ministry of Labour Training Centre (opened before the war in 1936) introduced courses for 600 ex-servicemen to qualify as draughtsmen, bricklayers, carpenters, tailors, typewriter mechanics and radio engineers. A 'Reinstatement Officer' was appointed by the Corporation to deal with the issues presented by the 2,000 Council employees now returning to resume their old jobs – among them teachers, policemen and transport workers (by March 1946, of the wartime staff only two female bus drivers remained in the employment of the City Transport Department).

The return of ex-servicemen to their previous occupations occasionally caused certain slightly bizarre situations. One such was the return to duties of Police Constable 77 John Cassie. PC Cassie joined the Leicester City Police in 1937; at the outbreak of the war he served first in the Scots Guards and later was commissioned into the 2/5th Battalion of the Leicestershire Regiment. Six years later he had seen a great deal of action, been awarded the Military Cross for gallantry at the Battle of Monte Cassino in Italy, and as a major was second-in-command of the battalion. (At one point, when the CO was killed, Cassie took command with the rank of acting colonel). When he returned to police duties in April 1946 it was common to see men who had served under him in the Tigers Regiment, on passing the ex-Major working point duty at the Clock Tower, to snap smartly to attention and salute him as they crossed the road.

Accustomed as they were to the vicissitudes of living in postwar Britain, the nation was not prepared for the hardships inflicted by the winter of 1946/7. It was the coldest in living memory, and fifty years on was still clearly remembered by those who lived through it.

Initial indications that Leicester was in for a hard winter came during the first week of 1947, when on Monday 6 January heavy snow began to fall on the city. Within two days a contingent of 250 men and 30 vehicles was busy clearing the streets. This in itself was not unusual, the seasons at that time were generally quite predictable. Leicester was accustomed to hot summers punctuated by heavy thunderstorms and flash flooding, followed by cold, sharp winters and a white Christmas and the 2in fall of snow cloaking the city streets was not seen as anything unusual. For those who had taken notice, however, the previous summer had been one of the poorest for years, the August holiday period being exceptionally wet.

Three weeks later conditions were beginning to give cause for concern. The night of 28 January was the coldest for sixty years, with a temperature of -32°F recorded at Moreton-in-the-Marsh in the Cotswolds. In the East Midlands and East Anglia trains with snow ploughs were out clearing the LMS and LNER lines; the River Thames was frozen over, as was the sea at Folkestone; at Falmouth the temperature was the lowest recorded since 1877.

Experiencing the coldest nights for two years (temperatures recorded at the Towers Hospital showed -19°F below freezing) Leicester emergency squads assisted by a contingent of 200 German POWs were employed trying to clear the city streets of snow and ice in order that the Transport Department could maintain a limited service. Eight water mains burst in the city in two days and the electricity supply was severely disrupted.

Snow very quickly closed all of the county's roads, isolating outlying villages. Ice building up on the Grand Union Canal at Husbands Bosworth prevented the movement of barges, and rising water levels burst the nearby culvert, causing a loss of 2 million gallons of water. With blizzards sweeping the Midlands, a military convoy of tank transports had to be laid up in the Square at Market Harborough. One of the column's two low-loaders with a Sherman on board made an abortive attempt to plough a path to Leicester along the A6. Skidding off the road at Kibworth Beauchamp, it had to be dug out by a working party of German POWs from the nearby Farndon Road camp. More POWs were kept busy clearing the drifts that had closed the A47 at Tilton-on-the-Hill.

On Monday 3 February the full implications for the city of the arctic conditions became apparent when, with coal stocks at a minimum and mining work shut down, the first three Leicester factories closed, unable to fire their boilers. By the end of the week many others were forced to follow suit. Some 5,000 building workers were laid off in the city and county; 300 men were idle on the City Council's New Parks housing estate project. The closure of the Leicester Brick and Tile Co.'s yards, with the consequent loss of 250,000 bricks a day effectively stopped work on twenty building sites across the city.

Food supplies in Leicester market dwindled rapidly. Vegetables could not be lifted from the frozen earth, and with road and rail links blocked, such produce as was available could not be delivered. Attendance dropped by 40 per cent in those city schools that managed to stay open.

By the second week in February 80,000 factory workers in the city (over half of the workforce) were laid off; 18,000 of the temporary signings at the Labour

Exchange were from hosiery factories. All of the shoe factories (with the exception of a few that generated their own power) were forced to shut down, resulting in the loss of between 3,000 and 4,000 pairs of shoes a week at a cost to the industry of £250,000.

Engineering firms also suffered. By the end of the week the British United Shoe Machinery factory had been reduced to 20 per cent of its capability. The closure of 1,200 factories in Leicester during the first two weeks of February, with the attendant loss in earnings, cost the city £3 million. On Saturday 15 February a special 'signing-on' centre was opened at the Granby Halls and at the end of the day figures showed that 20,000 men and women in the city were temporarily in receipt of benefits. Projections were that by the end of the following week the figure would exceed 50,000. Wherever possible workers were employed by factory managers on maintenance work and painting, but this had little effect on the overall figures.

Leicester was not alone in its situation; around three-quarters of the country was similarly affected. Due to the shortages of fuel, the City Council agreed to make some of its stocks of coke available for domestic use. During the morning of Saturday 15 February, when the supplies were allocated, a queue of never less than 500 people was to be seen outside the Aylestone Road Gas Works from 7 a.m., when it opened, until the gates closed at noon.

City-centre shops, while being encouraged to remain open for as long as possible, were prohibited from using any form of heating. Cinemas no longer held matinée performances and City Transport was running only 20 per cent of its normal services. In an attempt to regulate the supply the Electricity Department initiated phased power cuts, and street lighting was reduced to one electric lamp in every three. Later, as these conditions continued, the supply of electricity was 'zoned', and districts received power on a rota basis at different times of the day.

Working in extreme conditions, towards the end of the second week in February the Leicestershire pits eventually managed to reopen and began a limited clearance of their yards. By close of work on Friday of that week 4,000 tons of coal had been dispatched by road. Over the weekend, using POWs, the railway line between Coalville and Leicester was reopened, allowing a further 3,000 tons to be moved.

As the third week in February began, conditions worsened. Temperatures remained constantly below freezing, the Channel ports were blocked by ice, and fishing was suspended. Royal Air Force planes patrolled the North Sea searching for icebergs, following the appearance off the East Coast near to Lowestoft of an ice floe 4 miles long by ½ mile wide.

By a combination of the zoned electricity supply and employers arranging for factories to work staggered hours (single or two-shift working), production in Leicester slowly began to come back on line. During the third week of February coal supplies – reduced by 70 per cent and restricted to industrial use – began to trickle back into the town. Already the City Council was beginning to count the cost. In addition to the loss by the private sector of industrial production due to almost continuous snowfall, 500 men were now employed on a 24-hour rota dealing with snow clearance alone; 783 tons of sand and gravel had been spread over the city streets, and the conditions showed no signs of abating. After more than a month of snow the blizzards were still continuing, and such rail traffic as there was in the district was being used exclusively for the movement of coal supplies. The number of temporarily unemployed in the city had reached 54,000 and there were now concerns as to whether or not the supply of domestic gas could be maintained.

Sunday night, 23 February, was one of the coldest ever experienced in the county. Thirty-five degrees of frost were recorded at Woodhouse Eaves, and 23 degrees at the Towers Hospital. (Nationally, temperatures were the lowest since the winter of 1917). Trains at London Road and Great Central railway stations were at a standstill, unable to move because, not only were the points frozen solid but also, despite fires lit under them, the water columns (tanks used to supply water to the boilers of the locomotives) had turned to ice.

The change in the weather, when it finally came, was sudden. The first signs of a thaw began in Leicester on 25 February (although some of the worst blizzards of the emergency were still sweeping the north of England). Temperatures at the Jarvis Street Depot suddenly lifted to 43°F, the warmest for thirty-eight days.

Inevitably, the change in the weather conditions brought further problems. The Water Department dealt with 120 burst water pipes in one day (since the beginning of January it had already repaired 2,516) and the City Gas Department received 700 reports of frozen gas pipes. Garages across the city were inundated with motorists who, trying to start their vehicles, found that radiators and engine blocks, frozen solid for a month, were now cracked and useless.

Although the worst of the weather was now over, conditions still gave considerable cause for concern. Heavy snowfalls continued and firemen from Lancaster Place struggled to thaw out the eighty underground water tanks situated across the city. At the end of the month the cost to the Corporation of snow clearance alone stood at £15,000 – 450 men a day, using 70 to 80 lorries at any given time were still working around the clock. On Saturday 1 March the queue waiting for coke outside the Gas Works began to form at 3 a.m., and by 7 a.m. numbered over 2,000. The thaw brought other dangers. At Blaby two 8-year-old girls, Ann Dorothy David and Patricia Oates, both of Hillsborough Road, were drowned when the ice on which they had played during the last month collapsed beneath them. Throughout the rural districts of the county melting snow and thawing rivers caused widespread flooding.

Improving conditions rapidly resulted in factories reopening and transport returning to some degree of normality. More men than ever were thrown into the clearing-up process throughout the city, and at the end of the first week in March the gangs of workmen numbered over 1,000 strong.

Determined not to be caught out again, during the ensuing summer months the Corporation, aiming to conserve resources, made elaborate projections to stagger working hours in factories during the following winter. (In October 1947 a prohibition was imposed on the heating of factories until after 3 November, and Leicester coal merchants were already pointing out that, on a domestic level, they were unable to supply the government's recommended six months' winter allowance of 30cwt per customer, and a maximum of 10cwt for the first three months was as much as they would be able to manage.) It was a clear case of closing the stable door after the horse had bolted, and met with a limited response from both employers and workers. On the one hand the proposals would severely disrupt production, on the other they would drastically affect earnings.

Fortunately for everyone concerned, the winter of 1947/8 was not exceptional, and despite threats from the Board of Trade that punitive action would be taken by the Ministry of Fuel and Power against factory owners who refused to comply with instructions, the proposals were largely allowed to lapse.

It was very apparent that apart from the issues presented by the re-employment of men returning from the forces, the major long-term problem facing Leicester City Council would be that of providing adequate housing.

As a short-term solution plans were made by the Leicester Reconstruction Committee during the initial phase in 1944 for the erection of just under 800 temporary 'Portal' houses (named after Lord Portal at the Ministry of Housing), or 'prefabs', as they quickly became known, to be erected at various points throughout the suburbs. The first of these began to appear on Hughendon Drive at Aylestone Road in April 1945.

Next, the War Office was persuaded to clear the armoured vehicle park on the north-west side of the city, and with the departure of the last Crusader tank on 27 September 1945 work was begun by German POWs, digging out the roads, drainage and service systems for the New Parks estate, which was to be the Corporation's postwar showpiece in modern housing. With the first brick laid in January 1946, work on the estate was finally completed in October 1949 when 2,748 houses in varying styles (including 120 prefabs) had been completed. (Blocks of flats along Aikman Avenue were to be added at a later date, with plans being laid in 1950.)

These beginnings were quickly followed in the early postwar months by further proposals. A development scheme for Braunstone estate included a community centre, baths, a health centre, three secondary schools, a Baptist church and two Roman Catholic churches. As time passed further attention was paid to the area when, late in 1949 with the future of Braunstone Aerodrome in the balance, it was suggested that the site was made available for a housing development.

The Scraptoft Valley Development Plan was first considered by the City Council in January 1946, followed by proposals for the building of the Thurnby Lodge and Goodwood estates. In accordance with John Beckett's 'Fifty Year Plan', the question of clearing slum properties from the city centre areas, such as Wharf Street, was examined and time scales were drawn up.

An additional incentive for the provision of housing was the fact that by September 1947, with the improvement in postwar living conditions, the birth rate in Leicester was higher than the national average. The Education Committee estimated that, combined with the raising of the school leaving age to 15, by 1952 an additional 2,400 infant and 6,000 junior places would need to be found in city schools.

October 1947 saw the return to England of the 2nd Battalion Royal Leicestershire Regiment. (A special Army Order, promulgated in December 1946, granted to the regiment the title 'Royal'.) After nine years' continuous duty overseas 23 officers and 506 other ranks arrived at Southampton docks from Bombay. Following a leave period of twenty-eight days, they took their first home-based posting at Long Marston near Stratford-upon-Avon, working on clearing up the backlog of stores left by the war.

The following month, the 1st Battalion disembarked at Harwich from Germany, to return to its base at Glen Parva Depot. Its stay was not a long one (it was customary for only one battalion of a regiment's two regular battalions to remain on

The sale of clothing, which had been on ration since June 1941, was one of the first things to become derestricted, in March 1946.

home service while the other performed duties overseas); after eighteen months, in May 1949, under Lieutenant Colonel S.D. Field the battalion left for service in Hong Kong. Its stay at Glen Parva was punctuated by a running battle for accommodation. There were only sufficient married quarters for twenty-six families, most of which were already occupied by members of the Royal Army Ordnance Corps, Royal Army Pay Corps, Royal Electrical and Mechanical Engineers, 8th King's Irish Hussars (now responsible for the training of armoured units at the Leicester East Airfield) and Records Office personnel.

On a day-to-day level, the routine of life in the city began slowly to settle down. The wartime National Fire Service (NFS) was about to be dissolved and Leicester was not only to revert to once more having a Leicester City Fire Brigade, the man who had previously been Chief Officer, Errington McKinnell, was to return to his former position at a salary of £1,250 a year.

Applications were being received at a rate of fifty a day for new business and telephone lines to be installed, resulting in the reopening of the old manual telephone exchange in Rutland Street – closed since 1926 when the exchange at Free Lane rendered it temporarily obsolete – under the name 'Granby'.

In November 1947 the local elections, reflecting the general mood of the country, secured for Labour thirty-five seats on the City Council (giving them twenty-five councillors and ten aldermen). With import duties being eased on commodities such as machine tools, textile machinery, clothing and shoes, the city was set to make the most of having won the war.

CHAPTER TWO

Early Recovery: 1947–9

Not unexpectedly, it took some time and a considerable amount of readjustment for life in the city to recover its peacetime aspect. Men and women who for the last six years had either been away fighting or working at home to keep the factories producing and the economy afloat, now found themselves having to adjust to the changed circumstances of postwar Britain.

Rationing, one of the greatest impositions on domestic life continued into the 1950s. Demobilised service personnel had to be reassimilated into the workplace, the military presence in the city had to be wound down, and six years of Civil Defence provisions put into mothballs.

In December 1946 the Auxiliary Territorial Service (ATS) left Glen Parva Barracks, Wigston, for Queen's Park Camp at Guildford in Surrey. Queen's Park, previously a dispersal camp, then took over as the only ATS training unit in the country, leaving Glen Parva vacant for occupation by the returning men of the Leicestershire Regiment.

Similarly, a month or so earlier, in May 1946 a decision was taken by the War Office to transfer the Royal Army Pay Corps from its base in the city to Perham Downs on Salisbury Plain. During the postwar years the RAPC was to have a long if somewhat fragmented association with the city.

Housed since its transfer to Leicester from Warley in 1939 in the old hosiery factory of T.H. Downing at 3 Newarke Street (which was to be transferred to the College of Technology), the RAPC as part of the combined staff of military, ATS and civilians, employed in its two offices at Newarke Street and Great Central Street (along with four other lesser sites) around 1,000 civilians. During the heaviest air raid over the city on the night of 19/20 November 1940 several members of its unit were killed when the house in which they were billeted in Highfields sustained a direct hit from an HE bomb.

In 1946 about 400 of those employed by the RAPC were local people, who became unemployed as a result of the move. Pressure from these civilians resulted in the location of the new offices being changed from Salisbury Plain to Nottingham, with a moving date of 20 October, which gave some of those affected an opportunity to move with the military staff rather than lose their jobs.

The removal was short-lived and in 1948 the Pay Corps returned, taking up residence in the Ministry of Labour Training Centre on Gipsy Lane (the premises had started out life as a nail-making factory). One of the drawbacks of this site was that it had no living accommodation and, other than a few allocations of married quarters at Glen Parva Barracks, all of the warrant officers and NCOs had to be billeted out in private accommodation. After a second spell in Leicester, the RAPC moved again, first in February 1961 to Brighton and Foots Cray, and then in 1963 to Bestwood in Nottinghamshire, before returning to the district in 1977, this time to Glen Parva Barracks. The unit remained at Glen Parva for the next twenty years until its dissolution at the end of March 1997, when it was absorbed into the Army Personnel Centre at Glasgow. Although spasmodic, over a period of almost sixty years the RAPC was a substantial employer in Leicester city.

One unique circumstance that the RAPC in Leicester could claim during its wartime presence in the city was the inclusion among its ranks of one Lieutenant M.E. Clifton-James. Clifton-James was Australian by birth, and bore an uncanny resemblance to Field Marshal Bernard Law Montgomery. Having been badly gassed during the First World War, he later took to an acting career and was 41 when the Second World War broke out. While he was appearing at a London theatre his similarity to Montgomery was picked up on by Military Intelligence, and he was quietly recruited to be used as a double for the Field Marshal as and when necessary. As a cover he was inducted into the army, given the rank of lieutenant and posted to the RAPC at Leicester. When the film of the subterfuge entitled *I Was Monty's Double*, starring Clifton-James alongside John Mills, was produced in 1958, one of the early scenes was shot in the Queens public house on Charles Street. (M.E. Clifton-James died at Worthing in Sussex five years later, in May 1963.)

As part of the process of standing down the armed forces units, various establishments were handed back by the War Office to local authorities, among them the various airfields around the city and county. One such not far from the city was Desford Aerodrome, which, having been used during the war as a repair depot for damaged aircraft and to train bomber and fighter pilots, became a training centre for the RAF Reserve. The airfield returned to civilian status and local men who had previously served as pilots and aircrew were recruited by the Air Ministry. This was very much a reversion to the aerodrome's pre-war function when it had been used to train RAF Volunteer Reserve pilots (Leicester Aero Club was formed there in 1929), and the aim was to recruit up to 300 men to set up No. 69 RAF Reserve Squadron. In October 1949 the Council's General Purposes Committee also decided that Braunstone Aerodrome on the city boundary would no longer be used for flying.

The site of Leicester East Aerodrome at Stoughton continued to be used for military purposes, and in February 1948 the 8th King's Irish Hussars arrived from Germany to take over the airfield as a new training ground for the 9th Armoured Brigade, Territorial Army, where it remained until January 1950. The following year, in June 1949, Ratcliffe Aerodrome came up for auction. With the lease due to expire in March of the following year, its occupants, the Leicester Aero Club, were given first option on the purchase, although from the outset the Chairman of the club, Roy Winn, was doubtful that the offer would be taken up because of financial constraints. As with almost every other airfield across the country, Ratcliffe had served its purpose, in this case being used by ferry pilots (many of whom were women) engaged in flying replacement military aircraft between UK air bases.

Relatively inconsequential items such as the Territorial Army huts on Victoria Park, which still belonged to the War Office, were left in situ until 1950. Bomb-damaged areas in Highfields and around the city centre, were to wait even longer for redevelopment. The Nissen huts erected on Victoria Park at the beginning of the war were demolished in June 1950 by a detachment of Royal Engineers. During the

A bomb site at the junction of Sparkenhoe and Saxby Streets, which was one of the last to be redeveloped when Highfields Infants School replaced the devastation caused in 1940 by German bombers. *(Courtesy: E.R. Welford)*

war they were occupied initially by a Home Guard Rocket Battery; the next tenants were the ATS, who in turn were succeeded by a unit of the 159 (Independent Armoured Brigade) Royal Army Service Corps (TA) along with a small unit of Military Police. The MPs moved out in May 1950, and when the huts were demolished the Territorials moved to the barracks at Brentwood Road. One of the problems associated with the high wartime levels of military presence in the district was that of live ordnance, which was left around in dumps on the outskirts of the city and in the county. In April 1944 during the Easter school holidays three schoolboys, Lawrence Mann, Alan Dilks and Eric Orton, while playing on an American Forces weapon firing range on the north side of the city, found an unexploded bazooka round which they decided to take home. While they were carrying the round along Fairfax road it exploded, killing Mann and injuring both of his friends, together with three young girls who happened to be standing nearby. During May 1948, three young Leicester men out for a cycle ride in the country stopped to examine an abandoned ammunition dump and were severely burned when a quantity of black powder exploded.

The postwar Labour government of Clement Attlee was dedicated to social and economic changes, bringing in, among other things, the nationalisation of the Bank of England, coal mining, civil aviation, rail and road transport, the steel industry, and above all the setting up of a national health scheme. The introduction in June 1948 of one of the government's most ambitious postwar initiatives, the National Health Service, had a mixed reception. The public – the prime beneficiaries of the scheme – were, not unexpectedly, elated at being presented with health-care provisions that previously they could only have dreamed of; for the professionals, however, doctors and dentists accustomed to the incomes generated by private practice, the proposals were not so attractive.

In Britain the concept of 'pre-paid medicine' was not a new one. A National Health Insurance Scheme had come into being in July 1912 under the Liberal government of David Lloyd George. At a time when all medical services were in the hands of private practitioners, this scheme was based upon individuals' ability to pay an insurance premium which entitled them to treatment on 'the panel' of a participating doctor. Twenty years later, in Great Britain and Northern Ireland 17.2 million people (11,369,000 men and 5,808,000 women) were enrolled on the panels of 16,000 doctors. Over 10,000 chemists' shops were fulfilling panel patients' prescriptions. (There were still many medical practitioners not involved in the scheme, who would fill out their own prescriptions at their surgery.) The population of Leicester at this time was just over 239,000 people, of whom 117,000 (49 per cent) were signed on to doctors' panels. The obvious conclusion to be drawn from this was that the remaining 51 per cent – the most needy, those too poor to pay the insurance premiums – were excluded.

The concept of a postwar national welfare scheme originated in 1941 when Sir William Beveridge was commissioned by the government to conduct an inquiry into the structure of social services in the country. In December 1942 he produced a document entitled *Social Insurance and Allied Services*, which became known simply as 'The Beveridge Report'. He proposed that all working adults, in return for a weekly contribution deducted at source from their wage packets, should be entitled to benefits if they were sick, unemployed, retired or widowed. (Under the new measures a man received 10*s* a week on reaching pensionable age, and on retirement was entitled to an extra 16*s*; the allowance for uninsured wives was 6*s* a week.)

The reaction of medical practitioners to Beveridge's proposals was, not unexpectedly, mixed. In February 1948, following Aneurin Bevan's declaration that the scheme affecting some 50,000 doctors would be implemented within a few months, the dissent was strong. Nationally, of those polled only 4,084 said 'Yes', while 25,310 said 'No'. The British Medical Association estimated that about 88 per cent of doctors were opposed to the scheme on the basis that it was not viable inasmuch as the government would not be able to put together an infrastructure capable of supporting it. Other underlying considerations were their loss of independence and private incomes. Bevan did a lot of negotiating in an attempt to bring them around. Family doctors would be known as General Practitioners, or GPs; hospital consultants, while being part of the NHS, would be salaried and allowed to continue treating some patients privately. Previously run by local authorities or charitable institutions, 1,143 voluntary and 1,545 municipal hospitals across the country were to be taken over by the government. (The Leicester Royal Infirmary was handed over to the National Health Service by its management committee in June 1948.)

Four weeks before the Health Service went live, doctors in Leicester called an emergency meeting to discuss whether or not to accept the terms of the new Health Service Act. Although the majority were opposed to the changes, they now faced a dilemma. If they stayed out of the NHS and obdurately continued in private practice while an overwhelming proportion of the city's population enrolled in it, they would be financially worse off. The result was that the National Health Service came into operation on 5 June 1948 and, accepting the inevitable, most practitioners in the city signed up.

There was, not unnaturally, a certain amount of initial confusion regarding the administration of the system. A list of the doctors in Leicester who had signed up to the NHS, which should have been displayed in public libraries, was still not available in the early weeks of July. The general consensus, however, was that 'panel patients' would remain with their panel doctor and others with their family doctor. In fact, by the mid-point of July one hundred and eleven doctors in the city had enrolled into the NHS, with local dentists and opticians following suit. Dentists experienced a huge upsurge in demand for their services through the NHS. Dental hygiene had previously been seen as a very low priority; during the First World War a group of Leicester dentists had actually volunteered to remedy (mainly by extracting) the teeth of local recruits to the army before they could be accepted as medically fit. The resulting problem was not that dentists could not cope with the volume of work, but that dental workshops in the town did not have sufficient technicians to produce the huge number of dentures suddenly required.

One important change was the manner in which medicaments were now to be dispensed. As from 5 June 1948, chemists took over responsibility for the dispensing of medicines. Doctors other than those with practices in remote areas where there was no chemist were no longer allowed to fill out their own prescriptions. (An exception to this was where practitioners were going to administer drugs in their own surgery.) The change saw the closing down in Leicester of the dispensaries and Friendly Societies around the town. This affected around 45,000 people who had used the Public Medical Service Central Dispensary in East Street, or the Oddfellows and Foresters dispensaries.

As with any other social development, there were those who found ways to turn the new welfare system to an advantage. Many years later Carl Bedford, who in the early years following the inception of the NHS was a dispensing chemist at Boot's in Gallowtree Gate, recalled some of the methods enterprising individuals found for exploiting the new pharmaceuticals goldmine. There was an early 'run' on surgical dressings, which under the new dispensing arrangements could be obtained free. Chemists were quick to realise, when presented with demands for half a dozen packs at a time, that 1lb rolls of white lint (used to dress leg ulcers, etc.) made excellent bed linen! One pound jars of 'White and Yellow Soft Paraffin' or, as it was later branded and marketed, 'Vaseline', made an excellent grease for items such as cycles and motorbikes.

From the chemists' point of view, there was also a slightly bizarre aspect to some of the legitimate prescribing. At a time when commercially produced items were not as readily available as in later years, some strong morphine-based painkilling preparations had to be made up in liquid form by the chemist on the premises. These contained brandy or another similar spirit, and it was not unusual for a junior to be sent out to purchase a bottle of brandy from the nearby Hynard Hughes shop. Storing it securely in the dangerous drugs cabinet, the pharmacist would set it against NHS expenditure.

An unfortunate result of the chicanery generated by the free prescription scheme was the introduction in October 1949 of a 1s charge for each prescription in an attempt to curb the abuses (except for OAPs and War Pensioners) resulting in the vehement protests and eventual resignation from the government of Aneurin Bevan.

In April 1948 the National Fire Service (a wartime measure) was dismantled and brigades returned to their old local status. The former Chief Officer of the Leicester City Brigade, Errington McKinnell, was reappointed to his former position at a salary of £1,250 and rejoined the brigade on 1 May 1948. He remained as Fire Chief until his retirement in February 1964. Seen here in October 1954 he is presenting the prestigious 'Silver Axe' award to top recruit Lionel John Warden. Having previously served in the Royal Artillery as a regular soldier in the Far East during the Malayan Emergency, John 'Stretch' Warden was himself to become a Senior Fire Officer, retiring as an Assistant Divisional Officer in 1986. *(Courtesy: J. Warden)*

It was in February 1947 that, for the first time, the emergency telephone system was introduced. By dialling a dedicated number, 999, the public were able to contact the emergency services, Fire, Police, and Ambulance, through an operator. (Previously, the caller would have had to look up the number of the nearest police or fire station in the telephone book.) As part of the reorganisation of emergency services in April 1948 the National Fire Service, a wartime measure that had amalgamated all fire brigades across the country under one umbrella, was disbanded and the old system of locally controlled individual brigades was reinstated. Leicester City Fire Brigade insignia swiftly reappeared on vehicles and uniforms and, to the accompaniment of a civic dinner at Lancaster Place, the former Chief Fire Officer Errington McKinnell returned to the city from his wartime post as Chief Officer for the South East London Fire Area. (On leaving Leicester at the beginning of the war, McKinnell first went to Sheffield before being posted to London where, during the heavy V2 attacks, he had the misfortune to see his own house destroyed by bombs.) The Chief Officer was to remain with the Leicester Brigade for the next seventeen years, until his retirement. Errington McKinnell began his career with the Newcastle upon Tyne Brigade in 1923, and served as a fireman for forty-one years. He died in March 1970 at the age of 66.

Although the war ended in 1945, it was not until November 1948 that the last of the German POWs held in the city and county were finally repatriated. (When Germany lost the war, its forces personnel still had to be disbanded through an administrative system; the POWs held in Allied camps continued, until demobilised and repatriated, to be serving members of the German Armed Forces.) Across the county there was a large number and variety of POW camps. Some housed Italians, others Germans, many of whom were employed in agriculture on Leicestershire farms or, as was the case with many of the German POWs, in the city on work parties, digging out drains and services on building sites such as the New Parks Housing Project. Later work parties were to be seen in the suburbs, such as at Clarendon Park, lifting tramlines on routes scheduled for closure. When the bad winter conditions of early 1947 were at their worst in February, 200 POWs were put to work clearing the main A47 road at Tilton-on-the-Hill and the A6 at Market Harborough. Later, in May that year, forty Germans dug the trench across Victoria Park to lay the mains voltage cable from Freemen's Meadow generating station to the new primary sub-station on Marina Road, off Evington Valley Road.

One of the largest camps, covering 50 acres, was on Shady Lane at Evington. Opened in 1944 to accommodate troops of the American Airborne Division in preparation for the D-Day landings, it was redesignated in late 1944, when they left, as a POW camp and occupied by Italian prisoners, followed by an influx of Germans, and used as a dispersal camp. It was not until late 1948 that the last of these men were returned to their homelands. Not all of the Germans wanted to be repatriated, especially now that their country was divided into sectors by the American, British, French and Russian Forces, and any returning to the Russian-controlled Eastern Sector faced a bleak future. Some who were lucky enough managed to secure permanent work with local farmers, others who had married English women were allowed to remain. These totalled 200, about half of the number still living in the district. The remaining 250 left Leicester from London Road railway station on 20 November 1948, many planning to return to England as soon as possible.

After they left, the camps that they had occupied either fell into disuse or, as often happened, became occupied by squatters. Some, such as the Farndon Road camp at Market Harborough and the German camp at Enderby, were taken over by the government to house a new group of people entering the country – the European Volunteer Workers or EVWs.

Immediately after the war the British government faced a severe shortage of labour. This was influenced by several factors: service men and women could not be immediately released back into the workplace; many women who had filled jobs during the war wanted to return to the domestic environment; men and women who, due to the exigencies of war, had worked beyond retirement age now removed themselves; the raising of the school leaving age from 14 to 15 took a whole raft of young people out of the equation. Additionally, countries such as Canada, Australia and New Zealand – themselves desperate for new blood – attracted many families tempted by the prospects of emigration.

Approaches were made by the British government to people in displaced persons (DP) camps in Germany. The response was overwhelming and 83,000 people from countries either wiped out by war or now occupied by the Russian armies flooded into Britain. They were immediately given the title European Volunteer Workers, rather than 'displaced persons' (the relevance of this being that because they had volunteered to come to Britain as temporary workers they could not subsequently

After the war Great Britain relied heavily upon European Volunteer Workers, who came into the country to fill the gaps in the British labour force. This group of men, mainly Estonians, are en route from displaced persons camps in Germany in July 1947. (*Courtesy: H. Raak*)

European Volunteer Workers Camp 756 at Enderby, in the summer of 1947, housed ninety Estonians, ten Latvians and one Lithuanian, all of whom were engaged in agricultural work in the area. (*Courtesy: H. Raak*)

A party of European Volunteer Workers at Enderby relaxing after a day's work. Hendrik Raak from Estonia (first left, back row) was just 20 years old when he came to England in 1947. Having initially worked on the land he later married and settled down in Leicester, working for Byford's in the hosiery trade. (*Courtesy: H. Raak*)

claim the status of asylum seekers). The one common factor in their assimilation into British society at that time was that, irrespective of qualifications or previous occupation, they were only directed into manual labour or agricultural work.

Run by the Ministry of Labour, and designated as a transit or dispersal centre, the Market Harborough camp, a former RAF aerodrome, was the largest in the county and served the needs of both Leicestershire and Nottingham. In August 1947 more than 1,000 East Europeans from Lithuania, Latvia, Estonia and the Ukraine were at the camp. There were very strict rules governing the employment of the EVWs. Inasmuch as occupations were restricted, they could not take any job for which a British worker was available, and in the case of a married couple both were obliged to take employment. However, once engaged, if the employer did not have living facilities for the worker or couple he was obliged to find accommodation for them. In the short period between the camp's opening in June 1947 and August of that year, 2,400 men and 5,800 women passed through the dispersal centre.

By March 1949 there were a recorded 1,597 foreign nationals living in Leicester. This figure included demobilised foreign servicemen (mainly Polish) and released POWs employed in the town. From an administrative standpoint, every non-British adult had to be registered with the police in the district where he lived, and was required to report to them regularly. In Leicester the Aliens Department was located in a small office on the Northampton Street side of the police station building on Charles Street. It was not until later years, at the end of the 1960s, that the Aliens sign over the door was replaced by one declaring the office to be the Nationalities Department.

As part of the plans for developing transport links within the East Midlands, in April 1948 Councillor Harry Bowerman, Chairman of the Leicester City Publicity Department and John L. Beckett, the City Engineer and Surveyor, made a trip to Elmdon Airport at Birmingham to meet with representatives of the Air Ministry. The purpose of the discussion was to examine the prospects for establishing charter air facilities from Braunstone Aerodrome to Elmdon as part of the link service that had been opened for businessmen to travel between Birmingham and Paris.

In 1956 a 'helicopter taxi service' enjoyed a brief if uneconomic spell operating between the city and Elmdon. British European Airways, in conjunction with the Helicopter Experimental Unit, based at Gatwick (where the Civil Aviation Authority had paid £250,000 for the purchase of the local racecourse with a view to a future airport development) wanted to experiment with linking airports through local services. Based on Saffron Lane Show Ground, on Tuesday 3 July 1956 BEA commenced two business flights daily to Nottingham and Birmingham – the cost of a return flight to Nottingham was £1; to Birmingham £2 2s. In the view of the City Council the programme was a promising one; with slum clearance under way in the town, if the scheme proved a success then some of the cleared areas could easily be diverted from industrial usage to the creation of a heliport; alternatively, heli-pads could be accommodated on the flat roofs of suitable buildings. However, the experiment was not a success. In the first six weeks after opening the venture carried a total of only 172 passengers, and BEA closed the service down, declaring it to be uneconomic.

In 1949, with a civil war being fought in China, the British Navy had a warship stationed on the Yangtze river near to Nanjing, in readiness for the evacuation of British citizens and embassy staff caught up in the advance of the Communist forces. On 20 April, as the frigate HMS *Amethyst* was steaming up the Yangtze to take up station, it came under heavy shell fire from the People's Liberation Army (the Communists) on the north bank of the river (the opposition, the Kuomintang, was on the other side) which killed twenty-two crewmen, including the ship's captain, Lieutenant Commander Bernard Skinner, and wounding a further thirty-one. The ship managed to send a signal to the effect that it was under heavy fire and had run aground. Leaving about fifty-two men on board, of whom twelve were wounded (the ship's surgeon and his assistant were among those killed), the remaining members of the crew, numbering around sixty-five, were ordered to abandon ship. Some were shot while in the water, but the remainder made it to nearby Rose Island and escaped to Shanghai. Serving on *Amethyst* at the time were three 17-year-old Leicester lads: Boy Seaman, First Class, Keith Martin of 5 Briton Street, and Boy Seaman Bernard Grazier of 91 Narborough Road (Grazier celebrated his 18th birthday during the ensuing action) who had both recently transferred to *Amethyst* from HMS *Norfolk*; and Seaman Norman Harratt (aged 19) of 42 Glenfield Road. Wounded on 21 April by the continued shelling, Keith Martin was one of those who escaped to safety and was transferred to Stevens Mission Hospital at Chang Chow for treatment. Of those seamen who were ordered ashore, ten returned to the ship and fifty eventually made it to Shanghai. On 28 April Alan Richardson, a 22-year-old sailor, contacted his parents at 29 Beaufort Road, Braunstone estate, to let them know that he was among those who had made it to safety.

The 'C' Class destroyer HMS *Consort* attempted to tow *Amethyst* clear, but she also came under heavy fire and was severely damaged before destroying the attacking shore battery with her own 4.5in guns. Eventually, badly damaged and under fire from 37mm anti-tank guns situated on the river bank, and having sustained heavy casualties, *Consort* was forced to withdraw. On 26 April, no longer aground but severely damaged, *Amethyst* managed to steam upriver to Fu Te Wei, where she anchored to await assistance. This came in the form of HMS *London* and HMS *Black Swan*, which attempted to reach the *Amethyst* but were both subjected to shelling and sustained considerable damage and loss of life. HMS *London*, a 10,000-ton cruiser, was holed twelve times and lost twelve seamen killed and twenty wounded. Two more Leicester men, 28-year-old Yeoman Signaler David Anderson, and Leading Telegraphist Tom Mackey (27) of 153 Prestwold Road, were aboard the *London*. Telegraphist Arthur Moore (20) who lived at 36 Martin Street, was aboard HMS *Black Swan* and served as duty communications operator throughout the action.

During the course of the day medical supplies and a doctor reached *Amethyst* from a Sunderland flying boat, and a new captain, Lieutenant Commander J.S. Kerans, the British naval attaché, took command of the ship. A stalemate developed while negotiations for the safe conduct of *Amethyst* were discussed between the British government and the Chinese. It was not until 31 July that Kerans, frustrated by the delay and with his ship still in a perilous position, gave the order and, slipping her cable during the night, HMS *Amethyst* made a final dash for safety.

Of the Leicester men, the first to return home on demobilisation leave, after serving in the Royal Navy for thirteen years, was Tom Mackey, in September 1949. Arthur Moore, Bernard Grazier, Keith Martin and Norman Harratt returned home on leave between October and November that year. In 1957 the story of the *Amethyst* and the other vessels on which the Leicester men served was told in the film *Yangtze Incident*, starring Richard Todd as Lieutenant Commander Kerans.

At the end of July 1949 the Leicester Water Department announced a major project to improve the supply of fresh water into the east and south sides of the city. To be completed by March 1950 at a cost of £110,000, 8½ miles of 27in water main were to be laid from Hallgates reservoirs at Newtown Linford, across the east side of the city to Evington Service reservoir on Coleman Road. The pipe would be routed from Mowmacre Hill to the junction of Gipsy Lane and Victoria Road East. As part of the work, it was intended to build a coffer dam (used primarily at harbours and docks, and not commonly used for inland projects) on the River Soar near to the Belgrave Road boat house. This would allow the pipe to be laid 8ft below the river bed, along with a duplicate in case of bursts. In order to complete this scheme a further pipe, at an estimated cost of £250,000, would need to be installed between Mowmacre Hill and Hallgates.

Christmas 1949 was a particularly eventful one. The City Council had decided to replace its tramcars with buses; a phased closure of routes began as early as Christmas 1946 with the cancellation of the Aylestone route.

On Wednesday 9 November 1949, decorated for the occasion, No. 58, the last tram to run in Leicester, carrying Council dignitaries and officials, departed from the Clock Tower shortly after 4 p.m., crewed by Motorman F. Timson of 49 Thames Street, and Conductor John William Bennett of 56 Marshall Street. Along the side of the tram was painted the declamation 'We mourn the loss of faithful friends from the streets of our grand old city. To move with the times we cannot have lines – So – Go they must – It's a Pity!' Since 1904, when the inaugural run of the first Leicester Borough tramcar was made, the system had carried 2,068.4 million passengers a total of 171.8 million miles. With an appropriate historical touch, the tram halted on its arrival at the Abbey Park Depot and for the final passage through the depot gates Motorman Timson handed over the controls to 88-year-old Jack White of Great Easton, who had driven the first tramcar out of the depot almost half a century earlier, on 18 May 1904.

The Tramways Depot on Abbey Park Road (opened in 1915) was converted to accommodate buses, and the tram sheds in Humberstone Gate, which had housed twenty-six trams, were altered for the use of twenty buses and designated an overspill for Abbey Park Road. The tram sheds in Humberstone Gate, owned by the City Council, were quite large and extended through to Belgrave Gate, a circumstance that would stand them in good stead in later years when the Haymarket Centre Project, occupying the entire block, was initiated. Built in 1839, the site of the depot was originally the Old Leicester Amphitheatre which could hold 3,000 people and was used for circuses; towards the end of its days political meetings were held there.

With the first fall of snow in the city and county on 9 December 1949 promising a white Christmas, Leicester's first civic Christmas tree, a Norwegian spruce supplied by Bradgate Woods Ltd, appeared in Town Hall Square in the second week of December.

Over the previous eighteen months living conditions had been gradually improving. Although meat and soap remained on ration, some other commodities had been derestricted. Potato rationing ended at midnight on 30 April 1948. As from 9 August that year coupons were no longer required to purchase footwear, swimwear, leather goods or household fabrics, and during April 1949 sweets and clothing were taken off ration. A side effect of this was that people were now becoming more careful with their money. By June 1948 most families had spent the demobilisation gratuities, small windfalls that had come with the returning servicemen. Some manufacturing firms were running on short time and elsewhere overtime was becoming increasingly scarce. The pound sterling had now taken over from the coupon, and instead of desperate shoppers being willing to pay almost any asking price for goods, they could now begin to choose the best bargains on offer. In June 1948 the government lowered purchase tax, the bane of every shopkeeper's life, on articles such as kitchen appliances, clocks, watches, radio sets and bedding. Purchase tax on gas-operated space- and water-heating appliances was reduced from 100 per cent to 66 per cent; other items such as paper towels, handkerchiefs, galvanised baths, paraffin and oil-burning lamps were exempted. The price of a man's suit fell to its pre-war cost of around £10. One of the commodities most in demand was household paint. The asking price in 1947 was 7s for a quart tin of varnish paint; twelve months later it would not fetch more than 5s. Car sales, which had boomed as soon as the war was over, began to fall off with the continuation of petrol rationing.

As an added bonus, during the last week of November full street lighting was reinstated for the first time in ten years. Because of fuel shortages, and the government being caught off-balance by the Arctic conditions of early 1947, the Ministry of Fuel and Lighting subsequently ruled that street lighting be kept down to a maximum of 70 per cent capacity. In reality, however, after midnight each night 70 per cent of street lights were switched off, leaving only 30 per cent burning. It was therefore a novelty for Leicester citizens to find all of their street lights lit once more for the festive season.

Christmas Day

HOME (Midland 296.2 m and London 342.1 m)

7.55: Weather   8.0: News
8.15: Orchestra   8.40: Carols
9. 0: Postman's Knock
9.20: Christmas Bells Greeting
9.30: Christmas Day Service
10.30: Melodies from Vienna
11. 0: Story for Children
11.15: Sunday Prom
12.15: Gardening Scrapbook
12.55: Weather
1. 0: News 1.10 Victorian melodies
2. 0: Commonwealth Christmas
3. 0: THE KING
3.15: Opera Orchestra
4.15: A Christmas carol
5. 0: Children's Hour
5.55: Weather. 6. 0: News
6.15: Bethlehem
7.45: Christmas Music
8.30: Algernon Blackwood reads His Story
9. 0: News 9.15:Scrapbook for 1899
10.15: Recital: Campoli
10.50 Epilogue
11. 0: News Summary

LIGHT (1.500 m and 261.1 m)

8. 0: Way Out West
8.20: Kaye Cavendish: piano
8.40: Sandy MacPherson
9. 0: News 9.10 Silver Chords
9.30: Family Favourites
10.30: People's Service
11. 0: "Have a Go"
11.30: Yuletide in the Old Log Cabin
12. 0: Billy Cotton Show
12.30: "Twenty Questions"
1. 0: Variety Bandbox
2. 0 - 3.15   As Home Service
3.15: Gracie Fields Christmas Party
4. 0: Wilfred Pickles Children's Party
4.30: Down Your Way
5.30: "Take it from Here"
6. 0: Tom Jenkins and his Palm Court Orchestra
7. 0: News 7.10 Sport
7.15: Christmas Party
9. 0: Hymn Singing
9.30: "Much-Binding-in-the-Marsh"
10. 0: News 10. 5 Welsh Rarebit
11. 0: Victor Silvester
11.50: Epilogue
11.56: News Summary

Television (Sutton Coldfield)
10.50: Christmas Service
3.20: Children's Film
6.30: "Toad of Toad Hall"
9. 0: "Miranda"
10.40: News (sound)

1949 Christmas Radio and TV.

The set you'll simply have to get **DEFIANT**

MODEL TR 947 (Television Set)

A.C. 200 250 volts.   9in. Cathode
Ray Tube, producing pictures of
supreme quality 7½in. x 6in.

Beautifully finished figured walnut
Cabinet 24¼in. x 15½in. x 16¼in.
£62. 0s. 8d. including tax.

Supplied through **CO-OPERATIVE SOCIETIES** *everywhere*

In Leicester BBC television began postwar transmissions at Christmas 1949 and city-centre electrical shops such as the Co-op offered TV sets from around 42 guineas. *(Courtesy: Midlands Co-operative Society)*

The great event, for those eagerly awaiting it in the city, was the news that television would be available in time for Christmas. The first public television broadcast by the BBC had taken place in August 1932 and some limited steps to develop it continued until the outbreak of war in September 1939. (By 1935, nationwide, there were approximately 2,000 'Baird Televisors' in use, costing £100 each, equivalent to the price of a small family car.) After the war, work on television programmes resumed in about 1946; however, reception was limited to certain areas, and it was not until early in 1947 that, with promises of a new transmitter station being opened at Birmingham, television would soon be available in Leicester city and the county. Eventually a date was set for the service to start operating in late 1949, and in anticipation of this, by the middle of the summer retailers were doing a brisk trade installing H-shaped aerials on chimney pots across the city. Cutting it fine for the Christmas holiday, the first broadcast from Sutton Coldfield (*The Winslow Boy*) was beamed into Leicester homes on Saturday 17 December. The quality of reception was mixed (unfortunately for the many householders who had invited neighbours into their homes to show off their new acquisitions with organised 'television parties') for a variety of reasons ranging from customers not understanding how to adjust their sets, to the engineer having failed to set up the aerial correctly. Irrespective, the following Monday morning proved a busy one for the television stockists. The 'mixed reception' to the latest innovation in entertainment was, quite literally, confined to the shortfalls in its technical qualities. On Christmas Eve, the day when most householders had their sets installed, 111 television licences were issued and by New Year's Eve the number of licence holders in the city numbered 1,131.

In the years after the war large areas of previously undeveloped land such as this ground lying between Narborough Road and the River Soar were used for allotments or simply allowed to stand unused. This particular piece was later purchased and developed by Gimson's as a timber yard. *(Courtesy: G. Fenn)*

CHAPTER THREE

Building and Restructuring: 1945–59

That the war was to all intents and purposes won, and that plans needed to be made for the postwar infrastructure of the city was apparent by the beginning of 1944. In January of that year Councillor Charles Keene accepted the task of forming the Leicester Reconstruction Committee. Keene (who became an alderman in 1945) was eminently suited for the job. Born in Leeds in September 1891, he came to Leicester as a child with his parents and began an association with the city that lasted until his death in 1977. A successful businessman (he was managing director of Kingstone Ltd, and of the Mutual Clothing and Supply Co.) and staunch Labour Party supporter, Keene was elected to the City Council in 1926, from which time he served in a number of capacities. From 1939 until July 1941, when he accepted the post of Deputy Regional Air Raid Precautions Commissioner, based in Nottingham, he was responsible both as Chairman of the Emergency Committee and as the city ARP Controller for many of the measures taken by the Council to ensure the well-being of the residents of the city.

The Leicester Reconstruction Committee was charged with formulating a strategy for postwar planning, and its prime aim was to provide adequate housing. Three initial projects were put in hand. The first was to build a council housing estate on the north side of the city that would be named the New Parks estate. The second was the scheme for the Scraptoft Valley Development, and the Thurnby Lodge estate on the eastern border of the town.

As early as January 1946 an outline plan for the latter was being advanced. The scheme provided for two self-contained neighbourhoods with a population of about 10,000 each, with the dividing line between them being Scraptoft Lane. In the centre of both would be shops, churches, schools and other public buildings. When completed the entire area was to contain around 6,000 houses, divided equally between council and privately owned properties. Following its approval by the Leicester and District Joint Advisory Committee under the Chairmanship of Alderman Charles Keene in September 1946, the Council announced:

[a] new Garden City Project proposed for Evington Valley district. From Evington Valley [a] new road to be built through Chesterfield and Ethel Roads, direct to Northampton Square in the city centre . . . the scheme involves 483 acres, of which 420 are owned by the City Council. Remainder owned by the Wakerley Trust and the Evington House Estate . . . proposed to build 1,200 houses. Rowlatts Hill allotments will not be disturbed for the time being, but provision is made for them later to be converted to 650 houses. Of the 1,200 planned for now, 500 will be put in the area north of the City General Hospital and 700 in the Valley area . . . will include two secondary schools and a county college. These schools will cater for the overspill from Highfields and North Evington districts.

Portal houses, such as this one on Hockley Farm Road, better known as 'prefabs', were built immediately after the war as a short-term housing measure. An early occupant in 1952 was Albert Layte and his family, seen here with his daughter Sherry. *(Courtesy: S. Nesbitt)*

In the spring of 1947, at a cost of £155 an acre, the purchase of 85 acres of land at Lodge Farm was approved, as were two other small packets in Thurncourt Road, one consisting of 855sq. yd for £55, and the other of 3,070sq. yd for £280.

The third and more immediate consideration was to erect just under 800 semi-permanent dwellings at various sites across the city in order to partially resolve the urgent housing needs that the end of the war would bring. From a design originating in America, the 'Portal' house was a single-storey bungalow structure built from plywood sections that were bolted together onto a steel girder frame. Quickly dubbed 'prefabs', these chalet-style dwellings were an ideal solution to the Council's short-term needs. Designed, in relation to the prevailing weather conditions in Britain, to last for ten years (although many of them tripled and quadrupled this figure) the prefab had a living room, two bedrooms, a bathroom and a kitchen, which was way

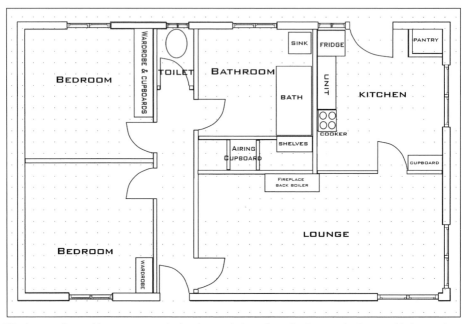

The layout of a prefab was extremely simple, consisting of two bedrooms, bathroom, kitchen and lounge. It was this simplicity that made them so easy and economical to construct in large numbers. *(Courtesy: S. Nesbitt)*

beyond the dreams of many occupants. Families who were rehoused from the overcrowded inner-city courtyard slums had had to share one outside toilet and tap with three other families. From the Council's standpoint their prime attraction was that of cost. In October 1944 the Council took the decision to buy in 750 Portal houses, to be delivered the following year, with an undertaking that the initial cost would be funded through a loan from central government, repayable over a fixed period.

Selecting sites on the Braunstone estate (140 on Hockley Farm Road, 200 on Hinckley Road East and West) the main New Parks estate (120) on the Groby Road side of the estate (141) at Wicklow Drive on the

Cheap to build and with a small garden at the rear, the prefabs provided excellent homes for families in the immediate postwar years. *(Courtesy: S. Nesbitt)*

Coleman Road estate (158) and at Aylestone on Hughendon Drive (31) all on land already owned by the Corporation, kept expenditure to a minimum.

The capital cost of the land involved was £19,000, with a further expenditure of £81,084 for the laying of sewers and access roads. As part of the drive to keep the venture economical due to the expected life of this type of structure being a mere ten years, the access roads were only of a temporary nature. The annual repayment from the local authority to the government for the cost of the dwellings themselves was £23 10s, per house, or £18,635 overall. For a total of 793 houses, albeit of a temporary nature, this was a sound business proposition. The whole scheme was intended to give the Corporation a reasonable period of time – a decade – in which to consolidate its financial commitments before moving on. It turned out to be a most successful undertaking, with work on the first group of houses, in Hughendon Drive, beginning in April 1945. Two months later, in June, they were ready for occupation. Allocation of the houses was based on a strict five-point system. First to be accommodated would be disabled ex-servicemen with families,

Only intended to have a ten-year lifespan, prefabs were far more durable than expected and in many instances the original occupants remained in them for more than double that time. *(Courtesy: S. Nesbitt)*

followed in order by men still serving in the forces; men recently demobilised from the forces; widows of ex-servicemen with families; other applicants with families who were presently living in rooms.

It is probably apposite at this stage to examine the reasons why Leicester needed more houses after 1945 than in 1939. Pre-war there was, apparently, sufficient housing and the postwar shortage cannot be attributed to bomb damage, which was negligible in regard to housing.

The reasons were basically attributable to an increase in population since the turn of the century and a change in the social structure of the city. In 1881 there were 122,376 people living in the town; by 1948 the number had risen to 278,000. Further, the average family in 1946 was only half the size it had been seventy years earlier, which meant that with an increased population but fewer people living in each dwelling, inevitably more houses were required. Thus the presumption that at the outbreak of war Leicester did not have a housing problem is essentially flawed (in 1931, with the years of the Depression looming, there were a total of 257,718 people living in Leicester city: 120,013 males and 137,705 females). True, there were sufficient houses for the upper- and middle-class citizens, but for the low earners, often living more than one family to a house in old, rented, terraced accommodation, overcrowding was definitely a problem. In a departure from traditional arrangements, there was a movement away from the extended family situation whereby, on marrying, a young couple would invariably live with one or other of the couple's parents. Elderly people remained in their homes while their children moved away after marriage, thus creating further pressure on available accommodation.

The problem was not a local one. Nationally, between 1939 and 1946, house building came to a standstill. If the figure of 200,000 houses a year (the average annual build) is taken, this means that the country lost 1.2 million houses during the period. The consensus of local authorities, including Leicester, was that there was now an opportunity to remedy the problem by putting in place long-term slum clearance and local authority building programmes.

A review of its housing needs by the City Council in January 1946 showed that 1,000 houses needed to be built to cover existing short-term needs, and a further 46,000 for long-term development purposes over the next thirty to forty years. To resolve the combined problem of need and development, 13,500 houses were required in the next ten years. Work was also to be instituted on clearing areas that were considered, by virtue of their age and condition, to be slums. Some areas of the city were at that time populated at a ratio of seventy houses to an acre, three and a half times the optimum density.

In order to facilitate new housing programmes, in February 1946 the government implemented a series of subsidies for local authorities, the object being to enable a three-bedroom house in the provinces to be let at 10s a week. A general subsidy of £16 10s per house per year, for sixty years, was granted by the Exchequer, plus a local subsidy of £5 10s for the same period.

Of prime consideration, so far as Leicester Corporation was concerned, was the question of where they could in fact locate new developments. Already more land was needed for building purposes on the Scraptoft side of the town. The only answer was to extend the city boundaries outwards, taking in some of the county's land contiguous to the city. Unsympathetic to the needs of its neighbour, and diametrically opposed to losing any of its rateable value, the County Council found itself engaged in an ongoing series of border conflicts with the City Council.

In March 1946 the first meeting of the Leicester Federation of Registered House Builders was held, following the announcement by the government of its plans to allow private contractors to purchase land for development purposes. Thus, apparently, the green light was given for mobilisation of another dimension within the construction industry. However, with the emphasis on monies being fed into local authority projects, the private sector of the building trade was not encouraged to the extent that it could

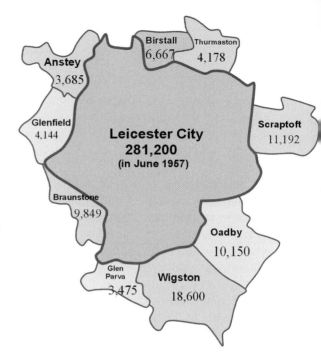

Some of the parishes administered by the County Council on the periphery of Leicester city in the period 1957–9 which were affected by movement of people out of the city. (The figures shown are of the population in 1959.)

have been. (This was in some measure attributable to local authorities wanting to establish a monopoly over supplies of building materials and labour.)

One person to discover the difficulties at an early stage was Tom Wheatcroft, the founder of Wheatcroft & Son, who in later years became the head of one of the country's largest building concerns and owner of the Donington Park racing circuit. After being demobbed from the army at the end of the war, Tom Wheatcroft set up in business as a house builder (with a restriction of £10 on any house renovation or maintenance work, jobbing building was not an attractive prospect). His first obstacle was to obtain licences from the local authority to build houses. This he surmounted in an interview with John Beckett, the City Engineer and Surveyor, who had ultimate responsibility for recommending the granting of permits by the Leicester City Council.

Sceptical of new applicants, Beckett asked Wheatcroft what his intentions were. Tom Wheatcroft replied that eventually he 'wanted to build one house a day'. The City Engineer, impressed by the young man's vision, granted his licence, and from that point the future of one of the city's major businessmen (and employers) was secured. However, Tom Wheatcroft and others had to compete with established builders such as G. Calverley & Sons, who had labour forces in place and an established reputation.

The process of becoming a house builder at this time was strictly regulated. First the contractor bought a plot of land, then he applied for a licence to build each individual property on the site. Once the licence had been obtained the plans filed under it had to be approved, and all materials required for the build were purchased accordingly. Additionally, new houses were built on a 'cost plus' plan, whereby materials and labour were costed out and a small percentage was added as a profit margin. Any errors in the costings came out of this margin. This situation prevailed until restrictions were eventually lifted. The first commodity to come off licence was cement. However, the purchase of an equally essential commodity, plaster, remained under control until 1950. Even at this stage, difficulties for the private builder continued. A government restriction of £1,000 on house prices was eventually lifted, but nervous building societies persisted in refusing to grant mortgages to the average house buyer in excess of £1,250.

Work on the New Parks housing estate – which was to be the City Council's flagship project in the early postwar years – was delayed somewhat because the site was being used by the War Office as a heavy vehicle park. It was not until 27 September 1945 that the last Crusader tank was removed, leaving it clear for the builders to move in. Money for the project was to be made available through government grants. Across a 90-acre area of land extending to Groby Road, the estimated cost of installing the sewage system was £39,000 and that of laying the roads £98,000. Working parties of German POWs under armed guard were used to dig out the storm drains and for other preparatory work.

In March 1946, at a cost of £307,000, tenders for the erection on the estate of 205 'Easi-Form' houses of three and four bedrooms, costing £1,205 and £1,493 respectively, were accepted, enabling the first phase of the building work to begin. The decision to use this style of 'all steel' building was taken because of a postwar shortage of bricks. A visit by City Architect J.S. Fyfe and members of the Housing Committee to a site at Northolt in Essex, together with the results of a previous experiment conducted in 1925 on the Portwey, indicated that this type of structure was eminently suited to the present needs. Designed by the British Iron and Steel Foundation, and costing more than a brick-built structure (the extra cost was mitigated by government subsidies) the three-bedroom house covered 882sq. ft with an additional 100sq. ft for outbuildings. Using an aluminium frame and four sections for the outer walls, the Easi-Form houses could be erected at the rate of four a day, and were ideal for the mass building of a new estate. Meanwhile, the Corporation had acquired a further 24 acres of land, including some farm buildings, in an area that had been designated for use as a golf course but was no longer required for that purpose. The first of the 'all steel' houses was ready in mid-October 1946 and twelve months later, on 31 October 1947, with the first Midland Red bus service due to run on the route into New Parks the following month, the keys to the last completed house in this phase were handed over to the Chair of the Housing Committee, Councillor May Goodwin.

Across the city by this time the Council's housing schemes were coming to fruition; 642 permanent dwellings had been erected and let, together with 572 prefabs, and with requisitioned properties this meant that 7,000 people had been accommodated. Over the next twelve months work on the New Parks estate moved on rapidly. Just prior to Christmas 1948 contracts had been let on 2,450 houses, of which 1,420 were already occupied, and tenders were being submitted for the building of a further 250 brick houses. At the beginning of March 1949 plans were put forward for a combined-levels school (360 infants, 480 juniors) on Charnor Road which, built on the aluminium frame system, including buildings, playground and drainage, would cost an estimated £40,000.

Work continued into the new decade and in January 1950 plans were formulated for the building of blocks of flats on Aikman Avenue. These were based on designs viewed during a visit to Copenhagen and Stockholm in late 1949 by members of the Council led by the Chairman of the Housing Committee, Alderman Geoffrey Barnett. The committee proposed to build seven blocks of flats, within a time scale of eighteen months to two years and at a cost of £544,710, which would house some 10 per cent of the 9,000 candidates on the council housing waiting list. The foundation work for the blocks was begun in late September 1950 and it was anticipated that work on the 388 flats would spread over the 1951–3 housing allocation periods. The completion of this phase of the New Parks project was critical to the Council's housing strategy, as the waiting list for houses now stood at 10,513 families. To date, since the beginning of the scheme 2,452 houses had been completed and let on this, the Council's major housing programme, whereas on the new Thurnby Lodge estate only 74 of a planned 392 houses were as yet occupied. The first of the New Parks flats, with a weekly rent of £2 7s for the two-bedroom and £2 12s for the three-bedroom, were ready for occupation by the summer of 1953.

Not counting the blocks of flats, when completed in late 1952 the 3,000 houses on the estate accommodated 12,000 people. The final accolade for those involved came in January 1959 when the shopping crescent on Aikman Avenue won a bronze design award from the Royal Institute of British Architects as the most outstanding building erected in Leicestershire and Rutland in the seven years up to 1957.

Work on postwar housing moved on apace in the latter years of the 1940s. Between 1946 and the beginning of 1949, 3.25 million people across the country were re-housed. Employing a total labour force of 521,500 men, in 1947 139,600 houses were built by local authorities, followed the next year by a further 227,616. In March 1947 Leicester City Council's declared targets for the coming year were the completion of 1,000 council houses in the public sector and 250 dwellings under licence in the private sector.

The Ministry of Housing Central Committee made some interesting observations on the situation in March 1949:

pre-war, in 1938, a house was built in sixteen weeks, now in 1949 it takes eight months. This is primarily due to lack of materials and the requirements for permits. It is quicker and cheaper to build a row of houses than a series of individual houses. With more materials [becoming available] and less administration, times should soon be reduced. Also, houses being built now are not as elaborate as in pre-war years. Materials, particularly wood are in short supply and design has had to change to accommodate this. In addition to the present council house applicants there are private builders who have their own lists of people waiting for houses to be built. As the allowance for houses depends on density of population, many of these private houses will go up on the outskirts of the city.

Work on developing other outer suburbs of the city did not progress as swiftly as New Parks. In May 1949 the Council was advertising for 'small builders to tender for the erection of 250 houses to be built on the Thurnby Lodge Estate', and later in October it was reported that, with work progressing on the roads and sewers, 392 houses had been contracted.

One of the reasons that progress in this particular area was slow was that, in order to achieve its aims, the City Council needed to push its geographic boundaries outwards into land owned by the County Council – something to which the county authorities were vehemently opposed. In December 1950 the animosity between the two authorities came to a head with the instigation of a public inquiry into what had evolved into a major boundary dispute. The basis of the quarrel was that the Leicester City Housing Committee was seeking to acquire land to extend the Thurnby Lodge estate between the upper stretch of Scraptoft Lane and the LNER (Great Northern) railway line, towards Thurnby railway station. The dispute had been simmering since the end of the war, and as an opening shot the City Council had already laid a sewer pipe as part of the Scraptoft Valley Development in preparation for further work, not later than a proposed date of 1953, with a view to creating housing for 4,500 Leicester citizens. Arrayed against the scheme were the Leicestershire County Council Planning Authority, Billesdon Rural District Council, the Leicestershire branch of the National Farmers Union and an assortment of private property owners.

John Beckett, putting the case for the City Housing Committee, submitted that there were in Leicester city at that time 8,358 families, constituting 19,128 people, living in shared accommodation. There was a waiting list of 8,700 applications for houses, and between 3,000 and 4,000 people were migrating into the city each year. In addition to any local authority provisions, it was anticipated that land needed to be acquired for the building of some 3,500 private-sector houses.

It was July 1951 before a decision in the inquiry was reached by the Ministry of Local Government and Planning. The adjudicator found in favour of the applicants and, much to the chagrin of its opponents, Leicester City Council was allowed to proceed with the Scraptoft Valley Scheme. Although further work could not be started for another two years, owing to practicalities in taking possession of the land (1,325 houses had already been completed), the success of the programme was now assured. It meant that on an area of ground roughly the same size as Braunstone, divided into two neighbourhoods lying to the north and south of Scraptoft Lane, a residential area of 4,725 homes and facilities would be created. Although it was not the last battle to be fought between the city and county administrations, the decision constituted a major political victory for the City Council.

While the creation of the New Parks housing estate was of prime importance to the Council, other matters were by no means neglected. In September 1946 the Town Planning and Reconstruction Committee announced plans for a development scheme on the existing Braunstone estate which included a community centre, swimming baths, a health centre, three secondary schools, a Baptist church and two Roman Catholic churches. This was in addition to the 120 prefabs that would be erected on the nearby Hinckley Road side before Christmas. Proposals were also put forward to build houses on 150 acres of the 400-acre site of Braunstone Aerodrome. The proponents of the scheme based their case on the fact that 1,000 houses could be erected on the acreage and there already existed a main sewer running from the edge of the aerodrome to the Braunstone estate. The opponents' view was that there was already sufficient housing in the area provided by the New Parks and

Braunstone estates, and as most of Leicester's industry was located on the east side of the city it would create an imbalance in the available transport system.

June 1950 saw plans to put up 500 concrete houses on Stocking Farm estate. The first tenders were submitted and seven months later, with the completion of the first phase of Easi-Form structures comprising three bedrooms, a bathroom, a kitchen with fireplace, and the remaining rooms being heated by modern wall-mounted heaters, tenants began to move in.

Five years after work began on the New Parks estate, work on the drainage system for the Eyres Monsell estate began. In June 1952 the Council decided to build 200 Easi-Form houses as part of a 600-house allocation on the estate. The cost of the 200 houses totalled £269,577 (an average of just under £1,350 each) and the project comprised 56 four-bedroom and 144 three-bedroom houses, plus 52 two-bedroom flats. Six months later, in January 1953, the Housing Committee was given permission by the Ministry of Housing and Local Government to build, in addition to these 200 houses, a series of three-storey Easi-Form flats based on exhibition blocks at Boreham in Essex. A further 334 brick houses were agreed upon at a cost of £342,093 (at a little under £1,024 per house this was slightly less than the average for the Easi-Form structures) together with a health centre costing £35,000.

With work under way on the Eyres Monsell estate, the Housing Committee totalled up its public housing programme in January 1953 and announced that since the end of the war 5,155 council housing properties had been completed in the city.

In September 1954, a plan to build 212 houses at Mowmacre Hill was put on hold, because sewers and roads were behind schedule, and it was decided to go ahead with plans to build 302 traditional-style council houses at Netherhall. The project, costing £358,069 and consisting of 184 three-bedroom, 8 four-bedroom and 52 two-bedroom houses and 58 bungalows, was undertaken by Drury & Co. of Wigston Fields.

Housing provision was, for postwar Britain, one of the major considerations in the regeneration of the country's social and economic infrastructure, and by the early 1950s local authorities such as Leicester were able to look back over their achievements and put them into an overall context.

At the beginning of 1951 Leicester Housing Committee was in a position to promise that during the forthcoming twelve months 1,500 council houses would become available for occupancy on sites at Steins Lane, Evington, Thurnby Lodge, Goodwood, Stocking Farm and New Parks estate. The previous largest comparable number of allocations had been in 1927 when 1,590 were allocated. (In 1925 the City Council obtained land on the south side of the city at Saffron Lane and Braunstone. Owing to the shortage of building materials at the time, a decision was taken to erect 1,500 houses at the Saffron Lane site, the first ones to be completed by 1926.)

Eighteen months later, exactly one year after the crucial decision to permit the city to absorb county land for the Scraptoft Valley Scheme, the City Council put the county authorities on notice that further expansion was inevitable. City planners projected that, with an influx of population and with rehousing needs due to slum clearances, there would in the long term be an overspill of an estimated 276,000 people from the city into fringe housing on the boundaries. The county for

In later years the area of Eastern Boulevard and Jarrom Street was altered considerably. This view shows, at bottom right, the Lowe and Carr building at the junction of Walnut Street and Eastern Boulevard. In the middle ground is the Polytechnic, later to become Leicester's second university. As yet the Magazine Barracks have not been pulled down, nor has the Leicester Royal Infirmary been extended to fill the landscape. *(Courtesy: G. Fenn)*

its part indicated that the acceptable figure would be 50,000 over a twenty-year period. Initially the City Council conceded this to be a reasonable estimate for the period up to 1971 only, however, by 1952 it had revised the figure to 60,500.

The city projections were that in the twenty years after 1953 the increases in population, plus a displacement of existing occupants from city centre properties due for demolition, would cost an estimated £46 million and require the incorporation into the city of several of the county parishes abutting the city boundaries. Additionally, to be treated as a separate issue and based on a figure of 300sq. ft of floor space per worker, industrial expansion would require another 432 acres.

Swift to pick up on the latter assertion, the county came back with the riposte that the calculation indicated the city was setting out to attract an additional 62,000 workers into its sphere of influence, and that these, with their families, would result in a population increase of 180,000 people, swelling the city population to an eventual half a million. This was clear evidence that the city authorities were attempting to create a city with that population. For each projection there was an objection, for every action, a reaction; it was unfortunate that the interests of the two authorities conflicted in this manner, as it soured their relations for many years to come.

CHAPTER FOUR

Slum Clearance

Ten years after the end of the war the government and local authorities, with the nation's immediate housing problems under control, turned their attention towards the long-term future of Britain.

In October 1956 the Ministry of Housing and Local Government laid out its plans for the future. The initial projection was that by 1975 half a million acres of land would have to be absorbed into new housing programmes. A broad view of the projections was that 400,000 people would need to relocate from London alone to green belt areas during the next fifteen years; similarly 200,000 would move out of Birmingham to the outskirts. Other major cities quoted were Manchester (200,000) Liverpool (160,000) Sheffield and Leeds (70,000 each). As an indication of the progress that was being made across the country in 1955 a total of 283,000 new homes were built, 39 per cent of them by private enterprise.

Significantly, during the early 1950s half of the local authorities in Britain (including Leicester city) had established slum clearance programmes to be implemented within the next five years – over 500 schemes had been given government approval. Of an estimated 13 million houses in England and Wales, 850,000 were declared unfit for human habitation. Through slum clearance projects 378,000 of them were scheduled for demolition; during 1955 over 25,000 were levelled and 75,918 people were rehoused.

This climate of change signalled for Leicester City Council two particular things. The first was that the odds in its running battle with the County Council were very much weighted in the city's favour. If the government was not merely comfortable with urban expansion, but was actively endorsing it, then they were virtually being given *carte blanche* to go ahead. Second, over the next twenty years the City Council intended to demolish 19,558 houses in the Gresham Street, Wharf Street, Charnwood Street, New Parks Street, New Bridge Street and Highfields areas, and early in October 1949 sanitary and building inspectors began a preliminary survey of 15,000 houses that fitted the criteria.

Envisaging the city's population in 1970 to be around 330,000, the clearance programme required new housing for 126,500 people, at a cost (with building by both the public and private sectors) of around £66 million. It was very obvious that relocation on this scale would have implications. First, the extension of the city boundaries was an essential factor in catering for the relocation of families. Second, it would present an opportunity to develop industrial sites – also on the outskirts of the city – and provide new employment.

Central to the clearance of city centre properties was the inclusion of many of the old Victorian factory premises located in the demolition areas. The dynamics of how the workforce would cope with the changes also needed to be addressed, because many of those being moved into new houses on the outskirts of the town had been used to walking a short distance from home to their place of work.

The postwar slum clearance schemes implemented by Leicester City Council, combined with a natural population growth, resulted in householders moving out to the suburbs of the city. Suburban estates were built by contractors to accommodate their needs. Seen here is the development by Wheatcroft's of Shackerdale Road on the boundary of Leicester and Wigston. *(Courtesy: Tom Wheatcroft)*

Others who were relocating to the outskirts were being moved miles away from their places of work. There were two solutions, both of which were eventually employed; one was to build new factories within striking distance of where the workers were rehoused, the other to invest in better local transport links between the outskirts and the city centre.

As was to be expected, the plans prompted another round in the city versus county battle over boundary extensions. On Tuesday 3 December 1953 the inquiry into the Leicester Development Plan opened to examine submissions by both authorities.

Representing the City Council's interests, Michael Rowe QC felt that the issue was quite clear-cut. Over the next twenty years it was the Council's intention to invest £46 million in housing; an additional £17 million would have to be invested in work outside the present city boundary to lay sewers and other services.

Counsel for the county authorities (which included the County Council and the Rural District Councils for Blaby, Oadby, Billesdon and Barrow upon Soar), Eric Blane, asked that, 'the Minister accept the suggestion that Leicester has adopted far too high a standard for the Housing Act's purposes . . .'.

With local authorities throughout the country engaged in similar wrangles, the government was inundated by local authority disputes – plans and objections, arguments over losses and gains of rateable land, allegations of authorities hyping expansion figures. Decisions were slow to come forward. A year later the Minister for Housing, Duncan Sandys, declared that the Leicester Housing Committee's application to build 1,500 houses in the following year would be limited to 1,000.

At that time the Council waiting list for houses was 7,564. However, the city's accomplishments to date were impressive. From the end of the war to August 1955 (when government cutbacks were proposing to restrict the Council's building to 1,000 houses), 8,640 council houses had been built in the city and a further 1,214 were under construction; plus 2,794 private dwellings had been completed and a further 412 were being erected.

Interestingly, in October 1958 the Leicester Housing Committee debated introducing a means test for those applying to become council tenants. Proposed by Councillor Philip Ashwell (Conservative), it aimed to impose a limit on applications from couples whose combined income exceeded £15 a week. This proposal was made on the basis that Norwich had already established a ceiling of £13 10s.

Obviously forewarned of the move, Alderman Mark Henig (Labour) destroyed the case by bringing in figures for the earnings of recent applicants. From a sample of 214 applicants, in only 59 cases did the wife work. From among this sample, 18 earned less than £5 and 126 earned between £5 and £10; 70 earned between £10 and £12 10s and 19 earned from £12 10s to £15. There were only 8 in the £15 to £18 15s bracket, all NCOs or warrant officers in the armed forces who were about to be demobbed, and did not yet know what their civilian income was likely to be.

It was not until early 1959 that matters relating to the boundary dispute began to crystallise. In March, under the aegis of the Local Government Commission for England, precise boundary changes were defined. It was announced that the changes would transfer 6,458 acres of land from the county to the city, the greater part coming from Oadby and Wigston, Barrow upon Soar, Billesdon and Blaby (the authorities that had been the prime objectors during the 1953 inquiry). The result would be a transfer of 31,500 people to the city from the county and of this number the largest single group affected would be 10,600 residents at Braunstone. However, in practical terms, the vast majority of those affected were already linked to the city in all but local government organisation.

An agreement was reached with Leicestershire County Council that an overspill population of 41,500 should be accommodated by 1972, with the understanding that the Leicester Development Plan was aimed at limiting the population of the urbanised area of Leicester (of which the city and the newly added areas formed a major part) to an ultimate population of 400,000. The city population at the time was estimated to be 280,000.

A local businessman and a Labour member of the City Council, Charles Keene was, throughout the war years and after, a pivotal figure in the regeneration of the city. As Chairman of the Leicester Slum Clearance Committee he was responsible for the rehousing of many families from uninhabitable areas such as Wharf Street.

Under the Chairmanship of the ubiquitous Charles Keene, the Leicester Slum Clearance and Redevelopment Committee now set to work bringing down the old Victorian backstreet housing of the inner city, the prime targets being Wharf Street and Highfields.

Wharf Street, as the district lying on the east side of the city and bounded by Belgrave Road, Humberstone Road and the Great Northern Railway was known, had since the mid-nineteenth century been viewed as an area of dense, enclosed housing and over the years had become enveloped in a mythology that in some ways belied its true nature. The romanticised view was of a tightly knit community, sharing a common bond of adversity and poverty, with a pub in every street and a shop on every corner; a place where justice was rough and policemen seldom ventured. Much of this was true. The inhabitants were universally poor, the houses in many cases were hovels without bathrooms, a shared outside tap and toilet the only token of plumbing or sanitation. Unemployment was high and it was a place where an outsider was immediately identifiable. Given the opportunity to escape into new and better living conditions, very few of those trapped in the area would have declined to move. (When the compulsory purchase of properties began, the local shopkeepers were always the ones to make bids for compensation, citing the mass exodus as being responsible for taking away their livelihoods.)

The history of Wharf Street went back to the late Georgian and early Victorian years, most of the properties having been built between 1828 and 1835 to house local factory workers, more being added in the 1860s when space for development was created by the removal of the Wharf Street cricket ground.

A 1948 class photograph of children from the Wharf Street district at St Matthew's Infant School in Upper Brunswick Street. *(Courtesy: M. & J. Zientek)*

A group of teachers and nursery assistants at St Matthew's Infant School, 1948. During pre-war years married women were not employed as teachers by the local authority and it was only during and after the war that this restriction was lifted. Back row, left to right: Mrs Margaret Handscombe; Mrs Jessica Brennan; -?- (Nursery Assistant); -?- (Nursery Assistant); Miss Norah Bloor. Front row: Miss Margaret Barrass (m. Zientek); Miss Norah Cresswell; Miss Doris Brown; Mrs Kathleen Kirby (Nursery Assistant). *(Courtesy: M. & J. Zientek)*

A network of public houses and shops within the area served from an early stage to create a closed community. As often happens with this type of district, many firms which over the years were to prosper beyond its tiny streets, began life in Wharf Street.

Charles Bennion, the benefactor who, having become the head of the British United Shoe Machinery Co., in 1928 purchased Bradgate Park and donated it to Leicester city, began business in Wharf Street as a sewing machine manufacturer and repairer in the 1880s. The Imperial Typewriter Co. was first established in Wharf Street in 1908; two of the city's most successful ice-cream manufacturers, Massarella's and Rossa's were at one time based in its side streets. William Carr produced his famous Carr's Fever Powders from premises at 168–70 Wharf Street.

Famous characters over the years had an association with its squalid thoroughfares. Joseph Carey Merrick, the famous 'Elephant Man', was born in Lee Street in 1862, and the gymnasium over the Jolly Angler Pub at 122A Wharf Street, was regularly used for training by well-known boxers such as Reggie Meen, 'Pop' Newman and Larry Gains.

One perception – that policemen only dared to venture into the district in pairs – does not necessarily hold true, as two of the Borough (later City) force's most formidable officers actually lived there. PC John 'Tubby' Stephens, who served on the borough police force for twenty-two years, lived at 84 Cobden Street until his death at the age of 48 in April 1908. An ex-soldier and veteran of the Zulu Wars, weighing in at over 24 stone, Stephens was reputed at the time to be the heaviest

Most of the properties in the Wharf Street district were built either between 1825 and 1835 to house local factory workers, or in about 1860 with a similar purpose in mind. By the middle of the twentieth century they were overdue for demolition. *(Courtesy: Urban Design Group, Leicester City Council)*

By the end of the war much of the old city was either bomb-damaged or simply uninhabitable because of the age of the properties. *(Courtesy: Urban Design Group, Leicester City Council)*

Demolition in the Wharf Street area viewed from Chester Street, with Christow Street leading off on the left. Further along Chester Street is St Matthew's Church, and next to it St Matthew's Junior School. At the rear are the remains of Wharf Street with the spire of St Mark's Church (Belgrave Gate) in the background. *(Courtesy: M. & J. Zientek)*

policeman in England. Broken only by his military service in the First World War during which Sergeant George Hankinson, probably the biggest man ever to serve in the force, lived in the middle of the area at 20 Gladstone Street, off Wharf Street, for eighteen years prior to 1932.

After the Second World War the area was a prime target for development and one of the first schemes to be implemented (with an anticipated commencement date of early to mid-1954) was for the demolition of 246 properties in Lewin Street (running at right angles to Lead Street and backing onto Benfield Street), at the back of Wharf Street. Reporting on the proposed Lewin Street Clearance Scheme on 7 January 1953 the *Leicester Mercury* made the point that 'most of Leicester's back to back housing will disappear under this scheme'. (According to Jack Simmons, one of the foremost modern historians of Victorian Leicester, while during the 1840s the town contained no back-to-back housing, there were thought to have been about 1,500 such dwellings by 1864. The *Mercury* report probably alludes to the area in general, as the Ordnance Survey map of the district for 1930 shows the properties in Lewin and Benfield Streets to be terraced, with small open yards between them at the rear.)

Overall this early measure was aimed at opening up a site bounded by Syston Street, Belgrave Gate, Cobden Street and Humberstone Gate. Initially a 6-acre section comprising Wheat Street, Benfield Street, Lewin Street, and Providence Place was pulled down. By July 1953 this had been dramatically widened to encompass all of the property enclosed by Taylor Street, Upper Brunswick Street, Wheat Street, Wharf Street, Russell Square and Lower Willow Street. The programme, once under way, proceeded apace, and with the end of the financial year approaching, at the end of March 1954 the Chairman of the Finance Committee, Alderman Hill, was quick to make the point that the compulsory purchase of plots in the area, including Lewin Street, had been achieved for £1,133 (each), which was the value of the land upon which the condemned property stood.

Plans for the redevelopment of the Wharf Street area were now announced. R. Langlands, the Leicester City Deputy Planning Officer, revealed that, with the first phase of clearance due to be completed by February 1955, the building of multi-storey flats was one of the options under consideration. The second phase of demolition was the old properties in the block comprising Wharf Street, Brook Street, Lead Street and Wheat Street, most of which dated back (with the exception of a few built in the 1870s) to between 1825 and 1835, and all of which were infested with vermin. As a parting gesture, before demolition the Lewin Street houses were used on the evening of 30 June 1954 in a combined RAF and Civil Defence exercise, in which they were subjected to an 'air raid' by a Canberra bomber from RAF Wittering. Explosive charges were detonated in the properties before Civil Defence and Auxiliary Fire Service crews began their exercise.

It was not long before an amendment was made to the proposals for the multi-storey flats. Towards the end of June 1954 the Chairman of the Slum Clearance Committee made a pronouncement that, for anyone with an eye to the future, was less than inspiring. Housing density was a crucial consideration, and because of the cost of land in the clearance area it would not be possible to rebuild at an occupational density as low as on other housing estates in the city. The density would be set at 95 habitable rooms per acre. (The first was a reference to housing on other estates, which was made up of conventional two-storey homes, and presumably the second would be by the simple expedient of reducing the proposed number of storeys of the blocks of flats). Some 727 dwellings were now to be built in the form of four-storey maisonettes, three-storey flats without lifts, and two-storey houses. Central heating, which had originally been seen as standard, was not now to be included. Having pulled down sub-standard, overcrowded housing, the Council now appeared to be well on track to repeating the mistakes its predecessors had made in the past. By the turn of the next century the estate had become one of the most depressed areas of the inner city.

November 1955, with only Russell Street, Christow Street, Dysart Street and part of Wharf Street left standing, saw the majority of the clearance of the Wharf Street district completed. In a ten-month period 720 premises (446 of which were houses) built between 1828 and 1835 without damp courses or bathrooms, and with shared toilets, had been pulled down, and 1,500 people had been moved out into the various council estates.

However, not all was going well for the City Council. By creating the new St Matthew's estate on the old Wharf Street site the Council would, under the government Housing Subsidies Bill, lose out substantially on grants – plus the fact that building costs were rising. (The name St Matthew's was first suggested much later, in May 1957, when, among other things, it was decided that the estate would be the city's first smokeless zone). The projected rents of £2 2s a week were amended, and a new figure of between £1 17s and £2 10s was deemed more realistic. (The rent paid by the first occupants for a two-bedroom flat was £1 16s.) The overall cost of the scheme, at £2 million, was becoming prohibitive and with the current housing applications list standing at 12,000 the local authority was in a difficult position.

A decision to continue with the programme was reached in late November 1958, when Charles Keene announced that consent had been given for the Slum Clearance Committee to go ahead with the project. Ideas, however, still had not coalesced into a clear vision of how the programme should proceed. Envisaged for the first phase were blocks of three- and four-storey flats, with an option to include others of eleven storeys if plans changed. Already concerns were being expressed over the lack of heating provision in the blocks. The second phase comprised 273 one-bedroom and 26 two-bedroom flats, along with 562 two-bedroom and 70 three-bedroom maisonettes. There was also now a suggestion, based on the need to provide new premises for companies displaced by slum clearances, that a road between Belgrave Gate and Humberstone Gate, following the line along Birstall and Stanley Streets, should form a buffer between the estate and 21 acres of land to be set aside for industrial development.

Whatever the financial reservations expressed by Alderman Keene, work continued and (to the protests of the remaining traders, who claimed that the disruption destroyed what little remained of their businesses) six months later underground cables were laid along Wharf Street itself in preparation for the new GPO telephone exchange that was to be built near to the junction with Humberstone Road.

From a promising start work slowed down. A tender of £1.35 million for work on the new estate (which had increased in value to £1,900 an acre and was now to house 2,500 people) from Sherriff & Co. Ltd, with John Laing & Sons as the sub-contractors, was accepted in March 1957, with a further contract put out to tender for £49,000 to cover the laying down of sewers and roads.

Meanwhile, the process of compulsorily purchasing the remaining properties that needed to be taken down continued; demolition orders were granted in January 1959 on 432 properties in Denmark and Curzon Streets; in July 1960, 352 houses in Willow and Spinner Streets were acquired; in October 1961, 131 properties at the eastern edge of the development were absorbed for building and for the widening of Humberstone Road.

Late 1962 saw a virtual end to the compulsory purchase of properties in what now remained of the district. The last block of orders (the third phase of the programme), relating to 250 properties in Birstall Street, Syston Street, Curzon Street and Cobden Street, was granted at the beginning of October 1962 with the epitaph that 'if these are cleared by 1964, this will end the slum clearance programme for Wharf Street area'. In all, a total of around 3,500 properties were demolished in the programme.

Plans to construct a £3 million industrial estate on the Syston Street/Cobden Street side of the estate near to Humberstone Road were put forward during the summer of 1963. Six months later the developers involved, Percy Bilton Ltd (London), served notice on the City Council of their intention to withdraw from the project on the grounds that it was financially unsound. Undeterred, the Town Planning Committee under the chairmanship of Alderman Kenneth Bowder elected to continue with the venture independently. To be completed in three phases, the project would create a letting area of 86,000sq. ft, and under the committee's latest proposals the entire scheme would cost an estimated £1 million as opposed to an original figure of £3 million. Each phase would take between eight months and two years to develop, the first phase to commence during the next financial year (April 1964). Although it was seen as a means of regenerating firms that had been forced by the slum clearance scheme to relocate, there were those who viewed the project with a jaundiced eye. Among some Council members there was a strong feeling that the properties, the first of which were to be ready for occupation in late 1966, could not be let at a viable rate and the small firms targeted by the scheme would not be able to afford the units.

In July 1963 plans were drawn up for two seventeen-storey tower blocks to be built (Marsden House and Goodwin House) as an extension to the estate. Scheduled for work to begin in March 1965, timed to fit in with the commencement of phase two of the estate, the chosen site was a 25-acre area to the north-east of the main project. Additionally, a shopping centre with underground parking was proposed near to the Humberstone Road/Dysart Street (later rebuilt as Dysart Way) corner.

From the time in 1954 that the initial properties in Lewin Street came under the ball and chain of the demolition teams, twelve years elapsed before the St Matthew's estate was completed and fully occupied in November 1966, allowing the planners to turn their attention to other things.

With the successful completion of St Matthew's estate the City Council continued to build on the same side of the city, utilising the 20-acre site between Coleman Road and Wicklow Drive, near to the General Hospital, to build the Rowlatts Hill estate, into which the first tenants moved at the beginning of 1966.

On Friday 3 July 1964 the *Leicester Mercury* announced that the first compulsory purchase order had been granted in relation to the clearance of properties in the Highfields District in preparation for the building of the St Peter's estate.

Highfields began life in the mid-nineteenth century, and by 1857 the construction of Sparkenhoe Street, running parallel to and just behind London Road, was well under way. The area originally grew up as a prosperous suburb of the old town, housing a professional and middle-class spectrum of the borough's citizens. Some of the municipality's most prestigious establishments were located there. St Peter's Church, after which the new estate was now to be named, appeared near to the corner of St Peter's Road and Gopsall Street in 1879, followed a dozen years later, and a short distance away, in 1891 by the red-brick edifice of Melbourne Hall. Just prior to the turn of the century, in 1898, the synagogue was built in Highfield Street. An earlier and more utilitarian institution, looking out over Swain Street in 1838, was the Union Workhouse, which by the time of the redevelopment scheme was known as Hillcrest Hospital.

Over the years, inevitably, the aspect of the Highfields district changed. During the inter- and postwar years large numbers of the traditionally upper- and middle-class occupants gravitated away to the burgeoning suburbs on the outskirts of the city. The exodus left an assorted concentration of houses to the east of the LMS Railway lines in a compact, 1-mile square of territory within walking distance of the town centre, ripe for the picking. Because of the mixed styles of the dwellings, ranging from the tiny terraced, to the large three-storey house, all were ideally suited for purchase and letting, and in many cases for multiple occupancy. Almost all of them had one thing in common – because of their age they were becoming rundown and cheap to buy. This dubious attribute made them attractive to one of the largest postwar communities in Leicester – the newly arrived immigrant families coming into the city from the Caribbean and the Asian subcontinent. Thus it was that the latest change of the face of Highfields came about and by the early 1960s it was primarily an immigrant area, with many properties in dire need of attention.

The compulsory purchase order granted in July 1964 was for the demolition of N. & F.H. Briggs, Victoria Tannery, at the bottom of Waring Street. The old tannery, founded in 1888 by Francis Bates Briggs, the father of the current owner, occupied 75,000sq. ft of ground and employed 100 people. Its levelling (which due to the size and structure of the place took several weeks) was the first chapter in what became a highly controversial development scheme. A block of Victorian terraced side streets bounded by Oxendon Street, Melbourne Road, Berners Street, Upper Kent Street, Upper Conduit Street and part of Sparkenhoe Street was to be evacuated (in later years the process engendered the more palatable word 'decanted') and a newly conceived housing estate, based on similar principles to the St Matthew's estate was to be built.

Compared to the Wharf Street clearances, this was a relatively simple task, and by the beginning of 1968 the required area, including housing at the junction of Sparkenhoe Street and Upper Conduit Street, had been demolished. To the dismay of the Council, as soon as the ground was cleared its first, uninvited, tenants moved in. In the depths of winter, in January 1968 a large gypsy encampment appeared overnight on the area between Berners Street and Oxendon Street. Occupants of the surrounding housing soon complained of thefts of coal and coke to keep the

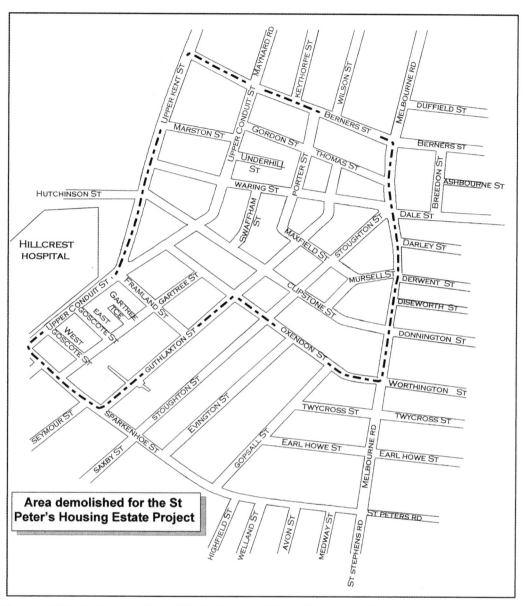

Begun in 1964 with the demolition of Briggs's Tannery on Waring Street, the St Peter's housing estate covered an area between the LMS Railway on one side and Melbourne Road on the other. Many of the old thoroughfares such as Framland and Goscote Streets disappeared only to be resurrected in the names of the multi-storey tower blocks that occupied their sites.

unwelcome squatters' fires burning, and the committee of nearby St Hilda's Church discovered that the pipes in the ladies toilets had been cut into to create access to running water. A swiftly orchestrated operation by the police and local authority officials resulted in the itinerants decamping after a relatively short period of time. The fact that the area was still undergoing a certain amount of tidying up from the demolition doubtless influenced their decision to move on.

The project was originally designated the Highfields North Redevelopment Scheme and a sum of £3.27 million was approved for it by the Ministry of Housing and Local Government. The estate was to comprise a mixture of high- and low-rise tower blocks, along with maisonette-style housing.

Building work, which commenced in February 1967, was to be carried out by the newly created Direct Labour Department, set up by the then Labour-controlled City Council in October 1964, which meant that all planning and building operations would be carried out by a workforce entirely employed and supervised by Council employees and officers. The decision to use this unit on an undertaking of such a scale was not unanimous, and was fiercely contested by the Conservative members of the Council, eventually being carried on a narrow vote of 27–21, and by the time the balance of power in the Council Chamber shifted to the Conservatives in May 1967, there was essentially no turning back. From the outset there were those in the private sector of the construction industry who expressed grave misgivings about the inbuilt potential for failure of the project.

The reservations all too soon proved to be well founded.

Although the construction of the St Peter's housing estate using the Council's own direct labour unit was controversial, the majority of the work was eventually completed by Wimpey and occupation began in May 1973. (Courtesy: Urban Design Group, Leicester City Council)

It was the brave new era of architects and designers, allegedly revolutionising housing concepts with the conviction that the best way to build was upwards, a philosophy underwritten by the fact that the Local Housing Act of 1956 ensured that the government paid a subsidy on each additional floor of housing properties that exceeded five storeys. Leicester City Council was not alone in its desperation to accommodate as many people as possible on the limited amounts of space available, when it embraced the notion of erecting high-rise flats in seventeen- and eighteen-storey tower blocks; local authorities all over Britain were doing the same.

With stunned disbelief, those involved in the provision of inner city housing across the country learned in May 1968 of the Ronan Point disaster. Standing 200ft high, Ronan Point was a newly built high-rise block of council flats in east London. On 16 May a tenant, Mrs Ivy Hodge, struck a match to light her gas cooker. The cooker was faulty, and the resulting explosion blew out the precast concrete panels of the building's outer wall, resulting in the collapse of the entire side of the block of 110 flats. Miraculously, Mrs Hodge survived, but four other people died in the disaster. The result of the incident was to place a huge question mark over the constructional safety of tower blocks.

Local authorities all over the country now had to reconsider their position in relation to this type of building. The use of precast concrete panels made building work extremely fast, but along with this now came the realisation that their use was also highly specialised.

On a local level disquiet was already being expressed concerning the way in which the St Peter's project was progressing. In July 1968 the Town Clerk, Robert Thornton, submitted a report to the Council voicing his reservations about the project. On 25 August 1969 when members of the Progress Committee, visited the site, they were appalled at the lack of progress and the poor standard of work-manship. (As its name suggested, the Progress Committee had been set up to monitor the progress of the building work; it included the Chairman and Vice-Chairman of the General Purposes Committee, who had responsibility for the management of the Direct Labour Department; members of the Housing Committee, on whose authority the estate was being built; and representatives of the Finance Committee who were responsible for the ongoing funding.)

That things were going decidedly badly was obvious. Budgeted initially at just over £4 million, the project was now standing at £5.94 million, almost 50 per cent over budget. A meeting of the General Purposes Committee was held on 8 September and three days later the Town Clerk went to meet government representatives at the Ministry of Housing and Local Government, where it was agreed that the Minister's personal adviser on housing, Mr Pymont (on secondment to the Ministry from John Laing's) would inspect the site, which he did on Friday 12 September.

Pymont's report was particularly damning. He was seriously concerned about a figure of £791,000 in the Direct Labour Department's estimate for strengthening of the tower blocks. He expressed the opinion that the organisational and management structures in place for the project were inadequate. While satisfied with the quality of workmanship on the low-rise blocks, he was perturbed generally by the enormous backlog of work and the sums of money required to remedy defects.

As a result of his report a memorandum was received by the City Council to the effect that 'the Ministry think it is a prudent course to seek independent advice by considering engaging a team of quantity surveyors to value and appraise the work completed to date, and in conjunction with our own professional auditors assess the financial position . . .'. The letter also recommended that the Council's own auditors make a similar examination of spending levels, and that the Direct Labour Department's activities be restricted to working on the low-rise blocks, where work above the foundations had already begun.

A worried General Purposes Committee under the Chairmanship of Councillor Bernard Toft realised the need to take action. The committee decided to bring in consultants to examine the situation, and while allowing work to continue on the low-rise sections, stopped all work on the high-rise blocks.

With what can only be described as much wringing of hands, the Town Clerk made the following statement in support of the Committee's actions:

> [it has been] a classic recipe for potential failure and a considerable act of faith would be required to believe it can succeed . . .

1. The original scheme was one of great magnitude, far in excess of anything previously undertaken by the Direct Labour Building Organisation . . . the architectural design made it impossible to phase the work, it was all or nothing . . . the method of construction, battery casting based on a rig invented by the Building Research Station had had only limited field trials and required to be developed. There was not in existence at the time a tried organisation supported by a system of cost control; in short, here was a classic recipe for potential failure and it could need something really exceptional to achieve success. The structural system employed on the St Peter's project utilised precast wall and floor panels, not blocks. (Smooth-sided on the internal face to receive a minimal finish, the panels were made on-site in batches, positioned side by side similar to the cells in a car battery – hence the name).

2. The cost of developing the system proved to be unexpectedly expensive. £50,000 was spent that was not in the estimate.

3. Constructional design has been extremely complicated and intricate, and this must be mitigated against high productivity which is dependent on simplicity.

4. Refinements intended to produce a richer architectural environment and to simplify fitting out later were introduced, the cost of which – still not quantified – cannot be carried out by 'contract' as had been envisaged.

5. Just at the time when the City Architect might have been expected to surmount his difficulties there came the problems of strengthening the joints in a way never anticipated. I cannot over emphasise the magnitude of those problems, but it will perhaps serve to illustrate it if I say that as recently as the end of June [1969], I was in grave doubt whether the problems were capable of solution at all, I am now assured, as I have said, that a solution will be forthcoming.

6. Much greater productivity must be achieved if the revised completion date of December 1971 for the low rise element is to be met. The position in regard to high rise and single person projects is even more uncertain. . . .

The assertion that the project was 'far in excess of anything previously undertaken by the Direct Labour Building Organisation' was something of an understatement. It was in fact the 'first, the last and the only' major project ever undertaken by them. The consultants, John Laing & Co. (themselves major contractors), whose role was to report back to the Ministry of Housing and Local Government, were deeply concerned over the quality of the work carried out. As a result of their inspection of the site on Friday 12 September, less than two weeks later on 22 September all work was halted, and the Town Clerk was instructed to begin negotiations with outside contractors for the completion of the job.

At a full Council meeting held the same night, a Special Committee under the Chairmanship of Alderman Kenneth Bowder was set up and given powers to appoint an independent architect, engage independent quantity surveyors, and arrange for the Council's accountants to examine and audit the project's accounts.

The Special Committee moved quickly and within four days 100 of the 120 workforce had been summarily dismissed, 13 of the 43 clerks, estimators and technical assistants were given a month's notice, and contracts with 100 suppliers of materials were cancelled. The firm of Pick, Everard & Kay was appointed as architects. This was followed four days later by the appointment of a company of independent quantity surveyors, Kenchington, Little & Partners, with a brief to measure up work already done and price the remaining work so as to establish the true financial situation.

That the project had become so sadly muddled, and consequently was allowed to deteriorate to the extent that it did, is a sad indictment of those involved. For the General Purposes Committee, Councillor Toft made the pronouncement that 'had any member of this Council been aware that a relatively untried system of building was to be used on St Peter's Redevelopment – a contract of £3 million – then the Direct Labour Organisation would never have been considered'. As was to be expected, recriminations and self-justification abounded. On behalf of his committee Councillor Toft offered the explanation that

> the City Council's Architect's Department has been concerned with new trends in building for the last ten years, but this new form of battery casting was a relatively untried system of building. . . . The Building Research Station [a department of the Ministry of Public Building and Works], who offered so much assistance and advice were relatively behind in experience and they profited by our mistakes. . . . That this Corporation has been used as a guinea pig in this project to gain experience for the future cannot be denied.

In fairness to the City Architect, Stephen George, he had made a complaint in July 1968 to the General Purposes Committee, which was later published in the *Leicester Mercury* (23 September 1969):

> the site is in a position to open out an erection of dwellings and move rapidly, provided that I can appoint staff and pay an acceptable bonus. The central problems, both of the site and of the organisation of labour are contained in these two matters which are not in my control. The situation is paradoxical to say the least. I am authorised to run a contract of over £3 million; I am

allowed to recruit as much labour as I require; I can within the contract sum buy or hire such plant as I see fit; I can purchase supplies and place sub-contracts where I consider it to be appropriate. But I have no power to appoint staff to control this vast expenditure, nor am I free in the matter of organisation of a bonus system; yet I have to compete for staff and labour in a sphere where no such bureaucratic control exists. . . .

Six months later, in January 1969, a cost accountant was engaged, with a brief to bring the accounts up to date. A bonus scheme was also introduced. It availed Stephen George little. Having joined the staff of the City Council as Deputy Architect in 1958, in which role he remained until becoming City Architect in 1963 on the retirement of his predecessor, J.H. Lloyd Owen, his position was no longer seen as tenable, and in March 1970 he resigned his post and left.

On 15 November 1969 the Special Committee concluded the first part of its brief by laying out the revised plans for the future of the St Peter's programme.

1. The proposed seven tower blocks would be reduced in height from twenty storeys to fourteen, with six flats per floor instead of three.
2. Two of the low-rise blocks would be demolished, owing to structural inadequacies. Completion of the ten shells of low-rise flats (each containing six units) which were in various stages of readiness would be handed on to local firms. There remained in the scheme another forty-six blocks of low-rise flats, some at foundation level, some not yet started. The construction of these would be left to the high-rise contractor, who had the right to change their style to either maisonettes or houses.
3. The walkway system, 85 per cent of which was yet to be started, would be discontinued. The completed section would be used as an operations centre for the Ministry of Housing Project Single Persons Tower Block.
4. Three contractors of prefabricated buildings: Geo. Wimpey Ltd, Concrete Ltd and John Laing Construction Ltd, were invited to submit tenders by April 1970 for completing the project.
5. Existing plant on the site was to be removed:
   Two of the three cranes, which had cost £28,000, would be advertised for sale;
   The third and largest crane, costing £40,000, would be kept in reserve until the appointed contractor indicated whether or not he wished to purchase it;
   The battery casting plant would be disposed of.
   The aspect of the estate could not be changed because most of the footings, sewers, and district heating systems were already in place.

With the assistance of the recently appointed consultant architect Hugh Smith and the quantity surveyor David Cox, the plans of the St Peter's Special Committee were concluded, and contracts arranged by the end of May 1970. The chief issue, that of finding a major contractor who was prepared to remedy the situation, was resolved when Geo. Wimpey Ltd agreed to complete the work for £3.24 million.

At a special meeting of the City Council on Wednesday 27 May, Alderman Kenneth Bowder set out the costs to the ratepayers. In January 1967 the projected cost of work to be carried out by the Direct Labour Department had amounted to £4.15 million. (In fact, when first approved by the Ministry of Housing in December 1966, as the Highfields North Re-Development Scheme, it had been costed at £3.27 million.) The new capital expenditure was now £5.9 million – a difference of £1.75 million. Kenneth Bowder made the point that 'had they [the Council members] been accurately informed of the price in January 1967 and then taken into account the effects of Selective Employment Tax, which was introduced that year, very probably the cost of the scheme would have come to within about a quarter of a million of the £5.906 million before the Council that evening . . .'.

Wimpey's projections were that, provided central government funding could be restored, it would be possible to restart work in a matter of weeks, during July, in which case the estate could be completed in two years, with some homes being ready for occupation in about six months.

The overall strategy now was for the estate to be larger than previously planned and to have only four tower blocks instead of seven. The height of these was still under discussion and it was possible that the original twenty-storey model would be retained for three of them and a twelve-storey structure be adopted for the fourth. Alternatively (as eventually happened), all four would be built to seventeen or eighteen storeys. The maisonettes would be four floors high, containing two- and three-bedroom flats, each of two floors. Altogether it was planned to build 254 three-bedroom, 190 two-bedroom, and 348 single-roomed maisonettes. It was intended with the combined building styles to provide 876 homes on the estate. A two-bedroom flat would be rented out at between £3 10s and £3 12s 6d a week.

Significantly, the Wimpey scheme was to be referred to as 'St Peter's Phase Two', and was entirely divorced from the building area started by Direct Labour, which was now scheduled for completion under private contract. For its part, Wimpey would take into account foundations, roads and services already laid, and merge its work in. Garages for 627 cars would be built around the perimeter and, in deference to the Ronan Point disaster, the entire development would use electricity rather than gas.

Unfortunately, Leicester City Council's difficulties (and continuing embarrassment) were not over. The Wimpey design team, under the company's design engineer, Lionel Roberts – already perturbed at the pre-tender stage by the quality of work achieved in relation to the monies spent – was now presented with a further major problem.

Following discussions with the consultant engineers, a decision was taken to run tests on the piled foundations for the twelve-storey block (designated E7) installed by an outside contractor, and on which Wimpey was due to work. The results caused it to reassess the quality of the workmanship it had inherited, and threw yet another shadow over the project.

The base area of E7 was approximately 90ft by 50ft and consisted of a 4ft thick concrete cap supported by 128 piles driven into the ground. According to the installation records, these piles penetrated the keuper marl, a hard, stiff, brown clay found in the Midlands. A series of tests was devised whereby one pile at each face of the foundation slab was exposed by excavating a hole; the top of the pile was then carefully removed in order that the length of the pile could be measured. Of the four piles measured, only one was satisfactory. The remaining three showed that settlement of four times the acceptable tolerance had occurred under working load. (The tolerance was ½in, and in fact they had settled 2in.) As a result, the full length of each pile was exposed and it was found that although the installation records indicated them to be between 18 and 19ft in length, one measured just under 17ft and the remainder less than 11ft. The three shorter ones, instead of penetrating into the clay level, were resting on top of it.

Wimpey's opening work was quickly re-scheduled, and it began to construct another high-rise foundation of its own nearby, on what should have been the site of a low-rise development, while the City Council entered into a dispute with the contractors responsible for the installation of the faulty piles.

With the foundation slab already in place, it was not practicable to conduct further tests on the piling, and the matter was allowed to fade into history along with the many other mistakes that had blighted the project's early history. Although E7 was not suitable for high-rise building work, it was totally safe for other aspects of construction and it was decided to erect a low-rise block on the site.

Thereafter work on the estate progressed apace and eventually four tower blocks, each named after one of the old streets buried beneath them – Framland, Goscote, Maxfield and Gordon Houses – were completed, along with the planned low-rise sections. They were occupied by early 1973.

Wharf Street and the Highfields developments, while being the largest individual areas to be cleared in the name of progress, were by no means the only ones. Across the city, houses, shops and factories were cleared at an alarming rate, often coinciding nicely with the construction of a new road system or other strategy. It was not until the beginning of 1976 that the process was finally halted. In January of that year an objection to the granting of demolition orders on fifty-eight houses in Leire Street was lodged by the Leicester branch of Shelter, the charity working for the homeless, on the grounds that during the previous five years, with 12,500 families waiting for homes, Leicester Corporation had pulled down 4,000 old houses and built only 3,000 new ones. On 15 April 1976 the Revd Kenneth Middleton, Labour leader of the City Council, announced that from then on houses would be renovated, not demolished – a move that was viewed by many of the members sitting on the opposite side of the Chamber as somewhat ironic, as twenty-two years earlier, in February 1954, a Conservative motion proposing the renovation rather than the demolition of repairable properties that had sewers and amenities already in place, had been defeated.

CHAPTER FIVE

Traffic Development Plans

It was inevitable that, postwar, there would be an urgent need to review the traffic situation in Leicester. An integral part of John Beckett's 'Fifty Year Plan' was the construction of three concentric ring roads radiating out from the centre of Leicester, with the main highways leading into and out of the city linking up to them. Sadly, while the building of this road system was inevitable if the city were to cope with the envisaged increase in vehicular traffic, the innermost of these roads created irreparable damage to Leicester's oldest and most historic district, around Oxford Street and Southgate Street. Some of the town's ancient buildings were lost when massive demolition was needed to facilitate the construction of the Southgates underpass and St Nicholas Circle.

In the middle and late 1950s the first steps were taken by the Highways Committee to improve the layout of the city's roads. In the summer of 1957 work commenced on the stretch from Burley's Lane to Great Central Street, 75 per cent of the £116,700 cost being absorbed by the Ministry of Transport.

In January 1959 approval was sought for the first 6-mile section of the outer ring road. The road was planned to run from the city boundary at Stoughton Lane, east of Evington, and cut across Spencefield Lane, on to St Denys Road and Colchester Road, then pass east of Humberstone village, across Abbott's Road and Steins Lane. From here it would continue to Thurmaston Lane and across Barkby Road to Melton Road and Loughborough Road, finishing at Red Hill Island. The expenditure would be heavily subsidised by central government, which would pay £650,000 of the £893,000 bill.

A catalyst for the completion of an adequate outer ring road was the fact that Britain was moving into the era of the motorway. If, as expected, the city was to find itself sitting midway along the country's newest main arterial route between London and Yorkshire, the volume of traffic accessing the motorway through Leicestershire, especially from the east coast and the Fens, would escalate rapidly.

Apart from the fact that the M1, as it was designated, was destined to influence the traffic flow through Leicester city and county, its actual route through the county became the subject of much discussion. Petitions were raised decrying the possibility that the road would pass through Charnwood Forest, and landowners protested over its incursion into their property. Work began south of Leicester, at Dunchurch, in May 1959. The Ministry of Transport, having rejected an alternative route proposed by the County Council, made the firm declaration that it would be routed northwards a few miles to the west of Leicester city and, passing near Markfield, continue to the Nottinghamshire border. The consulting engineers, Sir Owen Williams & Partners, proposed to start work on the 37½ miles of the Leicester section, at a cost of £200,000 per mile, during 1962–3.

George Wimpey & Co. commenced work on the first phase of the motorway to enter Leicestershire in August 1962, and work progressed quickly. As the engineers

As housing was redeveloped and new road systems were laid down, so many old-established business premises disappeared. One such was T.H. Wadsworth's, ironmongers, in Northgate Street. Seen here are the proprietor Thomas Wadsworth with son Tommy. The shop later achieved city-wide renown as Tommy Wadsworth's fishing tackle shop. Thomas Wadsworth's grandson Tony later became a well-known presenter on Radio Leicester. *(Courtesy: T. Wadsworth)*

moved north, past the site of the proposed Leicester Forest East Service Area, construction at Lockington, near to Loughborough, was halted for a day by an unexpected problem, the discovery of an unexploded wartime bomb. On a cold winter's morning in February 1964 the driver of an earthmover, unwittingly working on top of the 100lb bomb, put a deep scratch in its casing before the true nature of the object was realised. A local farmer identified it as one of a stick of five that had been dropped by a German bomber, of which only three had exploded, and the bomb, which was fitted with a 'tuning fork' detonator, was defused the following afternoon by an army bomb-disposal team from Horsham.

The first traffic to use the new Leicestershire section of the motorway, led by two white County Police Jaguar patrol cars, travelled from Misterton to Crick at 7.30 a.m., on Thursday 1 October 1964 for the official opening of the £5 million section. Three months later, on 23 January 1965, snow ploughs cleared the next 18½-mile stretch between Misterton and Markfield in readiness for the Ministry of Transport representative, Tom Fraser, to open it at 2.30 p.m. (The motorway project had begun while Ernest Marples was Minister for Transport.) Construction of the section passing through Leicester was completed when the last 11-mile stretch, which had required the removal of 7 million tons of earth and rock, came into use on Friday 3 December 1965.

One final phase – a £600,000 service area – needed to be completed before the entire project could be signed off. Leicester Forest East services, with a commercial drivers' café on either side of the motorway, a cafeteria area for general use and a bridge-top restaurant – 'The Captain's Table' – opened for business at midnight on St Valentine's Day, 14 February 1966. The first private car driver to be served, a Leicester man, Andrew Thorp, was presented with a £25 voucher for a meal at the services, valid every year on 15 February for the next 25 years. The first lorry driver, Derek Lashbrook from Greenwich in London, received an identical voucher.

This 1955 picture of the High Street bus stand shows a much slower pace of life. There is very little traffic, and no yellow lines. The bus, fleet No. 158, has its entrance at the rear, denoting a double crew of driver and conductor. Seen boarding are Ernst Silla (who came to England from Estonia after the war as a European Volunteer Worker) with his daughter Margrid (right) and the daughter of a family friend. *(Courtesy: M. Ford)*

With the tramlines removed and vehicles parked along the side of the road outside Lloyds Bank, the High Street in the early 1950s was a much quieter road than in later years. *(Courtesy: Midlands Co-operative Society)*

Work on digging out the Southgates Underpass, 1,150ft long, was begun in August 1966 and the completed tunnel was opened to traffic by the Lord Mayor, Alderman Sir Mark Henig, on 2 May 1968. *(Courtesy: E. Selvidge)*

The year 1960 saw the beginning of work on John Beckett's master plan to lay down a ring road system. Beckett envisaged that the outer road would follow the city boundary. In the south, at Welford Road, it would link the A50 with the A426 Lutterworth Road, then continue in a clockwise direction over Narborough Road (A46 south), the A47 westbound at Hinckley Road, to the A50 at Groby Road, before swinging back southwards over the A47 east coast route and the A6 at London Road, rejoining the A50 to complete the circle.

The inner ring road would run from London Road to Uppingham Road before swinging across to Melton Road, then join Abbey Lane, and turn back along Henley Road and Fullhurst Avenue. Passing the new prefabricated housing on Hughendon Drive, the line would continue along Knighton Lane to rejoin London Road.

The innermost of the three, the central ring road, was designed to allow vehicles to circumnavigate the city centre. In Beckett's own words in 1944, this would take motorists along

Oxford Street to the Magazine, [the] archway with surrounding buildings removed will stand as an island to divide traffic. Next island – straight road from West Bridge presents a tree surrounded vista of the Old Guildhall and Cathedral. Next island, point where a curved road from Upper Churchgate goes across to the Great Central Station. Near to the island is suggested a Central Baths site, omnibus station and car park. Next island, Churchgate reaches the Ring Road at this point, south of St Margaret's Church. An extended Churchgate will cross St Margaret's Pasture, skirt Abbey Park and join Abbey Lane near to Grundon Street. Thence the road cuts across old or partially cleared property passing the west end of Christ Church to the crossing of a widened Humberstone Gate near to Nichols Street. On the way down to the island at the junction of Granby Street where Charles Street now emerges, will be a small island marking the spot where it is suggested a road should be taken across the railway to join up with Clipstone Street. The road now completes the circle by skirting the museum grounds and Holy Trinity Church to the island near the Infirmary.

Beckett's detailed description of the route does not include what came to be the cause of the destruction of one of the city's most historic suburbs – the Southgates underpass. This commenced near to the junction of Castle Street, was tunnelled under the soon-to-be-created St Nicholas Circle, and emerged into what would become Vaughan Way. A host of ancient buildings, including premises such as the Blue Boar Inn that stood in Southgate Street, were destroyed during the excavation. The original Blue Boar, which dated back to the Middle Ages, was said to have been where Richard III spent his last night before the Battle of Bosworth, and although it was demolished in 1838, another tavern had been built on the site, which in itself was of historical importance.

Historian Jack Simmons later commented bitterly in respect of the refurbishment in the city centre:

> In the course of the last fifteen years – no more – the Old Town of Leicester has been almost entirely destroyed. In the late 1950s its medieval street plan was clearly visible, and it was dominated by the industrial buildings that summarised and embodied the town's Victorian prosperity. Now nearly all this has gone: not merely the streets but their very names – Applegate Street, Blue Boar Lane, Bakehouse Lane, Red Cross Street; and almost all the chief commercial buildings, notably Everard's Brewery at the top of Castle Street, and Preston's boot factory with its double-curved front, in Bakehouse Lane. In their place we have a huge swathe of concrete, taking the traffic through the city north and south, with windy and desolate stretches, of concrete again, on either side of it. . . .

The Blue Boar was not the only licensed premises in Southgate Street to come under the contractors' hammer. Two other public houses, Everard's the Golden Lion and the old Shakespeare's Head belonging to Shipstone's Brewery, were lost at the end of June 1962. The licence for the Shakespeare's Head was transferred to a newly built premises of the same name overlooking the underpass, the Council paying £8,450 towards the relocation costs. Work began in the summer of the same year on the section of road running from Great Central Street to St Nicholas Street, and thence on to the Newarke. Linking into the new approach road that connected to West Bridge, this phase cost £1.08 million. Excavation work on the 1,150ft-long underpass section was commenced in the middle of August 1966.

In November 1964 Konrad Smigielski's Planning Department published the Leicester Traffic Plan, which made three assumptions. First, that the traffic strategies for the city needed to be based on long-term projections – it predicted that by 1995 there would be 1.2 cars per family in Leicester, a fourfold increase over current levels. Second, that the population would increase over that period from 285,000 to about 340,000. Third, that there was a conflict between the use of land as traffic generators (roads) and the available traffic accommodation (car parks). The conclusion was that Leicester should be the first city in the kingdom to say 'No' to the motorcar. The recommendations of the report were firmly in favour of what it called an 'Integrated Transport System', based upon an elevated inner motorway and interchange car parks, improved road networking and, crucially, changes in public transport which included a prohibitively expensive monorail system. Without the elevated motorway and monorail, more conventional solutions needed to be considered.

One component of the traffic-flow programme was to be the introduction of a one-way system on the feeder roads into and out of the underpass area on the south side. On Sunday 8 May 1966 the former network of two-way roads became a one-way system. Beginning at the Magazine Arch, traffic now flowed in a giant circle up Newarke Street, along Welford Road, to Granby Halls, from where it could either break out of the loop and travel up Welford Road towards the cemetery and away from the city, or continue round and back along Oxford Street. Side roads feeding into the system, such as Regent Road, Carlton Street and the lower part of Lancaster Road also became one-way streets.

This system was extended four years later by the inclusion of an additional road, Almond Way, which cut through from Welford Road just below the cemetery along the line of the Cattle Market, to Aylestone Road near to Brazil Street, thus extending the loop further.

Almost nine years elapsed from the commencement of work on the inner-city ring road at the beginning of 1960 until the opening of Southgates Underpass to traffic on Thursday 2 May 1968 by the Lord Mayor, Alderman Sir Mark Henig.

New plans to alleviate congestion on completion of the St Margaret's Way stretch of the ring road were submitted by the Leicester Traffic Committee in September 1970. After deduction of grants from the £2.58 million expenditure, the cost of this phase to the Leicester ratepayers was £728,000. In addition to the flyover at the junction of Burley's Way and Belgrave Gate, a second one was proposed for the intersection at St Margaret's Way and Vaughan Way. Sanvey Gate was to be widened at its junction with Churchgate, to form the first part of the new St Margaret's Way, and a new road laid down to link East Bond Street with Churchgate.

The development of St Margaret's Way involved a final spate of demolition work in the area of Heanor and Friday Streets – while the housing and other properties, such as the Heanor Boat public house, were pulled down, street names were retained and land that was not affected by the new roadway was redeveloped. The £2.58 million scheme was completed in September 1970.

As part of the Leicester Traffic Plan, the City Council gave approval in February 1967 for another £30 million road programme, spanning the next twenty years. Costing £1.5 million, it would be implemented in two stages, beginning in 1971. The first stage, costing £750,000 (of which central government would pay £563,000), was intended to alleviate the bottleneck at the West Bridge entry to and exit from the town.

It was proposed to realign Hinckley Road, cutting across a mass of streets from Fosse Road Central and bypassing Braunstone Gate, with smaller roads leading off to King Richard's Road. The new section of Hinckley Road was to pass over the junction of Fosse Road Central, cross the adjacent side streets and emerge near to Western Boulevard before swinging away alongside the railway line in the direction of Dun's Lane and West Bridge. A spur from the new Hinckley Road, leading to King Richard's Road and thence to Groby Road, would effectively link the A50 north directly to the town centre via the 'West Bridge Motorway', scheduled for the 1970–8 phase.

Along with the widening of West Bridge from its current 30ft width into a five-lane carriageway, a gyratory system (which created St Nicholas Circle) affecting St Augustine Street, Applegate, St Nicholas Street, Highcross Street and Redcross Street came into being on Sunday 7 January 1968.

The second stage was intended to deal with the ingress and egress of city traffic along Belgrave Road. Once more heavily subsidised (£600,000 of an estimated £800,000 bill was to be met from government funds, the eventual cost rising to £2 million), the junction of Abbey Park Road and Belgrave Road was to be replaced with a flyover (as had been agreed in 1962). A dual carriageway, to be known as the St Matthew's Peripheral Road, was to carry traffic between the A47 Humberstone Road and the A46 Belgrave Road, emerging at a 200ft traffic island between Birstall and Syston Streets. (Initially the idea of including an underpass and creating, with the flyover, three levels of traffic, was examined, but it was not adopted. This may have been because it would have been necessary to include a large culvert under the structure to carry storm water and water from the Willow Brook.)

Work on the flyover and island began in late summer of 1973. In June 1975 the £2 million link road, stretching from Burley's Way, across Belgrave Gate, to Humberstone Road completed the project.

The Traffic Development Scheme heralded the demise of the familiar figure of the policeman on point duty. Historically, since the early years of the twentieth century, working a 'traffic point' had been part of a constable's daily routine. The term derived from the fact that in the early days of the electric tramcar, policemen directing traffic often stood on the rails and points in the middle of the road, and had to stand aside from the 'points' to allow tramcars to pass. In the years between the wars a squad of City officers, wearing distinctive white helmets, was formed, whose sole task was to regulate traffic. The new one-way and gyratory systems at a stroke rendered this function obsolete, releasing a large number of men for other duties.

One of the less-successful inner-city schemes (along with the monorail project) was an abortive project to build an inner-city motorway stretching 3 miles from Melton Road to London Road.

In October 1969 the City Council gave its approval for initiation of the project, which had first been discussed in 1964. Included in the Ministry of Transport Programme for the years 1970–8, the scheme, which entailed the demolition of eight blocks of newly built flats on the St Matthew's estate and numerous other properties along the proposed route, bore all the hallmarks of the head of the Town Planning Department, Konrad Smigielski. The twin three-lane carriageways of the 'Eastern Motorway' would cut a swathe across the St Matthew's estate and through the Highfields district to its destination near to Mayfield Road and would require fifteen years to complete.

Also affected by this project would be the new St Mark's housing estate that was to be built on ground enclosed by Belgrave Road, Dysart Way, Birstall Street and Catherine Street. The City Architect's Department had already announced that an outline scheme for the estate, with 420 dwellings and parking provision for 360 cars, could start during 1970, with a completion date of 1973. Occupying 25½ acres, 14½ of which were to be housing, the estate was to have an occupancy figure of 111 people per acre. Some 30 per cent of housing was to be made up of two-bedroom dwellings, 30 per cent three-bedroom, and 40 per cent one-bedroom. All of the family housing would be at ground-floor level, with the remainder in three-storey blocks.

Integrating the plans for the new estate and the motorway was once more either challenging or extravagant, depending upon the viewpoint. Although it was not anticipated that the motorway would become a reality for another fifteen years, design work to accommodate it would be in place from the outset. The Housing Committee's plan was that 'seven lifts will be positioned at strategic points throughout the three storey estate and the blocks of one, two, and three-bedroom dwellings will be connected by centrally heated, elevated corridors . . . in order to combat noise from the motorway high tree studded, landscaped earth embankments will be thrown up to flank the motorway . . .'. Additionally, a pedestrian bridge would enable residents to cross over the motorway from one side of the estate to the other.

Still pursuing Smigielski's monorail dream of interchange car parks feeding an inner-city highway, a suggestion was also submitted that a car park for residents and users of the motorway should be sited at the old Great Northern Railway station.

Opposition from those affected by the scheme was swift and vociferous. At one end, the St Matthew's Community Association enlisted the support of the Leicester North West MP, Sir Barnett Janner; at the other end, organised by the Revd J.W. Josephs, the vicar of St James the Greater Church (situated at the exact point on London Road where the motorway would emerge), a 28,000-signature petition was raised in 1972. Constant efforts by the groups fighting the scheme resulted, in July 1973, in the government agreeing to an official inquiry being convened for April the following year.

In the event, matters did not reach that stage. By the beginning of the year pressure on the Council was becoming intense, because, even with no clear mandate to complete the project, in preparation for putting the road through they had already acquired 169 properties along the route by means of compulsory purchase orders. The consequent loss of business to shops and firms, and the hardship caused to dispossessed householders, created much bad feeling – especially when it was realised, with the growing prospect of the road project failing, that the properties would not be used for the intended purpose. The Council countered by announcing that unexecuted compulsory purchase orders would be allowed to lapse, and that where property had already been acquired it would either be held for highway purposes or be let. In April 1974 the Council declared that, for financial reasons, the Eastern Ring Road Project was to be abandoned as impracticable.

Equally thorny as the problem of traffic flow into and out of the city, was that of what to do about parking of vehicles once they were actually in the town centre.

During 1935–6 a system of 'waiting regulations' was implemented along certain streets to deal with what was, at the time, considered to be major congestion. Although by later standards the amount of traffic was not then substantial, the passage of tramcars down the centre of main roads such as Gallowtree Gate and High Street, combined with vehicles parking outside the shops, often led to disruption. Also, until after the Second World War, horse-drawn delivery vans were still common in the city centre. The enforcement and effectiveness of the regulations was poor, and in the long term made little difference to the situation.

So far as the local authority was concerned, off-street parking was a mixed blessing in the immediate postwar years. Bombed sites, hastily filled over with rubble, and demolition sites still awaiting redevelopment under the slum clearance projects, provided a useful if unsightly short-term solution. In 1949 one such place where the motorist could leave his car for 1s a day was the Lee Street car park. An open area of rough land providing parking for 1,200 vehicles and flanked on one side by Wharf Street and on the other by Humberstone Gate, it was encircled by a band of concrete and in the middle of it stood a small block of single-storey buildings that housed the wartime British Restaurant.

In October 1959, in another of its by now familiar ten-year plans, the Corporation, this time under the auspices of a Special Traffic Committee chaired by Alderman Mark Henig, set out a series of proposals for the future of Leicester city and the motorcar. Once again, some of these came to pass and some did not.

The committee began by outlining that there was a ratio of one motorcar to every three and a half families in the city and that the question of parking should be addressed by the development of multi-storey car parks, the construction of street-level car parking on giant ring-road traffic islands and the installation on city streets of parking meters, government approval for which had already been sought.

Suitable sites for the multi-storey car parks had been examined by the City Surveyor and were now under discussion. The options centred on five sites. The largest was in Lee Street, with a capacity for 1,080 vehicles, followed by St Peter's Lane, which could hold 1,070. Next was Dover Street where a 1,030-capacity car park could be built on bombed ground; next came a site at Magazine Square that could hold 740 vehicles, and finally came King Street where the capacity was still to be decided. Ring road island parking sites were suggested at the Welford Road/Carlton Street junction and in the Newarkes. The Newarkes scheme would hold 350 cars while the anticipated number at Carlton Street was 560. The entire plan for all of the venues would cost £3.9 million.

Two further suggested locations were never pursued. One was a platform car park over the market place at a cost of £¼ million and, more significantly, involving the loss of 82 market stalls. The second was an underground scheme in Town Hall Square, which at a cost of approximately £102,000, would have accommodated the relatively small number of 100 cars.

In March 1960 plans for a six-tier car park in what was to become Lee Circle were submitted by Fitzroy Robinson & Partners of London, the consultant architects of a consortium that was building a multi-storey car park in Bristol. The plans were accepted and work began in early 1961. An addition to the original proposal was the construction at ground-floor level, beneath the car park, of a thirty-six-lane American-style bowling alley for Associated British Cinemas, to be

The City Council decided in the early 1960s to build multi-storey car parks in the centre of the town to alleviate traffic congestion. Built in 1961, Lee Circle was the first of these. *(Courtesy: Urban Design Group, Leicester City Council)*

Complete with a Tesco shopping centre and an American-style bowling alley, Lee Circle multi-storey car park, built at a cost of £750,000, opened in December 1961. Capable of accommodating 1,050 cars, its charges were 6d an hour for a minimum of two hours.

Apart from a few cars on the first deck, the car park is virtually empty while what is left of the old Corporation car park in the foreground is full. Note the banner along the fourth-floor wall which reads 'AUTO MAGIC SHOPPING PARK'. *(Courtesy: Urban Design Group, Leicester City Council)*

Built after Lee Circle and Abbey Street car parks, St Peter's was the third of the city's multi-storeys. Seen in the background is the old Fielding Johnson Mill, which was demolished as part of the Shires shopping centre complex. St Peter's car park was pulled down in 2006 as part of the John Lewis development of the Shires shopping centre. *(Courtesy: Urban Design Group, Leicester City Council)*

opened at Christmas. Both the bowling alley and the multi-storey car park were completed on time and opened on Tuesday 12 December 1961. The structure provided parking for 1,050 cars at *6d* an hour (minimum of two hours) and was built at a cost of £750,000. A short time later the company announced its intention to invest in a further parking facility in Abbey Street. This development, when completed, housed the Abbey Motor Hotel.

Enthusiastic over the success of the Lee Circle venture, City Engineer and Surveyor, John Beckett, announced that his department was negotiating to build two more car parks, one at the junction of Wellington Street and Dover Street (no doubt intended to service the Albion Hill Civic Centre, which was never built) and another, as previously planned, on St Peter's Lane.

There now came a significant blip on the radar screen of the Council's parking strategy, with the arrival of new Chief Constable of Leicester City Police, Robert Mark.

Robert Mark came to Leicester in January 1957 from his home city of Manchester, where, except for the war years, he had been a police officer since 1937. The Watch Committee and in turn the City Council during his predecessor Oswald John Buxton Cole's term in office, had an extremely easy time – Cole worked for them. Compliant with their wishes and directives, for the past quarter of a century Cole had been an able and 'steady' Chief Officer, whom Mark, in his autobiography, described as 'a fine old man and a very nice person'. They were in for something of a shock with the new Chief Constable.

Once he had settled in, Mark began a long overdue review of the organisation, something that the Watch Committee applauded. He emerged as a man of ideas, intelligence and a strong will, which was not necessarily to their advantage. After leaving Leicester in 1967, he was to become, next to its founder Sir Robert Peel, the most famous Commissioner ever to rule over the Metropolitan Police Force.

Concerning the matter of parking in Leicester's streets Robert Mark had rather strict views (strangely, when he arrived in Leicester he could not drive, and he only passed his test shortly after taking office). An early scheme to introduce parking meters had been tentatively appraised in November 1953, when it was decided, as an experiment, to purchase sixty-two parking meters at a cost of £2,500 from an American manufacturer. The idea was dropped within a couple of weeks when it was realised that, unlike in America, there was no legislation on the issuing and payment of fixed-penalty tickets.

On learning of the City Council's plans to go ahead with the installation of parking meters, the Chief Constable decided that, as the person responsible for the enforcement of law and order in the city, he should assert his authority in the matter. In 1958 he had made the point that in 1947, immediately after the war, there were 3.5 million motor vehicles on the roads in England and Wales and that the number had now increased to 7.5 million. In Leicester there were now 47,000 vehicles licensed by the local authority, an increase of 161 per cent since the end of the war. Mark's stance was that

it is the right of every citizen to pass freely along the highway, whether on foot or in a vehicle, and it is the inescapable duty of the police to see that this freedom is maintained. Whenever the problem of concentration of traffic is encountered in its more severe form the enforcement of law can generally be said to have two objectives, namely the maintenance of free traffic movement along essential routes and the sharing as fairly as possible of the space available for parking. . . .

His basic objection to parking meters was that, in his opinion, it was unfair to impose an additional charge on the motorist for the privilege of using the road. His preferred option was for the Council to create workable 'no waiting' regulations, and for the police to enforce them. This approach, which resulted in 1961 in the creation of the country's first traffic warden force outside the London Metropolitan Police District, led to much criticism and acrimony towards Mark on the part of other, less progressive, chief constables around the country, who found themselves in a 'Catch 22' situation when their own local authorities successfully pressured them to set up similar enforcement procedures. (The first traffic wardens were employed in London in the Metropolitan Police District in 1960; in Leicester members of the fifty-strong force were paid £10 a week, and a fixed-penalty ticket cost £2.)

The parking meters were consigned to the scrapheap (for the next forty years at least) in favour of on-street parking regulations. The change in policy upset nobody more than Auto Magic Car Parks, the company managing the recently opened Lee Circle multi-storey car park. In August 1962, sixteen months after the first traffic wardens appeared on the city streets, they proclaimed sourly that they were operating at a loss and were distinctly unhappy with the situation. Estimating that by the end of the year the company would have lost £40,000 in revenues, Hilton Lowndes, the managing director of Auto Magic Car Parks, made the statement that

> Corporation surface car parks need to raise their prices to the same as the Lee Circle project, and consideration needs to be given to on-street parking meters to drive motorists off of the streets . . . [Lee Circle], not being used to capacity in the week and at the weekend, usage is down to 10 per cent of capacity . . . the company had been led to believe that the Corporation were going to install parking meters in the streets, but the Council had opted for Traffic Wardens. . . .

Lowndes' statement did little to ease the tension caused (if his assertion about assurances relating to the use of parking meters was correct) by the situation now existing. City Engineer John Beckett declared for parking meters as the cheapest option for the rate payer; Alderman Charles Worthington of the Traffic Committee stood resolutely behind the Chief Constable and declared that 'operators need to be patient, in a short while the whole of the city centre will be controlled by Regulations and motorists will use the multi-storey'.

Charges to use the multi-storey were in reality very reasonable, even for that time – 6d per hour, 3s 6d a day, and 12s 6d a week (an average weekly wage at the time was about £12 a week). Lowndes also stated that his company had spent £400,000 setting up Lee Circle as a car park and had no intention of reducing its charges. In fairness, motorists who wanted to park in the town centre for longer than the new parking regulations permitted now had a choice between the Corporation's surface parks, which were always going to be of a temporary nature, and which one observer described as 'axle breaking demolition sites', and the security of a multi-storey car park. In March 1963 the Corporation announced that parking fees on their sites would be doubled from 1 May: 1s for four hours, 2s for a day, and 8s for a week.

Given the City Council's long-term development strategy, the end result was inevitable. Bombed sites and demolition areas were eventually cleared and built on, parking regulations came to be accepted as the norm, and the obvious place for the motorist to park in safety was a multi-storey car park – which, as time progressed, increased in number. In February 1963 Multideck Car Park Developments announced their second project in Leicester, with the building of the Abbey Street complex. In January 1969 the Traffic Committee recommended that the Council grant a 99-year lease on the site bounded by St Peter's Lane, East Bond Street and Causeway Lane to the company of Parking Management Ltd (who were also the tenants of Abbey Street car park) for the erection of a 915-capacity multi-storey car park.

In relation to traffic flow and parking in any city centre it is virtually impossible to please everyone. Addressing any one set of needs will always satisfy one group and alienate another. With the immutable law of cause and effect, the solving of one problem will ineluctably create another. From the 1950s onwards the imposition of no-waiting restrictions in Leicester brought happy smiles to the faces of the town planners and howls of dismay from motorists and from owners of city-centre shops, who claimed that their businesses were being ruined. The imposition of parking fines meant that an entirely new system had to be set up for their enforcement – at a cost to the ratepayer. And while multi-storey car parks removed vehicles from the streets, an unforeseen problem was that, in later years, they would become high-risk crime areas.

CHAPTER SIX

Early Postwar Economic Decline
1945–59

That Leicester, after the late 1850s, enjoyed a period of roughly 100 years of economic growth followed by a sharp decline in its fortunes is an indisputable fact. Similarly, how such growth began is well understood – it is the cause of the decline that is not quite so clear-cut. In recent years economists and historians have put forward various explanations, quoting demographic studies and surveys. For the lay person, the solution is often as confusing as the problem. While facts and figures are an inescapable factor in any discussion, an attempt is made here to present answers in as uncomplicated a manner as possible.

The city's economic decline after the Second World War was the result of a series of interrelated factors, which it would have been difficult, if not impossible, to have avoided. The one thing that should not be overlooked is that, while of little comfort to those directly involved, the situation was not peculiar to Leicester: all over the country a host of trades and businesses suffered in a similar manner, to a greater or lesser extent.

The first stage in obtaining an overall picture is to look at reasons behind the economic stability of Victorian Leicester.

During the first half of the nineteenth century the borough was an unremarkable municipality of around 60,000 people, the only claim to fame of which was a high mortality rate, primarily attributable to the town's polluted water supply; a reliance on the income generated by a somewhat tenuous framework knitting industry; and, until the passing of the Municipal Reform Act of 1835, a notoriously corrupt and venal Tory-led Corporation. With the passing of this particular piece of legislation came the first step in the upturn of the town's fortunes. The Act enfranchised all male ratepayers, entitling them to vote in local government elections, as opposed to the previously existing situation whereby only freemen could vote. The new situation enabled many wealthy local businessmen, almost without exception of Liberal persuasion, who had hitherto been excluded from standing for election to the Corporation, to become involved in the town's affairs. In the first elections held after the passing of the Act, the old Tory Council was removed and political power was transferred into the hands of a group of men who had a genuine concern for the town's well-being.

Efficient management by the new Town Council successfully stabilised the borough's long-term finances; many of the public health problems caused by poor sanitation and inadequate water supplies were resolved during the second half of the century (in 1853 piped water was brought into the town for the first time from the nearby Thornton Reservoir); and Leicester began to attract its share of the new industries that were a hallmark of the late Victorian era.

High Street viewed from just above Cart's Lane on a warm summer's day in the late 1950s. To the left of the picture is the Co-operative building on the corner of Union Street and on the other side of the corner the Magnet Stores. *(Courtesy: Midlands Co-operative Society)*

Although for many years traditional framework knitting remained in place as a major cottage industry in both the town and surrounding district, it was structured in such a way as to create a very rich élite (who controlled the supplies of yarn and owned and rented out the frames) while keeping the vast majority of operatives in a state of acute poverty. Not surprisingly, factory-based employment quickly became far more attractive.

The two trades that from the 1860s onwards became predominant in the town were boot and shoe production and hosiery manufacture. By the outbreak of the First World War there were listed in the borough (Leicester did not become a city until 1919) 187 boot makers, 163 boot and shoe manufacturers and 105 hosiery manufacturers.

The advertisement of one firm, Pool, Lorrimer & Taberer with a factory in King Street, in the Leicester and District Trades Directory of 1911 gives a broad contemporary view of the scope of local hosiery manufacture '[we are] manufacturers of all classes of hosiery, rib vests, combinations, men's and boy's sweaters, Norfolk golf jackets, honeycomb shawls, aprons, children's muslin, costumes – also spinners of knitting and hosiery yarns . . .'.

As a natural progression, related trades also proliferated – heel makers, lace producers, boot and shoe knife manufacturers and last makers; lamb's wool and worsted spinners (such as the firm of Fielding and Johnson with its large factory in West Bond Street), hosiery trimmers, and needle and guide makers.

The lifeblood of any factory-based industry is machinery, and very quickly machine manufacturers, alongside tool-makers and other ancillary trades, sprang up.

Built in 1891 and once one of the largest shoe-producing factories in Europe, the Co-operative Wholesale factory, the Wheatsheaf, in Knighton Fields Road East was by the turn of the twenty-first century a derelict building, production at the plant having ceased in 1990. During the war years part of the factory was given over to munitions production, when Bren-gun components were manufactured in purpose-built workshops. *(At the time of writing, no photographs of the Wheatsheaf as a working factory seem to exist. I am indebted for the background information to Edna Welford who worked during the war on production of Bren-gun parts, David Kylie, a long-term employee at the factory, and Karen Ball of the Midlands Co-op, Customer Services Department.)*

Tanners, leather factors and manufacturers appeared; a tradition of elastic web manufacture had, along with boot and shoe production, existed for many years. In 1911 there were eleven box-making factories across the town, providing packaging for the goods that were being turned out.

As time passed and more people settled in the town (in the forty years between 1861 and 1901 the population increased more than threefold, from just over 68,000 to 211,579) and other businesses flourished to service the growing township. At the beginning of the 1910s there were, in addition to the public houses and hotels in the town, 17 breweries and 127 beerhouses; in a society dependent on the horse for transport, 24 blacksmiths and 19 saddlers had premises in the town. Support industries with the potential to become major employers were also firmly established, including concerns such as the British United Shoe Machinery Co. (originally the locally owned firm of Pearson and Bennion, as early as 1899 this company had become the subject of a takeover by an emerging American Corporation), G. Stibbe's in Newarke Street and Grieves & Co., whose Queen Street Works were destroyed by bombing in 1940. The town boasted fifty-three engineering companies, many of which specialised in producing hosiery machines.

Paradoxically, in relation to trade, the high point of the years following the turn of the century was the First World War. With munitions being defined as anything from gun shells to soldiers' boots, trade flourished. For the first time many local companies found themselves caught in a circle of supply and demand. Large numbers of men were required at the front to fight, but in order to maintain those men an equally large workforce was necessary to ensure that the factories at home kept up full production. For the first time workers were paid substantial amounts of overtime and war bonuses; on the shop floor women replaced the men who went into the forces, giving rise to Leicester's subsequent reputation for employing a large female workforce. (Although in the interwar years and after, the city was famous for its working women, the common impression that the First World War was generally a watershed for female emancipation in the workplace is not correct. Nationally, strict agreements were in place between employers and the unions from a very early stage, that where female labour was engaged in shops, factories and transport, it was only 'standing-in for the men' and that immediately the war ended, they would relinquish those positions. In Leicester the difference was that, after 1919, many places in the hosiery and shoe industries came to be perceived as belonging traditionally to women.) Another factor in the town's prosperity at this time, that is often overlooked, was its central location in the Midlands, at the heart of a prime network of rail and canal transportation that facilitated the reception and dispersal of manufactured goods across the length and breadth of the country.

Despite the fact that by the 1920s Leicester had achieved a pre-eminent position in the country in relation to its main trades of hosiery and footwear manufacture, it was not immune to the hardships of the decade that saw the General Strike of 1926. Those who had jobs prospered, but there were still many without work. In 1921 unemployment in the city was 7,419, 5 per cent of the workforce. The situation of many was so desperate that on Friday 30 September, 600 unemployed men led by Bertram Ley, himself unemployed, besieged the Poor Law Offices in Rupert Street and had to be dispersed by a large contingent of baton-wielding police.

Worldwide during the period known as the Depression, few escaped from the vicissitudes imposed by financial crisis. However, with its firmly established tradition in the manufacturing field Leicester survived, and as things improved across the board, so the city's fortunes began to rise once again. By 1936 Leicester was described in one publication as being 'the city of a thousand trades'. There were, in fact, at that time 250 hosiery manufacturing companies and 200 boot and shoe manufacturers in the city and county.

So what was it that, in the middle years of the twentieth century, went so dramatically wrong? The first thing to be understood is that not 'everything' did go wrong. Many areas, such as service industries, prospered and, in fact, continued to expand throughout the economic downturns of the later 1970s and 1980s. In trades where businesses (some of them very large concerns) collapsed, others that adapted, or that avoided the pitfalls of recession, survived and grew.

The demise of the Leicester boot and shoe trade was not an overnight thing; it took many years of slow decline, but at a time when everything appeared to be booming, the seeds of the decline were firmly planted by the end of the Second World War.

One of the fundamentals of trade in the city before the war was that a high proportion of companies and retail outlets were family-owned – albeit some, such

Worthington's stores, owned by Charles Worthington, was one of the most famous grocery chains in the city during the postwar years, with its 'Sam & Pete' logo and the slogan 'Let Worthington's Feed You', over the door of each of its shops. *(Courtesy: C. Chesterman)*

as the Bentley Group and G. Stibbe's, were considerable concerns employing large numbers of people.

In March 1941 the beginnings of a sea-change came about with the introduction by the government of a wartime measure known as 'Concentration of Industry'. The scheme, critically for a city such as Leicester, was directed primarily at the hosiery and shoe trades. Many smaller companies were beginning to feel the effects of the reduced labour force resulting from conscription and the decline in commercial trade as supplies of raw materials were directed into the production of munitions. The only viable way for such companies to survive was to bid for government contracts which, if secured, gave them access to much-needed materials and allowed them to have a percentage of their workforce classified as being in reserved occupations. The Concentration of Industry Scheme was specifically designed to reduce the number of such firms by declaring a minimum requirement to qualify for contracts. Large manufacturers were classified as 'nucleus firms' and given the government work and then simply absorbed their smaller rivals through a process of buying out their contracts.

The inherent flaw in this arrangement was that in one respect it was self-defeating. After the war small companies often could not afford to invest in new equipment and premises, consequently they did not start up again, for the first time in 100 years causing the demise of small manufacturing units in the city.

Preparations for the rebuilding of Britain's industrial infrastructure began immediately the end of the war was in sight, and a decision was taken to impose a national policy, to be overseen by regional controllers. While the activities of small traders such as shopkeepers and other one-man businesses would be virtually unaffected by the restrictions of a common policy (other than the need for individuals to obtain licences and permits for various areas of trade) the effect on medium and large-sized companies was significant. The actual processes of decommissioning industrial concentration, and the control of labour posed many difficulties.

Within this structure, Leicester was placed in the Board of Trade, North Midlands Region. Other regions were designated for Bristol, Cardiff, Birmingham, Cambridge, Nottingham, Manchester, Leeds, Newcastle upon Tyne and Glasgow. The regional offices were to have four specific functions:

1. Reconversion of industry generally, and the engineering industry in particular, to peacetime working practices;
2. Derequisitioning of factory and storage space, along with the allocation of surplus government factories (this function itself had the potential for massive controversies);
3. Distribution of factory functions as outlined in the government White Paper on employment policy, together with surveys and information-gathering generally (a catch-all to allow regional controllers wide latitude for discretion);
4. Deconcentration of civilian industries, along with the release of raw materials and labour for civilian production and employment.

While in essence totally necessary, the scheme inevitably led to anomalies and inequitable decisions, as in the relocation of business premises, which in later years had detrimental consequences for businesses in the town.

The Board of Trade restrictions specifically prevented new companies from starting up in existing areas of industry. On the face of it, the provision was intended to allow pre-war businesses to commence trading again with as little competition as possible. However, rather than stimulating regeneration it actually created a degree of stagnation. This is evidenced by the fact that in 1939 there were 120 boot and shoe firms in Leicester, and in 1947 the Concentration of Industry Scheme had reduced the number to 94. The remaining factories relied heavily on the return of female labour, much of which, during the war years, had been directed onto the shop floors of engineering firms that had relocated to Leicester from high-risk areas. These new engineering factories, with improved facilities such as works canteens, were a far more attractive prospect than the dingy Victorian premises the workers had previously known, and few showed a desire to return to their old trade.

Similarly, from an early stage, in an ever-developing market the textile industry struggled to attract labour back into its factories. Pre-war Leicester and the surrounding district employed 130,000 workers in the hosiery trade; by July 1946 the number had dropped to 68,000, of which over 47,000 were women.

It is worth noting that at this time, and for many years after, there was a substantial difference between the earning powers of men and women. It was not until the introduction of the Equal Pay Act 1970 that a woman performing the same job as a man became entitled to the same wages. Postwar, for a 48-hour week in a hosiery factory a woman would be paid a minimum wage of 50s against a man's 80s. Many factories were unable to re-employ men in various departments so long as there were insufficient women to complete the finishing work in other departments. Desperate to build up their labour forces, firms such as Wolsey and N. Corah started training schemes to encourage new recruits. In May 1946 Wolsey was forced to announce that the company had taken a decision not to reopen its factory at Fleckney. Used as a machine store since its operational closure in 1941, prior to the war the factory had employed a workforce of 300.

In many ways the 1950s were austere for the individual, primarily owing to the inevitable shortages of raw materials and foodstuffs while Britain, along with the rest of Europe, strove to rebuild its economy. Locally, a factor came into play that, more than any other, proved destructive for the economy of Leicester. There were more jobs than there were people to fill them.

After 1945 a huge workforce was needed to rebuild the country's resources. In Leicester more than anywhere there was an abundance of men and women to provide that workforce. The demobilisation rate from the armed forces was high, and by early 1946 between 90 and 100 Class 'A' men were returning to the city every month, looking for jobs. For many, the restrictions of factory work were now unpalatable, and while the employment exchange had 5,000 vacancies across the board, many applicants showed a preference for outdoor work on building sites or in transport. In March 1946 a significant number of the vacancies were for women in hosiery and clothing factories. In July 1946, fourteen months after the war's end, with 130,000 people in full employment in the city, there were only 400 men unemployed and claiming benefit; returning ex-servicemen had filled 4,000 jobs since May. Even so, the labour exchange still had job vacancies for 3,000 women on its books.

During the first four years of the postwar period the general employment situation in the UK stabilised; in 1949, with an estimated population of 270,000, there were only 229 people registered as unemployed in the city (207 males and 22 females).

However, by the early 1950s the employment situation was beginning to change rapidly, for two very important reasons. Along with the rest of the world, Britain was still struggling to bring her economy back up to pre-war levels, and in many respects was being overtaken by other countries in the race for trade domination. Nowhere was this more relevant than for the two industries upon which Leicester's economy was based – hosiery and footwear. The abundant supply of manpower available in the city now became a recipe for disaster that prevailed through to the 1960s and 1970s. Too many people for the available jobs meant that individual firms had to pay higher wages to attract workers, pushing up production costs, which in turn made it more difficult for manufacturers to compete with foreign trade.

Alarm bells began to sound as early as 1950, when a local MP, Captain Charles Waterhouse made a statement in the House of Commons to the effect that

in Leicester there are signs of a slow down in the prosperity of the last four or five years . . . wholesale and manufacturing warehouses are becoming full with unsold stock, short time is being worked in some factories, mainly in the boot and shoe trade . . . the reason is that costs are too high as a result of devaluation and we have lost sight of the fact that two of Britain's major competitors, Germany and Japan, are now recovering from wartime stoppages. . . .

Despite this doom-laden warning, life for the average worker continued uninterrupted, bolstered by a short-lived upturn in the figures for 1951. There was still full employment and a decent pay packet at the end of each week. In the summer of 1951 the working population of Leicester was 180,000 and there were still 2,123 job vacancies for men and 1,039 for women on the labour exchange books.

In the late summer of 1951, for the first time since the war, workers began to come under pressure. In August, Bairnswear Ltd in Nottingham laid off one-fifth of its 1,000-strong workforce. Three weeks later, at the end of the first week in September, two Leicester firms, Wolsey and H. Tomkins & Co. of Countesthorpe, announced that, with yarn piling up in their warehouses, they would cut the hours of 200 half-hose workers from a five-day week to a 36-hour week. Deeply concerned over the future of their industry, Leicester manufacturers complained bitterly to Westminster that while they were putting workers on short time, the government was giving away armed services contracts for the supply of jerseys, tanktops, and underwear to companies in Denmark, Germany, Belgium, Greece and Holland. The government response was that granting overseas contracts was a matter of expediency. In simple terms, British manufacturers, and those in Leicester in particular, were no longer competitive.

This first taste of the effects of foreign competition was compounded a few months later when, in an attempt to rationalise its own trade deficits, one of Britain's closest trading allies, Australia, reduced its imports from the UK by 80 per cent. In the resulting slump, which hit the hosiery industry hard by the end of 1952, 3,500 operatives, 2,700 of them women – 13 per cent of the hosiery workforce in the city – were lost to the industry as firms restructured, struggling to stay in business. A downturn in the boot and shoe trade during the same period resulted in many factories going onto short-time working. Unemployment figures in the city began to climb – to 1,214 in June 1952.

There was, however, another factor in the economic equation that played a critical role in the years after the war in determining what happened to Leicester: the absorption of many medium-sized, locally based companies, by larger, national and international groups. Individually, there were sound reasons behind such mergers. A small, ailing, local company taken over by a larger organisation could, on the face of it, be beneficial to both the owners and the workforce. A prime example of this was the Bentley Engineering Co., which in the immediate postwar years acquired firms such as Wildt & Co. Ltd, George Blackburn & Son of Nottingham and, in March 1950, Clarendon Engineering Ltd, whose Parker Drive factory became one of its prime sites. Formed in 1910 as a family business, Bentley Engineering began manufacturing knitting machines from the 1920s. The firm acquired Clarendon Engineering from the liquidators, an acquisition which established the Bentley Group as one of the largest privately owned enterprises in the Midlands.

A small hosiery factory could be set up for a relatively small capital outlay, whereas to establish and maintain an engineering shop required a far larger investment. Consequently the owners of small- or medium-sized engineering concerns who could not afford to retool in order to remain competitive, were often more than willing to become part of a bigger group. Large firms that had expanded to the limit of their resources amalgamated with similar companies to create more powerful organisations. In this process, though, there were grave dangers. Another reason to buy out a company was to eliminate a potential competitor, a practice which on occasions led to the stripping-out of the newly acquired firm's assets, followed by its summary liquidation and the dispersal of its workforce.

After hosiery and the boot and shoe trades, engineering came a close third in the league of Leicester's main industries. In 1956 there were 21,229 workers (19,634 men and 1,595 women) employed in engineering in the city, many of them at one or other of the main Bentley Group plants in New Bridge Street or Parker Drive. Founded in premises on Clarendon Park Road in 1910 by Percy Bentley, the firm moved to a larger site on Queen's Road in 1916 to undertake government war work, and in 1921 built its first knitting machine. The company remained firmly in family hands for the next thirty years until, in July 1952, the shareholders discovered to their horror that, over a period of time, 1 million of the company's 3.8 million shares had been quietly bought up by a concern trading as Prince's Investments.

With the price of ordinary shares standing at 7s on the stock market, Prince's offered to sell back to the Bentley family the million that it now owned at 10s a share. The managing director, William Bentley, personally owned 500,000 shares, but due to trading losses the previous year by one of the group's subsidiaries, William Cotton Ltd, of Loughborough, he could not raise the necessary £½ million asked by Prince's. To the general public this was the first indication that the group was carrying a weak subsidiary; it was not, however, a fact of which predatory developers would have been unaware.

In April 1953 the *Leicester Mercury* carried a short piece to the effect that Charles Clore of Prince's Investments, along with one of his co-directors, Leonard Sainer, was to join the board of Bentley Engineering, the value of which was estimated at £5 million (later figures amended it to between £3.5 and £5 million). It also mentioned in passing that two months earlier Mr Clore had taken control of J. Sears (Tru-Form Boot) Co., which itself owned 900 retail outlets and several factories, along with its main subsidiary, the Leicester-based firm of Freeman, Hardy & Willis. For the general public, most of whom had never previously heard of Charles Clore, this latest piece of financial manoeuvring passed by almost unnoticed. It was, however, one of the most important economic developments of the century in the history of the city.

Described as a 'small elegant man with cold eyes', one of a family of seven children, Charles Clore was born on Christmas Eve 1904, the son of Israel Clore and Yetta Abrahams, Russian immigrants who lived in the Mile End district of London. After leaving school and working for a while in his father's textile factory, in 1924 the young Clore set off to South Africa where he remained for the next three years. On his return to England he became involved in several business ventures, including buying into a prosperous South African gold mining company. By the end of the Second World War Clore was an extremely wealthy man (in 1946 he was in a position to buy up the Richard's Shops chain) and by 1951 was dealing in multi-million-pound investments. His acquisition of control of the Bentley Group through the back door became the hallmark of his controversial and totally ruthless style of business. Buying out J. Sears was a development of first importance on his road to becoming one of the most influential entrepreneurs of his time, and to establishing an undisputed power base in Leicester.

Sears already owned 99 per cent of one of Leicester's biggest shoe manufacturers, Freeman, Hardy & Willis, along with its national chain of 500 shops, which immediately passed to Clore. Typical of his buccaneering management style, the new proprietor of Sears immediately removed the chairmen of both Sears and Freeman, Hardy & Willis, appointing himself in their places and bringing in as directors on both boards two of his own men, accountant J.C. Gardiner and lawyer Leonard Sainer, to vouchsafe his interests. In an early move to consolidate his latest investment, Clore transferred the business side of Sears to Freeman, Hardy & Willis, leaving Sears as a holding company which thus owned the entire equity capital of Freeman, Hardy & Willis, along with its surplus cash resources. Within the next two years Clore had restructured the original company to form Sears Holdings, and consolidated his position by further absorbing companies such as the retail giant Dolcis, with its 250 shops, for £5.8 million.

By 1958 Sears Holdings owned, in the shoe industry alone, Freeman, Hardy & Willis, Tru-Form, Dolcis, Manfield's, Phillips Bros, Character Shoes, and Curtess Shoes, giving the group six manufacturing plants and 1,500 shops. These holdings, which in 1954 declared trading profits of £990,000, within four years had more than tripled to over £3 million. In January 1962 a £30 million bid for the Saxone-Lilley & Skinner Shoe Group brought two more Leicester factories (George Green & Sons, Ash Street and Parker Shoes, Bardolph Street) along with a further 475 shops into his empire.

The amalgamation of his shoe interests during the 1960s, by the formation of the British Shoe Corporation, with 2,000 shops and a massive warehousing complex on the outskirts of Leicester at Braunstone, allowed Clore to establish a hegemony over a previously independent British shoe industry. Overall pre-tax profits of Sears rose from £1.4 million in 1953, to in excess of £90 million in 1979, the year of his death.

Whether the acquisition of Freeman, Hardy & Willis with – as well as its chain of retail shops and war-damaged factory premises in Rutland Street – additional land for development in the Walnut Street area (the firm had purchased 60,000sq. ft of business premises from William Buckler & Co. in March 1952) alerted Clore to other attractive business opportunities in the city, or whether it was all part of a much wider grand plan, is a matter for speculation. The fact is that, by subsequently gaining control over the Bentley Engineering Group, Charles Clore made his position unassailable.

In a city incontrovertibly bound to two main trades, possession of Bentley Engineering, one of the country's main producers of textile knitting machines, provided Charles Clore, already a major player in one industry, with the key to the eventual control of the second. Under the umbrella of a firm called Investment Registry Ltd, in March 1954 a swift and 'impossible to refuse' offer of 15s for every 2s share secured for Clore and the Bentley Group the textile machine-building enterprise of Mellor Bromley.

Mellor Bromley were builders of industrial knitting machines, fully fashioned hose machinery, and other textile accessories, and the parent concern in a group that included Samuel Pegg & Sons, the Leicester builders of dyeing and finishing machines, and Pegson Ltd of Coalville, who produced quarrying and mining plant. Their incorporation into the Bentley Group was a major coup and at a stroke removed one of Bentley's leading British competitors.

Manufacturers in the city were not slow to realise the implications of these latest developments. In a speech to the National Hosiery Manufacturers Federation in April 1954, Donald Byford, Managing Director of D. Byford & Co., one of Leicester's largest manufacturers (the firm was taken over in 1970 by the Coates Paton Group), made the prophetic point that 'every day, every week, hosiery machines are being shipped abroad to help our export trade, but they help our export of capital goods and in the same breath take away our exports of consumer goods'.

This was a Leicester businessman referring to local industry. The golden goose was being killed – in trading terms, frighteningly rapidly. Two industries that previously had enjoyed a cosily mutual interdependency in the city were now sprung apart, and one was in the process of destroying the other. Already high, labour costs in Leicester forced manufacturing prices to spiral upwards. By supplying the same or improved machinery as their own to foreign competitors, which had inherently cheaper labour forces, the knitting machine manufacturers were destroying the ability of the hosiers in the city to compete.

The pressure imposed by foreign trade began to make itself felt more and more as time passed. Styles in shoes and clothing were changing, earnings in general were gradually rising, and items that had previously been in short supply were once more becoming freely available. Many manufacturers struggling to cope with the deluge of imported goods found themselves unable to afford either to keep up with the new technology that was emerging, or to re-equip with the new machinery needed to produce the constantly changing styles that the public wanted.

One emerging market proved particularly dangerous. In 1955 Hong Kong suppliers exported to the UK 11.5 million pairs of wellington boots and the new, cheap 'bumper style rubber soled shoes'. At a trade price of 3s 8d a pair, British manufacturers could not begin to match the price of this latest import.

In November 1955 a not unnatural demand by shoe hands for better pay and working conditions was grudgingly conceded by the employers. A man working a 42½-hour week in a Leicester shoe factory earned a minimum rate of £7 a week; a woman in the same trade earned £5 3s. By reducing the working week to 40 hours and increasing wages by 10s and 8s respectively, the price of a pair of men's or ladies' shoes was pushed up by 4s, and a child's by 1s.

Not all trades and occupations were subjected to this downward trend. Those not associated with the staple industries survived and many prospered. With emphasis on the regeneration of housing in both the public and private sectors, the building trade prospered (in 1954 a building worker was paid 7s 4d an hour for a 44-hour week), as did engineering and the service industries. Indeed, even in the affected areas, those that were big enough or had the flexibility to adapt – such as the old-established firm of N. Corah & Sons with their massive production plant at St Margaret's – passed through these years in relative stability.

A useful snapshot of the overall situation in the Midlands is given in this report by G.E. Ball, the Regional Controller for the North Midland Regional Board for Industry, in January 1955:

At the end of 1954 there were four job vacancies for every registered unemployed person in the North Midlands Region. Unemployment at the beginning of December 1954 in the region amounted to less than 8,000, the lowest figure since the end of the war. High levels of expansion in the engineering and aircraft industries has led to them increasing their labour forces in recent months. During October and November engineering employed an extra 950 operatives and the motor industries about 750.

In the clothing and textile industries there has been a downturn losing 800 [operatives] from clothing and 350 from textiles.

There are a total of 30,000 job vacancies in the region.

The hosiery industry is going through a downturn, some firms have sufficient orders while others are struggling. Clothing, and boot and shoe manufacturers have lost around 800 workers in November and December.

Engineering has seen a rise of 950 workers in the first six months of 1954, followed by 1,900 in the next three months, and a further 950 in November and December.

This gain did not extend to the textile industry which lost 350 workers in November after being static for some months.

Presenting a picture of swings and roundabouts for the economy of the region during the first ten years after the war, the author of the report would doubtless have cause in later years – with the car production plants becoming hotbeds of industrial action, and the manufacturers of aircraft parts such as Beagle Aircraft Co. of Rearsby, and Rolls-Royce, going into liquidation – to ponder his optimism.

CHAPTER SEVEN

The Austere 1950s

In February 1950 the government of Clement Attlee was returned for a second term, to continue the task of creating a better Britain. The new decade, while holding the hope for a brighter future, also presented many difficulties, certainly in the early years.

There were still shortages. Britain owed a huge amount of money to America – $650 million for materials supplied under the wartime 'Lend-Lease Act'; and there were the costs of revitalising the economy and putting into place massive rebuilding plans. Many goods were still 'on coupons' and for most people money was tight. Grave concern was growing among Western politicians concerning the ambitions of the Russian ruler Joseph Stalin, and a situation of mistrust and tension led to the Cold War between East and West, giving rise to Winston Churchill's description of an 'iron curtain' being drawn across Europe.

The austerity of the coming decade was presaged on the last day of January 1950 by heavy snow, cutting off electricity supplies in Stoneygate and heralding a typically hard winter. Although at that time the seasons were more clearly defined than they are now – as in the arctic winter of 1947 – snow and freezing conditions combined to create difficulties. Coal, the basic essential for domestic heating and industrial power, was still in short supply. Leicester coal merchants at the beginning of 1950 were only receiving 80 per cent of their needs and were thus unable to supply the government allocation, with the result that many of the poorer Leicester households, who had not been able to hoard any small supplies, found themselves without fuel. The situation did not ease during the coming year. In February 1951 the city suffered selective power cuts, and at the beginning of the following winter it was announced that a household coal ration between November 1951 and January 1952 would be 12cwt.

Leicester's population in 1951 stood at 285,061 (134,858 males and 150,203 females), and despite the enforced rigours of the early 1950s, progress was being made in many respects. The last tramcar ran in 1949, and in January 1950 a £260,000 scheme was put in place to remove the tramlines from the streets and to resurface the roads. The chief disruption caused by this programme occurred from July to October 1950 when work was carried out on the High Street and Belgrave Gate area of the Clock Tower.

Unfortunately, the Corporation bus service, which would have been expected to prosper from the closure of the tramways, failed to do so in the initial years. In July 1950 the department was losing money, the managers attributing the cause to the costs of taking over from the Tramways Department. Twelve months further on, General Manager John Cooper blamed the deficit of £19,000 in operating costs on a fall of 20 per cent in passenger numbers, combined with the cost of fuel, tyres and maintenance, and increases in wages (in 1954 a Leicester Corporation

Transport bus driver's basic wage was £7 3s, which could be made up to £9 with overtime). In 1949–50, the last year of the tramways, the buses showed a profit of £29,455. Subsequently, with the occasional exception, City Transport ran at a loss until 1957. In July of that year the figures showed that its 232-strong fleet had carried 95,052,783 passengers and for the first time the department's turnover had exceeded £1 million, of which £29,000 was profit. The following year, for the first time since 1949, it was free of debt.

Moves were also made to improve the city's hospital services. It was decided in 1950 to redevelop the John Faire Hospital in Countess Street, owned by the No. 1 Hospital Management Committee, and in late 1957 the Bond Street Maternity Hospital opened its doors. (Born in Derby in 1843, John Faire came to Leicester in 1851 and later, with his brothers Samuel and Arthur, founded Faire Bros. During the early twentieth century he was a member of the Board of the Leicester & Leicestershire Provident Dispensary, which had been founded in answer to the needs of 'paying patients with moderate means', and later became the Faire Hospital.)

In September 1950 the Sheffield Regional Hospital Board put in hand plans to build a casualty and X-ray wing at the Royal Infirmary. The project had been on a stop-start footing for some years, and as early as 1938 the Leicester and County Saturday Hospital Society had launched an appeal which collected £140,000 to fund the new department. Handing the money over to the government when the National Health Service came into being resulted in administrative and financial constraints, which meant that the scheme was postponed. However, with the Infirmary handling 45,000 cases in 1955, matters became pressing and in October 1956 the new Casualty and X-ray Department, costing £250,000, was finally opened.

In April 1951 a major improvement in the city's water supplies was made by the Derwent Valley Water Board, when the supply into the Ladybower Reservoir in Derbyshire, from where 85 per cent of Leicester's water was drawn, was augmented by the damming of the River Noe and diversion of its flow into the reservoir. With Leicester's needs amounting to 12.5 million gallons a day the increase was critical if the extra demands imposed by the city's expanding housing programme were to be met. Over the next few years Councillor Mark Henig was deeply involved in Leicester's membership of the management of the scheme. The project, which was shared by Trent River Board, ran into difficulties from an early stage in a dispute concerning how much water each partner was allowed to draw, resulting in the opening of a public inquiry on 14 July 1954, with the River Dove Management Committee's interests being represented by Sir Hartley Shawcross QC. The project envisaged taking water from the River Dove at an intake works at Stretton, for storage in a reservoir at Staunton Harold. Trent River Board's objection was that in times of drought, abstraction of water from the Dove would raise pollution levels in the Trent, compromising water supplies in its area. After a great deal of haggling over the niceties of quantities, the scheme was given the go-ahead in November 1955.

One of the most important events of the early 1950s was the outbreak in June 1950 of the Korean War between the United States and North Korea, which quickly escalated to involve the forces of the United Nations – including Britain on the side of the Americans and the Chinese on the other. On 26 July 1950 the Minister of Defence, Emanuel Shinwell, told the House of Commons that a British Commonwealth Division comprising one brigade each of troops from Britain, Australia and New Zealand would be sailing to join the conflict.

On the home front, in January 1951 Prime Minister Clement Attlee decided to call up for training purposes 235,000 men on the 'Z' Reserve list who had served in the army prior to 1948, during the coming summer. A large number of Leicester men found themselves recalled to the colours in May for a fifteen-day training period. Of these, many went to the Leicester City Fire Brigade for training with the Auxiliary Fire Service. Nationally, 80,000 went to Territorial Army units, 40,000 to Anti-Aircraft Command, and 115,000 to active service units (such as fire brigades). Additionally, 10,000 officers and men were recalled to the RAF ('G' Class Reserves) for three months, and 6,000 fleet reservists to the Royal Navy for eighteen months' service. In relation to the 235,000 'Z' Reserves, it is difficult to understand the reasoning behind the fifteen-day recall. The logistics of kitting them out with uniforms and equipment far outweighed any possible benefits.

It was October 1951 before the 1st Battalion of the Royal Leicestershire Regiment (40 per cent of whom were National Servicemen), at the time stationed in Hong Kong, received orders to embark for Korea on the troopship HMS *Empire Halladale*. On their arrival at Pusan on 13 October they travelled north to take up positions on the River Imjin where, along with the Shropshires, the Royal Australian Rifles and the Canadian Royal 22nd Regiment, they entered into a period of continuous action until relieved on 22 November by the Seventh Regiment, 3rd US Infantry Division, against the Chinese forces who were supporting the North Koreans and were trying to recover territory before the Panmunjom peace talks became effective.

The majority of the battalion returned to Leicester at the end of July 1952 to march through the city led by their commanding officer Lieutenant Colonel G.E.P. Hutchins. The streets were decked with bunting and lined with crowds as the troops marched through Town Hall Square to be reviewed by the Lord Mayor. The remaining seventy-five officers and men returned to Liverpool a month later on board the troopship HMS *Devonshire*. On 14 September 1953 the troopship *Asturias* arrived at Southampton with 500 British POWs who had been released by the North Koreans; these included twenty-one men of the Leicester Tigers Regiment.

Life for many in Leicester during the early 1950s was gradually beginning to improve. Booking through the Co-operative Travel Service, 11 Union Street, in January 1950 the Workers Travel Association Ltd began running advertisements for seven-day motor-coach trips to Devon, the Yorkshire Moors and the English Lakes, staying at first-class hotels, for £13. That summer rail fares to Leicester's traditional east coast resorts of Hunstanton, Skegness, Mablethorpe and Sutton-on-Sea were 10s return, and a local run from London Road to Market Harborough by train cost 2s 3d. A return ticket for Leicester–St Pancras was 19s 11d. (British Railways paid its workers an average of £4 12s to £4 19s a week at this time; public sector wages were more favourable, with the starting pay for a policeman being £7 12s 10d and that of a fireman £6 18s 6d). A pint of beer cost 1s, and in May 1950 the derationing of many sweet stuffs led to a scramble for such indulgences as chocolate biscuits, golden syrup, raisins and sultanas. The release from controlled sale of tinned fish resulted in a huge demand for the ultimate in luxury – tinned salmon. For many years to come a host of housewives who had weathered the difficulties of feeding a family in the 1940s and 1950s kept a store cupboard where they hoarded away tinned foods such as salmon, corned beef, spam, pilchards and a variety of tinned fruits, against a rainy day. Another essential commodity, soap, came off ration in September.

One of the major postwar requirements for freeing up the country's transport system was the derationing of petrol, which came on 26 May 1950. The subsequent increase in fuel prices was not welcomed. During the last month of rationing a gallon of petrol at the pump cost 2s 3d; in the first month of derestriction it jumped to 3s ½d.

Meat remained on ration until July 1954. This was a controversial area as far as the government was concerned (Britain being the last country in Europe to have meat rationing), and with the unpopular move of cutting the allowance per person in January 1951 from 10d worth per week to 8d, many Leicester butchers closed their shops two days a week in protest. In an effort to alleviate the situation caused by the continued rationing of meat, in April 1950 Attlee had removed the control on the price of fresh fish, which had been in place since 1941. (It had hardly been necessary during the war to ration the supplies of fish to the public, as they were severely depleted, due to the fact that deep-sea trawling had been virtually impossible as a consequence of U-boat activity.) The result of this move, intended to be conciliatory, was counterproductive because the price of fish escalated overnight – in Leicester the price trebled, with a devastating effect on the city's fish and chip shops. When meat finally became freely available in July 1954 the scenes at Leicester's cattle market were chaotic, vehicles standing nose to tail as butchers tried to get in to buy carcases. As with other prices, meat prices rose dramatically, best steak going up from 3s 6d per pound to 5s; topside was 4s 6d per pound and sirloin 3s 10d. Even such cheap cuts as shin of beef increased from 2s to 2s 8d.

For those who could afford it, a television set could be bought from Wigfall's in the High Street, for 42 guineas, including purchase tax; a haircut was 1s 6d, and the new Austin A40 Somerset motorcar, when it came into production in 1952, was priced at £467.

For others, however, life was not on the up, and their condition presented a continuing source of embarrassment to the local authorities of both the city and the county.

In August 1946, two months after the camp on the Thurnby–Stoughton Road was vacated by the military, two families of squatters moved into the empty huts. Bill Beesley, who had seen six years of war service between 1940 and 1946 and was now homeless, moved in with his wife and 8-month-old baby. Along with them came Neville Poxen, his wife and two children. Poxen, a miner by trade, and his family had in the past two years lived at eight different addresses, and on Saturday 10 August they were forced to leave a one-room flat in Sparkenhoe Street to make way for the family of a returning serviceman.

Originally an army gun site occupied in turn by the RAF and ATS, the camp had stood empty for two months and the families, desperate for accommodation, decided to take possession of them. The two couples and their children occupied what had been the officers' quarters. Although the War Office, which still owned the camp, protested volubly, it dared not risk the political furore of forcibly ejecting the squatters, and within less than a week fifty other families had joined them, filling the camp to capacity. A month later, in return for an offer of the services (water and sanitation) into the camp being restored, the squatters agreed to pay a rent of 10s a week to Billesdon Rural Council. The offer does not seem to have materialised. In the depths of the harsh winter of 1947, during which the weather conditions closed down most of the industry in the country and 250 men with thirty lorries were employed on a daily basis to clear the city streets, conditions in the squatters' huts were described as desperate. With no heating or electricity, the occupants used candles for lighting and boiled snow over paraffin heaters to make tea. Seven years later, in September 1954, four families, totalling twenty-four people, were still living in the huts.

In the immediate postwar years squatting became a major problem nationally, and in September 1946 the Minister of Health, Aneurin Bevan, instructed local authorities across the country to cut off water supplies to installations taken over by squatters, and to use the police to evict them – eviction, fraught with legal problems, seldom being a practical option. Locally both the City and County Councils had problems. In September 1946 Melton Council cut off the water supply and other services to sixteen people squatting in a six-roomed cottage at Craven Lodge, and a month later the empty NFS huts at Market Harborough were invaded, while a camp sprang up at the deserted American camp at Gaddesby.

In the immediate postwar years squatter camps, such as this one in Shady Lane at the side of the Leicestershire Golf Club, near to Evington village, were set up across the country in disused military establishments by homeless people desperate for accommodation. In perpetual conflict with the local authority, the Shady Lane squatters remained firmly in situ for ten years until the site was finally cleared in 1958. *(Courtesy: Leicestershire Record Office)*

Following the example of those at Thurnby, in April 1948 seven homeless couples moved their families into the empty huts (used first as quarters for the American airborne troops before D-Day, then as a dispersal camp for POWs) adjacent to the Leicestershire Golf Club at Shady Lane, near to Evington village. Workmen were hastily sent by the Corporation to demolish the remainder of the huts before others could occupy them, but they were too late and the local authority was forced to capitulate. Accommodation across the country was at a premium, housing plans still on the drawing board could not be implemented fast enough to alleviate the situation of those who could not find homes or live with relatives, and to have evicted the squatters would have created an embarrassing situation, forcing councils to concede that they could not provide alternative living quarters. At Stoughton, seven months later in November, with no water or electricity, seventy-five families were squatting in the huts. (As soon as the camp ceased to be used for the dispersal of POWs in the district, the Ministry of Works removed window glass and doors for use in the construction of the European Volunteer Workers' Centre at Market Harborough, in an unsuccessful attempt to prevent occupation by squatters.)

A virtual siege developed at Shady Lane, with local residents continually pressuring the Council for the eviction of the squatters and, whenever possible, buildings being reclaimed. On Wednesday 17 November 1948 the *Leicester Mercury* reported that

> residents of Shady Lane [are] complaining about the state of the squatters camp in Shady Lane, [they are] complaining of the state of the Stoughton ex-Prisoner of War camp which since the Germans have left has fallen into disrepair . . . when the Germans were there they had cultivated the gardens and decorated the huts . . . a few months ago men of the Royal Engineers removed all doors, partition panels, and window frames, and disconnected the piping to the larger huts. Soon the camp will again be used by the Services and the amenities will be restored. This plan may be postponed because of the damage caused by the present squatters. A caretaker, Edward Wilcox has been appointed to guard the camp. As many as possible of the huts have been padlocked to prevent any further pillaging, [and] the camp is patrolled at night by the 8th Hussars.

The 8th King's Irish Hussars had been posted as a training unit to the nearby Leicester East Aerodrome in February 1948.

In August 1949 seven newly arrived families were evicted by Messrs Noel Clay, Nottinghamshire – a demolition firm which had obtained a contract to pull down the huts they were occupying and to dispose of the salvaged building materials. The fifty families in the remaining huts that were not due to be demolished were decidedly unsympathetic to the situation, maintaining that they had been in the camp since the beginning, and that the newcomers were playing the system, having arrived during the last few weeks and taken possession of the huts in the knowledge that they were scheduled to be destroyed.

A compromise of sorts seems to have been arrived at following this incident, for in November 1950 the occupants of Shady Lane, with the holes in their roofs patched with brown paper, were paying a rental of 4s a week – this time to the

Ministry of Health – to legalise their position and for the maintenance of one stand pipe at the camp gate as a water supply.

The end of the occupation of the Shady Lane camp came about in a manner that can only be regarded as ironic. At the beginning of March 1958 it was announced that a visit to the city by HM Queen Elizabeth II and HRH the Duke of Edinburgh was planned for the month of May, and that the royal aircraft was scheduled to land at Stoughton airfield – within clear view of the squatter camp. The Leicester City and County Councils decided that the presence of the squatters was no longer acceptable, and a hastily brokered arrangement was made, whereby five of the remaining six families on the site (one of whom had been there for eight and a half years) were housed by Oadby Rural Council, and the sixth by Leicester City.

On the other side of the city a similar set of ongoing circumstances developed in relation to the deserted US 82nd Airborne Division camp on Braunstone Park. This time, however, the Corporation was prepared, and rather than go against the flow it decided to regularise the situation from the outset. The army, glad to be rid of the responsibility, handed over the site, which contained 100 Nissen huts, to the Corporation and in August 1946, in order to control the influx of squatters onto the site (the Council's housing application list stood at over 15,000 at the time), it was decided to allow the occupants to pay a nominal rent and to designate the camp as a temporary housing estate, termed a 'Housing Transit Camp'.

A distribution list was drawn up for the allocation of the Nissen huts to between 120 and 150 people with priority needs. The first three families were moved in on Monday 26 August and during the next two weeks they were joined by a further thirty families, bringing the occupancy up to 150 people. The smaller huts were converted into housing units with a living room and two bedrooms, while the larger ones had four bedrooms each. Existing coke stoves, temporarily left *in situ*, were to be replaced as soon as possible with proper stoves. Plumbing would also be dealt with, and sinks installed in the huts. Until these jobs were completed the occupants had to use a communal kitchen, along with shared toilets and washing facilities. The camp's NAAFI canteen was to be turned into a community centre.

The occupants of this official camp fared only marginally better than the squatters at Thurnby and on Shady Lane during the first winter (in February 1947 the numbers had risen to 106 families), with complaints that, with the water turned off at night to prevent pipes from freezing, there was no sanitation and it was impossible to keep clean. The following July a live-in warden, Thomas Burrell, was appointed.

Braunstone Park continued as a Housing Transit Camp until, in January 1951, the Council decided that the 113 families living there should be rehoused. The decanting process was a gradual one, the huts being demolished as soon as they were vacated in order to prevent reoccupation.

True to the old adage that countries always prepare for the last war, in November 1949, with the East–West political situation deteriorating, the government began an intensive campaign to reinstate the discontinued wartime Civil Defence Corps. A Leicester Civil Defence Committee was formed under the chairmanship of Councillor Charles Worthington, who had served for a great part of the war as

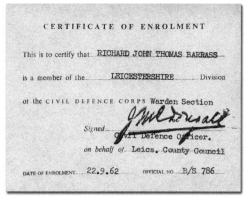

The Civil Defence Corps Armband was bright yellow, picked out with blue lettering; the King's Crown was depicted in red with blue and white stitching. Members of the Corps also carried a buff-coloured identity card. *(Courtesy: R. Barrass)*

Air Raid Controller for the city. The public response to the campaign, both in Leicester and nationally, was not encouraging. In the first six months the strength of the Civil Defence Corps in England and Wales was 22,188 men and 9,261 women, with a further 3,915 volunteering for the Auxiliary Fire Service. In Leicestershire, initially a mere 450 people offered their services (the wartime figure had been 4,300). However, the outbreak of the Korean War in June 1950 provided a much-needed impetus for recruiting, and numbers began to improve. By 30 September Leicestershire had recruited 1,375 members, which equated to 4.1 recruits per 1,000 of population. In the city things improved at a slower rate; by the end of September 303 people had joined the organisation, representing 1.3 per 1,000 of population, although on 16 October the Civil Defence recruiting office in Belvoir Street reported that, with 43 recruits coming in during the last fourteen days, it was achieving just over three new members a day.

With the threat of nuclear attack foremost in its mind, the government wanted to put together some form of trained and equipped mobile defence force that could spring into action in the event of an enemy attack, the prime aggressor always being viewed as the Soviet Union. A fairly basic uniform was devised (cost, as always, being a governing factor, the complete uniform was priced at £10, with the government contributing £7 10s towards the cost), comprising for men a greatcoat, beret, battledress blouse and trousers and for women a beret and greatcoat, skirt or slacks, jacket and shoes. Although this was the designated uniform, materials were still in desperately short supply. For instance, in 1948 the Home Office had issued an instruction that police forces were to discontinue the wearing of closed-neck tunics in favour of the modern open-neck style. Owing to the shortage of cloth few forces were able to implement the instruction, and in Leicester city it was not until 1950 that regular police officers made the change; for special constables it was later still. Consequently, civil defence sweaters with a cloth badge on the breast were generally substituted for the men's battledress blouses and women's jackets. While the authorities were purchasing through official channels at £4 13s 7d, with supplies available from army-surplus depots, it was still possible for an individual to buy a greatcoat for £2 14s 6d and dye it dark navy or black.

At the beginning of November 1950 Dr Elfed Thomas, the Director of Education for Leicester city, was appointed Civil Defence Welfare Officer with responsibility

The large, colourful badge worn by Civil Defence Corps members on the sweater and tunic (right) was woven in gold and red on a black background. The instructor's enamelled metal lapel badge was somewhat less eye-catching, in blue and grey.

for the coordination of evacuation and welfare centres. The logic behind the appointment was that, historically, schools had always been the obvious locations for such activities, and the school meals service was eminently suited to the preparation and distribution of food on a large scale.

One of the reasons for the slow rate of recruiting to the Civil Defence was that Attlee's recall to the colours of men who had been discharged from the armed forces prompted many of those who might otherwise have signed up for the Civil Defence to wait and see whether the old wartime Home Guard would be reconstituted – which was, in fact, what happened. In January 1952 recruiting began for the newly re-formed Leicester City Section of the Home Guard, under Lieutenant Colonel H.E.H. Ward, based at the Magazine.

Meanwhile, a house-to-house recruiting drive for volunteers for the Civil Defence Corps was held in the city. Primarily targeted were males aged between 16 and 30 who were not on the reservist list for the armed forces, and women between 18 and 30 for training as wardens and for headquarters work. At the same time, candidates were sought to become special constables or auxiliary firemen. The campaign began to meet with some success and by midsummer of 1952 Leicester city was one of twenty-three Civil Defence Divisions across the country to have reached their peacetime establishment. Nationally at this time, with British soldiers serving in Korea and the Cold War situation deteriorating, 201,349 men and 97,476 women volunteered to become Civil Defence workers, while 12,171 joined the Auxiliary Fire Service (AFS). Also, mobile defence columns, established in January 1953 for the purpose of providing mutual aid to any area of the country subjected to an attack, were manned by army and RAF personnel. One such column, made up of 54 motor vehicles, 6 motorcycles, 12 officers and 168 other ranks, passed through Leicester in September 1953, travelling from Yorkshire en route to Bedford. To service the needs of the defence columns, provision was made at the same time for the formation of eleven strategic food convoys. The expenditure of the organisation remained surprisingly moderate. In 1952–3 the Leicester committee managed to only spend £4,095 and asked the City Council for a budget the following year of £8,205, explaining that the increase was due to an influx of recruits requiring uniforms (the city now had 1,000 Civil Defence members, rising in 1957 to 1,547) and the equipping of proposed new control rooms. Civil Defence exercises, such as the one in June 1954 when a 'blackout exercise' across the city was run, followed two days later by an RAF Canberra 'bombing' demolition property in Lewin Street in order that Civil Defence and AFS squads could practice firefighting and casualty clearance, became commonplace. The largest such exercise, in October 1954, was a combined six counties exercise centred on Leicester when 2,400 Civil Defence workers, along with 100 vehicles, provided demonstrations and mounted a parade of 1,500 personnel.

So far as Leicester was concerned the only occasion when its Civil Defence unit was given any practical application was in February 1953, when flooding caused by a tidal wave devastated much of the east coast and assistance of every kind was sent to the area from the surrounding districts.

The government was determined to continue the strategy of maintaining an organisation to ensure the well-being of the country following a nuclear attack. In a reshuffle of senior posts, in January 1958 Charles Worthington was appointed the Group Controller of Civil Defence for Leicester, Leicestershire and Rutland (he was succeeded in July 1960 by Lieutenant Colonel G.L. Aspell). A further addition to the resources of the organisation came in the summer of 1960, with the

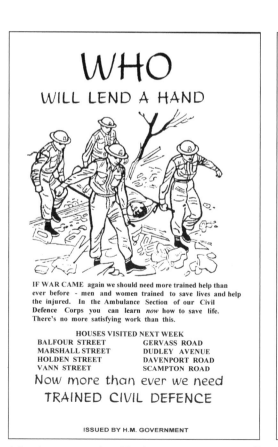

Advertisements produced by the government as part of its national recruiting campaign for the Civil Defence Corps.

The Green Goddess fire-fighting units were an integral part of the Civil Defence Corps's equipment (they were designed to pump water at the scene of a fire). *(Courtesy: J. Warden)*

formation of police mobile columns. These were (in the Leicestershire district) a relatively short-lived phenomenon. Made up of police officers drawn from the boroughs, cities and counties of Leicester, Northampton, Nottingham, Derby, Peterborough, Lincoln and Grimsby, the first of these columns passed through Leicestershire in September 1960 and spent a day at Mallory Park motor-racing circuit, 'searching for saboteurs'. The last, in June 1964, under the title of the 'North Midland Region Police Mobile Column', made up of 150 men from the same group of forces, took part in a similar seven-day exercise ranging across the North and East Midlands.

However, interest was waning at both individual and organisational level. Coventry City Council had already ceased funding for the Civil Defence in August 1954, on the basis that the eventuality of a nuclear attack was negligible and it was no longer prepared to waste public money. A decision was taken nationally that, as from April 1963, Civil Defence training would no longer be undertaken by the police and the organisation would become responsible for its own members. By this time numbers in Leicester had dropped to 944 active participants. Five years later, in March 1968, the government finally accepted that the Civil Defence Corps was no longer viable and announced that its vehicles and equipment would be put into storage (the Corps's Green

Following the collapse of the Civil Defence Corps in 1968 the Green Goddess firefighting units were put into storage. They were brought back out during the firefighters' strike in 1977, when they were operated by army personnel under the guidance of senior fire officers.

During the 1950s and 1960s a major August bank holiday event each year, attracting thousands of Leicester people, was the Abbey Park Show, opened by the Lord Mayor. *(Courtesy: M. Ford)*

Goddess vehicles were kept garaged until the firemen's strike of 1977, when they were used by the army in a firefighting role), and the organisation was stood down the following month.

In many respects the beginning of the first decade after the war saw the start of a return to normal life. Abbey Park Show, a favourite with adults and children alike, opened its gates on the August bank holiday of 1950 for the fourth time since the end of the war, to a record crowd of 55,000 people. A month later the annual Battle of Britain Parade was held in Victoria Park, and John Beckett stamped his name indelibly on the city by installing down the centre of London Road and along Charles Street a series of ornamental flower troughs, ever after to be known as 'Beckett's buckets'. Eight months later the Duchess of Kent made a visit to the city to open the Leicester Industries Exhibition and Trade Fair at Granby Halls. In February 1952, HM King George VI died, and on 18 February, the day of his funeral, all of the city's factories switched off their machinery and observed a two-minute silence. Shops closed for three hours, and maroons were fired on the city parks, followed by an open air service held in the Town Hall Square.

The following year is always remembered as Coronation Year. One particular incident cast a dark shadow in the month before the event, and at the same time provided a historical punctuation mark. In the early evening of Friday 22 May 1953 Janet Warner, a 12-year-old schoolgirl, was walking her collie dog in Blue Banks Spinney near to her home at 141 Leicester Road, Glenhills, when she was attacked and murdered by Joseph Christopher Reynolds, a 31-year-old Irish labourer. Arrested later in Leicester city centre by a patrolling uniformed officer on night duty (PC Jack Milner), Reynolds, who admitted killing the girl, was tried on 26 October before Mr Justice Pilcher and sentenced to death. Joseph Reynolds had the distinction of being the last man to be executed at Leicester prison, being hanged on 17 November 1953, his body later interred in the prison grounds next to the wall by the mat shop.

The main civic event of the decade marked the coronation of Queen Elizabeth II, and the City Council allocated a budget of £10,000 for decorating the city in readiness for the great day. The procession on 2 June 1953 took an hour to pass through the Leicester streets and was punctuated by showers of rain. At 3.45 p.m., with all of the City Transport buses stopped, the Quorn hounds approached the Clock Tower, heralded by a fanfare of trumpets from the Royal Leicestershire Regiment. After this came a cavalcade of lorries with displays of Elizabethan personalities such as Drake and Shakespeare. These were followed by a 1,000-strong parade made up of the bands of the Royal Leicestershire Regiment and the Territorial Army; a naval contingent from HMS *Gamecock*; the band of the Royal Canadian Air Force pipes and drums from No. 1 Fighter Wing, North Luffenham; the Leicester City Fire Brigade; and the Civil Defence and Red Cross. Planned festivities at Abbey Park had to be cancelled because of the heavy rain; however, an evening bonfire and fireworks display went ahead at Victoria Park.

In one form or another 1953 was a year for celebrities. On 1 July a leading member of the City Council, Geoffrey Barnett, was knighted. A fortnight later Frank Sinatra gave a concert at the De Montfort Hall. Two months later, on Sunday 13 September, by order of the Watch Committee the same venue was prevented from having the comedian Bob Hope grace its boards on the grounds that 'his performance might, under the Sunday Observance and Entertainment Act be classed as making the Demontfort Hall a disorderly house . . .'.

A children's favourite at the Abbey Park Show was the tiny model railway, which despite its diminutive size was capable of pulling at least two carriages loaded with passengers. *(Courtesy: M. Ford)*

In the early years after 1945 a Battle of Britain Parade was held each September to commemorate those who had died in the conflict. For this occasion City Police officers who had flown as aircrew during the war were allowed to wear RAF wings on their tunics. An example of this shown here in the 1956 parade is the Inspector (Ronald Wigley) marching second in line, who flew Sunderlands in both the Atlantic and Far Eastern theatres, and is wearing full pilot's brevets. The officer leading the parade, Inspector John Todd (ex-Warrant Officer, Scots Guards) is the holder of the Croix de Guerre medal for gallantry. *(Courtesy: K. Wigley)*

Convicted in 1953 of the murder of schoolgirl Janet Warner, Joseph Reynolds was the last man to be hanged at Leicester gaol. Working at the prison at the time as an electrician's mate, William 'Bill' Collins (inset) was present when Reynolds's body was interred inside the prison grounds. *(Courtesy: W. Collins)*

The summer of 1953 saw the city preparing for the coronation of HM Queen Elizabeth II. Seen here are some of the Leicester City Police officers who went to London to participate in the celebration parade. Front row, left to right: Inspector D. Hackett; Sgt J. Todd; Sgt R. Wigley; -?-; PC 116 J. Broughton; PC 61 W. Sims. Back row: Sgt T.F. Sandall; Sgt J. Pomfret; PC 194 D. Bush; PC 89 G.A. Noble; PC 167 R. Hunt. *(Courtesy: Leicestershire Constabulary)*

A different type of notoriety fell upon Albert Hattersley, a 31-year-old colliery shot-firer who, while serving a seven-year sentence for a post office raid at Birstall, escaped from Leicester prison on 19 December 1953. In order to escape Hattersley scaled a 25ft-high courtyard wall inside the prison, worked his way along the parapet to the main gate on the Welford Road side of the building and across the gateway, onto the roof of the Governor's (Mr J.R. Truswell's) house, and dropped 30ft to the ground before making his way over the Governor's garden wall and onto Welford Road. Following the break, the Press was full of speculation that he had been assisted by accomplices and that a waiting vehicle had whisked him away. In truth, the prison break was unaided, and Hattersley, having broken his ankle in jumping from the roof of the Governor's quarters, made his way to the nearby railway line. After splinting his injured leg with a piece of wood, he stowed away in a railway wagon. The escape, which attracted a great deal of publicity, ended ignominiously. Hattersley left the railway truck to hide in a field near to Long Eaton. His cries for help as he lay injured attracted a nearby policeman, who arrested him.

The second half of the 1950s, along with 'Teddy boys' and the brief appearance on the city streets of the 'bubble car', saw a fundamental change to the way in which people chose to pass their time outside work. Music Hall was long dead and buried; however, live theatre and the cinema had continued to prosper. There was now a sea-change. On Friday 17 February 1956 Associated Television (ATV), broadcasting from Lichfield, went live in the Midlands to a 1.5 million audience. Very quickly small toast-rack-shaped additions appeared, bolted onto the existing

H-style BBC television aerials across the city. Christmas viewing figures were stolen by the new company, with its classic six-part Saturday night science fiction thriller, *Trollenberg Terror*. The new form of home entertainment heralded the demise of local cinema, series such as *Trollenberg Terror* and the earlier BBC *Quatermass Experiment* (July–August 1953) also being the forerunners of the modern science fiction genre that was to signal the virtual end of the traditional cowboy movie. (The lenses for the first television cameras used at the BBC's Shepherd's Bush Studios were made in Leicester by Rank, Taylor and Hobson, at their Stoughton Street works.)

With television in the ascendancy, the decline of other forms of entertainment came rapidly. R.S. Theatres announced in October 1956 the imminent closure of the Theatre Royal in Horsefair Street. In May 1957 the premises were sold to the Leicester Permanent Building Society (later the Alliance & Leicester), and work was begun on demolishing the building. On Saturday 14 February 1959 the Palace Theatre held its last performance, followed a few weeks later by the closure of the adjacent Floral Hall cinema – demolition work began in September. The Essoldo cinema in Granby Street, which had started life as the Temperance Hall before becoming first the Cinema de Luxe, then the Princes Cinema, closed on Saturday 2 July 1960. It had specialised in long runs of popular films, and in 1954 the box office favourite *Three Coins in the Fountain*, starring Frank Sinatra, was screened there for nine continuous weeks. The list of cinemas that closed down in both the city centre and the suburbs was long and depressing, the Gaumont (originally the City Cinema) in the Market Place, the Picture House on Granby Street, the Sovereign in Woodgate and the Knighton Kinema on Welford Road, were but a few. In November 1959 Arthur Black, owner of the Regal in Havelock Street, unsuccessfully offered his cinema to the City Council for use as a civic theatre.

The city's remaining theatre, the Royal Opera House in Silver Street, survived a little longer than its contemporary, the Theatre Royal. Following a disastrous incident at Christmas 1952, when a large amount of masonry supporting the ceiling over the stage collapsed onto the cast and into the orchestra pit during the Boxing Day pantomime performance, the building was declared unsafe for public performances and closed down. It remained closed for the next six years and then reopened with the pantomime *Sinbad the Sailor*. The reprieve was short-lived, and in June 1960 the theatre closed for good.

Britain had for some time, in collaboration with the American administration, been building airfields at various locations across the country for use by the United States Army Air Force as bomber bases, and in February 1951 the House of Commons was told by Arthur Henderson that American bombers, supplemented by fighters, were already stationed in this country. One of the locations to be seconded to the USAAF was the wartime RAF Station at Bruntingthorpe, a few miles south of the city.

Bruntingthorpe was retained on 'care and maintenance' by the RAF from 1945 until its transfer to the USAAF as an auxiliary to their base at Alconbury in January 1957. A new 3,400ft-long runway was laid down to accommodate the B-47 aircraft of 3912 Combat Support Group and the Strategic Air Command 100th Bomb Wing, which took up residence in January 1959, to be joined in August of that year by the

19th Tactical Reconnaissance Squadron (10th TRW). This was much to the irritation of local farmers, who complained bitterly about the presence of the Americans preventing them from using the airfield roads as shortcuts, and the installation of automatic signals on the local roads disrupting traffic when aircraft came in to land.

As a result of the American presence a large number of servicemen could be seen in city-centre pubs. The local police and American Military Police (commonly known as 'Snowdrops' because of their white helmets and cravats) were kept busy with fights most weekends between American servicemen and locals.

Bruntingthorpe Air Base, converted for use by the United States Air Force at a cost of £3 million, was closed down as part of an economy drive by the American Administration in late 1962, when it was handed back to the Royal Air Force. At the time of its closure 80 officers and 860 servicemen, approximately 10 per cent of them married to English women, were stationed at the base. The closure caused a brief blip in the local economy, inasmuch as around 100 Leicester people who had been employed by the Americans became redundant, businesses such as local shops, taxi firms and city-centre places of entertainment experienced a significant loss in revenues, and the price of accommodation dropped appreciably. The rental of flats in the surrounding area (including the city suburbs), demand for which had from the outset exceeded availability, dropped from the inflated price of around 6 guineas a week, to around 4½ guineas. A semi-detached house, rented to an American for around 8 or 9 guineas a week, suddenly returned to its normal price of 5 guineas. On the positive side, dwellings that had been built by the Americans to house personnel on the base, known as 'tobacco houses' because they had been paid for by the sale of surplus US goods to the British government, were auctioned off to Leicester house buyers in October 1964 by the firm of Shakespeare, McTurk and Graham, with a reserve price on each of £2,000.

Once the base was back in British hands it was converted back to UK standards (electrical circuitry had all been altered to American specifications) and after April 1963 it was used as a reserve RAF base with flying facilities. This was mainly a public relations exercise to dispel rumours, prevalent during the time of its occupation by the USAAF, that the station was in fact a missile base.

Just as the first half of the decade had seen the outbreak of the Korean War, so the Suez Crisis was to have an effect on life in Leicester during the decade's latter half. In July 1956, to the outrage of the canal's joint French and British owners, Egyptian leader Gamal Abdel Nasser took possession of and nationalised the Suez Canal. Fearing that Nasser might close the canal and cut the main supply route for oil between the Persian Gulf and Europe, the British and French governments, along with Israel, mounted a short-lived and unsuccessful military action against the Egyptians which ended on 22 December with the withdrawal from Egypt of British, French and Israeli troops. The direct effects on Leicester were twofold. First, a number of men who had served in the armed forces returned to duty when, on 2 August 1956, Prime Minister Anthony Eden decided to recall 'A' and 'AER' Category 1 Reservists and officers of the Regular Army Reserve. Second, and more widespread, was the introduction of petrol rationing, which was necessitated as from 17 December by the failure of the military action. As was to be expected with such a rushed measure, the situation was chaotic, with many garages in the city not

During the immediate postwar years and into the early 1960s, conscription into the armed forces was a fact of life for young men. Seen here in 1957 is a group of young soldiers of the Royal Leicestershire (Tigers) Regiment. In the back row, second from the right, is Pte 23405196 Neville Gunby, who served with the Tigers from July 1957 to July 1959 as a Regimental Signaller. *(Courtesy: J. Gunby)*

being certain as to their allocation and Leicester firms who had not received coupons for their vehicles unable to obtain petrol and diesel. Fuel shortages inevitably resulted, bringing hardship to a number of transport firms such as H.V. Day & Sons Ltd, which, with only seven out of a fleet of twelve lorries operating, began to lay off drivers on New Year's Eve. The confused situation continued into the spring of 1957. In April, with garages now holding an excess of fuel that they were not allowed to sell, it was announced that rationing would end on 15 May.

Running in tandem with the Suez Crisis was another situation demanding military action and in which the Royal Leicestershire Regiment was directly involved, commonly referred to simply as 'Cyprus'. During the early 1950s the leader of the island's church, Archbishop Makarios III, agitated for the island to become independent of British rule. In 1955 his cause was espoused by an organisation entitled Ethniki Organosis Kypriakon Agoniston (EOKA), the National Organisation of Cypriot Fighters, under Colonel George Grivas.

With the political situation deteriorating, in October 1955 the 1st Battalion of the Royal Leicesters was transferred to the island from Sudan, arriving at Famagusta on 16 October aboard the troopship *Charlton Star*, to take up barracks at Golden Sands (the same name as a popular Leicester holiday destination at Mablethorpe), which until recently had been a rest camp for troops on leave from the Suez Canal zone. A month later, amid a series of terrorist attacks against Britons, two of the Tigers' soldiers were injured in a bomb attack on the barracks. With a state of emergency declared, the battalion settled down to a prolonged period of anti-terrorist duties on the island. Six months later John R. Webster, Assistant Chief Constable of the Leicestershire and Rutland Police, temporarily took the position of Assistant Commissioner of Police as second-in-command to Colonel G. White. Officers from both the County and City Police forces were seconded to Cyprus for the duration of the emergency, along with men from other British police forces.

The 1st Battalion of the Leicesters spent the next two and a half years in Cyprus. When they returned home, arriving at London Road station on 24 May 1958, they had lost sixteen men and one officer in the emergency.

Education after the war was viewed as a priority, and 1957 was a particularly important year in this respect. On Friday 15 March Leicester became a university city. At that time the university had a staff of 100 providing for the needs of 830 students studying the arts, education, sciences and social sciences. In October it was announced that starting in 1960 a new College of Art was to be built on the 2½ acres of demolition land next to the existing premises in the Newarkes; on 1 acre of ground cleared by the levelling of Asylum and Fairfax Streets an extension would be added to Gateway Boys' School. (In Cardigan, Gray, Middle, Asylum, Goswell, John, Cromwell and Fairfax Streets and in Mill Lane 213 houses were pulled down.) Additionally, at the end of the year in November it was proposed to spend £½ million on a new teacher-training college for 420 students at Scraptoft. On 9 May 1958 HM Queen Elizabeth II opened the Percy Gee building at Leicester University. Future development work at the university included a hall of residence for female students later in the year, a chemistry building costing £½ million to be ready by 1960, and a £400,000 physics building and lecture theatre for the following year.

On an everyday level, talk of creating a major airport at the Leicester East Aerodrome was allowed to lapse in favour of a proposal to spend £¼ million utilising the old RAF base at Castle Donington for the purpose. The old age pension for a married couple was between £1 14s and £3 5s a week, while a war pensioner on a 100 per cent disability allowance was entitled to £3 7s 6d. Smog that blanketed the country in January 1956 prompted a motion from Alderman Fred Jackson, Chairman of the Leicester Health Committee, to create the city's first smokeless zone.

Following the furore of September 1956 over proposals to build a new civic centre in Victoria Park, money was allocated and the new pavilion, to replace the one destroyed by a land mine in 1940, was opened on 16 December 1958.

James Albert Downe, a 31-year-old Antiguan who had worked for Leicester City Transport as a conductor since February 1956, became the first West Indian bus driver in the city in August that year.

An innovative if short-lived scheme to provide bus travel to India made its one and only trip in March 1959. Trading as B&S Coaches, T. Broughton and Dalys Singh undertook the journey with a 33-seater coach travelling through Belgium, Germany, Austria, Yugoslavia, Greece, Turkey, Iran, and Pakistan, eventually arriving in India. It catered for the newly arrived immigrants to the city – a single fare was priced at £45, and a return at £90.

A gent's haircut cost 2s 6d. A 'Stella' four-valve portable radio cost 12½ guineas including purchase tax; costing less than ½d a mile to run and with a cruising speed of 25mph, a Mk II Raleigh moped from Halford's for 51½ guineas provided an independent mode of transport to and from work.

CHAPTER EIGHT

Acquiring a Civic Centre

As in the closing years of the nineteenth century the Borough Corporation had turned its attention to the provision of a new Town Hall, so, after the Second World War, Leicester City Council set in motion a series of programmes, plans and projects to furnish the city with a civic centre commensurate with the city's status as one of the wealthiest in Europe.

In March 1944 City Engineer and Surveyor John Leslie Beckett created his 'Fifty Year Plan' for the future development of Leicester as a modern city. Included in the plan was a scheme to demolish parts of the city centre in the area surrounding the existing Town Hall and to replace them with a 'civic and cultural centre'. The radical scheme called for the removal of 'wrongly placed industry', and for the cleared areas to be zoned into sectors that would include civic administration, law courts, a library and a theatre (the existing Town Hall, built in 1876 was to be retained). Unlike Beckett's scheme to demolish the oldest and most historic part of the town around Southgate Street in the interest of traffic flow (which did come to fruition) this particular project never left the drawing board. To have attempted the compulsory purchase of the necessary business properties in the area enclosed by Granby Street and Belvoir Street up to Welford Place would have been economically impracticable, and political suicide. Time, however, was on the side of the authorities. Along with other cities Leicester, prosperous and expanding, was in the throes of implementing many postwar measures. The new civic centre could be put on hold while other more pressing matters such as housing and road-building schemes were addressed.

Thus, it was not until, under a banner headline in the *Leicester Mercury* on Tuesday 11 September 1956 declaring 'SECRET CIVIC CENTRE PLAN TO COST £3,000,000', that an early scheme to rehouse the City Council was brought to the attention of the Leicester ratepayers. The front-page leader, written by the editor, launched a vitriolic attack on the City Council's Labour group.

We are able to disclose that the new civic centre now being considered by a secret committee of the City Council would cost three million pounds.

Three million pounds – the price is as fantastic as the whole plan which cuts right into Victoria Park and appropriates six and a half acres of playing grounds for the purpose.

And all this is top secret! The most elaborate plan of swearing the members of the committee to secrecy has been resorted to. Now, after a year of conspiracy, this committee has not said a word to the members of the City Council or to the public. What a load of mischief it has up its sleeve!

We are telling the people of Leicester today because it is our duty as a newspaper. We are also saying that it is an eccentric conception of duty to keep such matters secret.

We go further than that. The oath of silence is bizarre, the filching of six and a half acres of Victoria Park is a serious violation of liberties and open spaces. It must not be allowed to happen. . . .

Accompanying the piece, along the top of the page, was a line of portrait photographs of those unfortunate councillors who, serving on the Administrative Offices and Civic Buildings (Special) Committee, were to be deemed responsible for the alleged piece of chicanery. The first shots had been fired in what became one of the longest-running and, on occasions, most acrimonious political disputes in Leicester's postwar history.

Given the sensationalist nature of the newspaper's revelation (an appraisal of the deteriorating situation in Suez on the same page was relegated to a one-quarter-column six-paragraph précis, along with the news that the Watch Committee at Blackburn in Lancashire had banned the showing of the Bill Haley film *Rock Around the Clock* on the grounds that the film 'contained matter that was likely to lead to public disorder'), what had actually happened?

While the *Mercury*'s sensationalist approach to the matter was in essence correct, and the Committee was being devious, the broad proposals had been known by many in the Council Chamber for some time.

The original pavilion in Victoria Park, seen here in 1937 when members of the Leicester City Police force were being inspected by His Majesty's Inspector of Constabulary. Described by many as a 'Gothic monstrosity', it was destroyed by a German land mine in November 1940. It was the matter of planning permission to rebuild the pavilion that provoked the first political debate concerning the scheme to site a civic centre in Victoria Park, in September 1956. *(Courtesy: Leicestershire Constabulary)*

The old Victoria Park pavilion had been destroyed by a land mine during an air raid on the city during the night of 20 November 1940, and as part of the postwar rebuilding scheme money was obtained from the War Damage Commission to build a new one. By July 1956, with finances in place (an estimated £30,000 to £40,000) and a site decided upon, the Parks Committee under Alderman Bertram Powell had for some time been pressuring the Town Planning Committee to give the go-ahead for the work. To all intents and purposes it was a simple matter: a building that had been demolished was to be replaced and there was the entire park to choose from. However, the Town Planning Committee prevaricated and delayed giving permission until Alderman Powell forced the position and the Planning Committee finally gave official consent on Friday 13 July 1956.

The Chairman of the Planning Committee, Councillor Albert Vesty made the following statement:

> the matter is now finished. The Parks Committee now have a site and they can get on with the job. A start could have been made two years ago, the complications that arose then were nothing to do with the Town Planning Committee. By the time the Parks Committee were ready to proceed, the situation had altered. We had commissioned a plan for a new civic centre and the pavilion had to take second place. The old pavilion site would have encroached on the site of the suggested new civic building parallel with Granville Road and mid-way between the Victoria Park Gates and the War Memorial. We have just moved [the pavilion] away from the corner of the new proposed civic building.

So the existence of a plan to site a civic centre in Victoria Park was known two months before the publication of the *Mercury* article.

Eight months before this, in November 1955 a local authority group that had been established under the title of the Administrative Offices and Civic Buildings (Special) Committee, was given permission by the Council to engage the services of an architectural consultant to examine the viability of building a civic centre. The remit of the Committee was to 'explore whether local government departments should be retained in or about their present positions and extended separately, or whether all departments should be brought under one roof in a new civic centre away from the central area'. In April 1956 architect Cecil Howitt presented to the committee a drawing for a civic centre in the De Montfort Hall area – almost exactly where the Parks Committee wanted to build the new pavilion. While the Special Committee firmed up their proposals it was necessary to deflect Alderman Powell and his group, a relatively simple matter because Councillor Vesty was Chairman of both the Special Committee and the Town Planning Committee.

At the meeting of the City Council on 1 August, Councillor Kenneth Bowder raised the question of the activities of the Special Committee and the veil of secrecy in which its members had shrouded themselves (at one point it was claimed by the Committee that the information it held was the copyright of the consultant architect, and as such could not be divulged). As Bowder pointed out, the Special Committee was duty bound to report to the full Council, and should do so.

Kenneth Bowder, leader of the Conservative group on the City Council, was opposed to the purchase of the New Walk Centre complex. *(Courtesy: Urban Design Group, Leicester City Council)*

Clearly privy to a leak of some of the Special Committee's dealings, Councillor Bowder next pointed out that, subsequent to receiving the architect's report, at a meeting on 11 May the Special Committee had passed two resolutions: first that there should be a new civic centre, and second that it would be in the Victoria Park area. These were decisions that should, as a matter of priority, have been reported to the Council in order for a balanced assessment to be made. While the Special Committee continued to prevaricate, the options presented by other available sites were slipping away.

The arguments were overridden, and a motion that the Committee be forced to produce a report was defeated by thirty-nine votes to sixteen. Councillor Vesty, his position for the time being safe, declined to comment on whether or not the proposed site would exceed the original ½ acre (a figure of 6½ acres was already being bandied about) and declared that it would be impossible for the Committee to make any report to the September meeting of the Council.

By now, however, despite the secrecy of its deliberations, the Special Committee's plans were being leaked to the press: the building would have a frontage of 190yd – as long as Gallowtree Gate – and be 160ft high, almost two and a half times the height of the municipal buildings in Charles Street; the cost was already put at £3 million. The *Leicester Mercury* article, accompanied by the row of thirteen cameo photographs of the Committee members, sealed the fate of the project, and following another hostile Council meeting on 25 September the project was dropped and allowed to fade into obscurity.

How could such an important issue have been dealt with in such an inept manner, and why? One factor that needs to be taken into consideration is that of party politics. The Administrative Offices and Civic Buildings (Special) Committee was primarily a Labour group, and it was in fact severely criticised for the fact that, while refusing to disclose any details of its dealings to the full Council, it reported in secret direct to the Labour members of the Council following the *Mercury* exposé. There is little question that the objective of the committee was never in any doubt on either side of the table. In the interests of efficiency local government needed to be centralised, and this involved new, centralised premises. However, the location was another question. Kenneth Bowder no doubt put his finger on the Committee's agenda when he made the point that, in a climate in which developers were snapping up all available prime inner-city sites, the longer the Special Committee extended matters, the fewer alternatives would be available and the more committed the Council would be to its recommendations.

Another site did exist, in the area just off London Road between Waterloo Street and Albion Hill. If that were to become lost to the Council the Victoria Park site would be much more attractive. Already there were suspicions that the scheme would expand from the proposed ½ acre (sufficient for an adequate building) to 6½ acres (the area needed for a complex) and the park would provide almost unlimited space.

It is ironic that, although this particular venture came to nought, twenty years later, in circumstances of secrecy and conflict almost mirroring this unhappy incident, Leicester City Council took up residence in New Walk Centre.

The possibility of building a civic centre in the Albion Hill area of the city had been tentatively discussed as early as October 1947, and once the furore raised by the Victoria Park débâcle had settled, this project was lifted down from the shelf, dusted off and put back on the table as a viable option.

On 29 July 1958 Councillor Vesty, again on behalf of the Administrative Office and Civic Buildings Committee, placed before the Council the results of the Committee's latest research.

The plan, which envisaged spending in the region of £1.6 million, was initially to build a six-storey block of offices along the southern edge of the new ring road at a cost of £280,000. This first phase, under the auspices of City Architect J.H. Lloyd Owen, would be built along a line parallel to Waterloo Street. (At this time Waterloo Street was still a relatively narrow thoroughfare, its main claim to notoriety was as a 'red light district', connecting London Road with Hastings Street.) Dependent upon the granting of government aid, work could commence within two years, and within five years would provide 36,500sq. ft of accommodation for the Surveyor's and Architect's Departments. Flexibility in the planning would allow for the building to rise to ten storeys if necessary, and by putting a bridge over New Walk a further three-storey block could be connected to

After twenty years of research and planning, involving proposed sites in Victoria Park and Albion Hill, Leicester City Council settled on the site at New Walk Centre for their main administrative headquarters and took up occupancy in 1976.

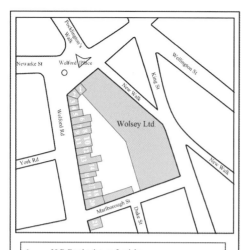

1	J&R Franks, house furnishers
2	E.W. Campion & Sons Ltd., cycle agents
3	Cyril Bramley, bookseller
4	Wellshod & Willwear, boot and shoe repairer
5	Joyce Wesly, wardrobe dealer
6	M.H. Staines Ltd., leather merchants
7	Martin's, herbalists
8/9	W&J Bogod & Co. Ltd., sewing machine fittings
10 / 11	Arthur Queenborough Ld., hairdresser
12	Geo. Green, (Leicester) Ltd., electrical engineers
13	Prince Leopold p.h, ('The Big Window')
14	Royal Arms p.h.
15	Geo. Green, (Leicester) Ltd., electrical engineers
16	Cyril Needham, confectioner
17	Welford Cabinet Supplies
18/19	F.H. Ross & Sons, auctioneers
20	Jobling's, confectioner
21	Marlborough Head, p.h.

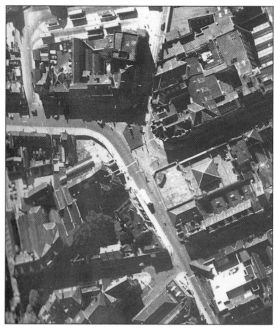

Taken in the late summer of 1971, this picture shows, at the centre, Welford Place with demolition work in progress on the block that was eventually to house the New Walk Centre. *(Courtesy: E. Selvidge)*

Left: Plan of the properties demolished to facilitate the building of New Walk Centre.

a custom-built Council Chamber, Committee Rooms and Mayor's Suite. Additionally, provision would be made for the parking of 700 cars.

The Vice-Chairman of the Committee, Councillor J.W. Taylor, made the valid point that, had the designing of this proposed complex been made the subject of an architectural competition, and the Council refused to accept the winning design, the project would have been set back to its starting point. The Committee's response was that it was 'more than satisfied that the City Architect's Department could do this worthily and efficiently'. There is little doubt that, in the circumstances, this statement was true; however, it displayed a closed-mind syndrome that in later years fuelled the political row that erupted over the issue of the acquisition of the New Walk Centre.

By the end of October that year, under a slum clearance programme, compulsory purchase orders had been made on 180 properties built in Ashwell and Wellington Streets during the period 1844–67 to facilitate preparation of the site.

The initial estimate of five years' work was just not practical, and in less than two and a half years, while the project was still on the drawing board, grandiose plans for an entirely new concept were once again being formulated by the Administrative and Civic Buildings Committee, now under the stewardship of Councillor John Taylor. At the beginning of February 1961 the Council was presented with an enlarged scheme which included a civic theatre, reception hall, art gallery and restaurant. While ostensibly drawing all of the local authority departments under one roof, designs were being laid out for a much more impressive enterprise. Geographically the proposals now encompassed the area bounded by Regent Road, the line of the proposed central ring road, London Road opposite to the Midland station and South Albion Street. To proceed with the venture it would be necessary to acquire the land at the corner of London Road and East Street.

With the proposals now having progressed openly to a much higher level, it was decided in 1960 to seek the advice of a consultant architect. Peter Chamberlin of the London firm of architects Chamberlin, Powell & Bon (who were also involved in designing London's Barbican Centre) was brought in. By October 1965, in Chamberlin's own words, plans for 'a new precinct worthy of Leicester's seat of government', had been arrived at. This latest draft went further than anything previously envisaged: accommodation for all of the City Council departments, including municipal offices, committee rooms, a suite for the Lord Mayor and banqueting facilities. In anticipation of a staff of 1,400 people, there would be underground parking for 1,000 cars. The plans provided for the insertion of mezzanine floors as needed, to provide extra accommodation. Around the perimeter of the complex were to be a new railway station concourse, a hotel, shops, a block of flats, an art gallery and a conference hall.

Because of the increased complexity of the recommendations it was envisaged that work would not begin before 1967. The estimated cost was now £7 million. In November 1967 the County Council's new administrative centre, County Hall on Leicester Road at Glenfield, was opened, built at a cost of £1.8 million.

The big question here is why was there was so much urgency on the part of the City Council to provide such a complex and expensive infrastructure. Given that

This rooftop picture (probably taken from Albion House) shows a mixture of laid-out car parking and undeveloped ground adjoining Wellington Street, and behind it the Catholic church in New Walk, 14 February 1974. In the background stand the two office blocks which, the subject of political conflict, were shortly to become the City Council's administrative centre. *(Courtesy: Urban Design Group, Leicester City Council)*

many of the authority's departments were spread in a somewhat disorganised manner across various parts of the city, they functioned effectively, and at a time when government pressure was for councils to cut back on expenditure, the justification to spend some £7 million was neither easy nor palatable in the eyes of the ratepayers. Since the end of the war Leicester City Council had been involved in a series of skirmishes with rural councils the boundaries of which were contiguous with the city's, and with an ever-increasing population and pressing needs to provide housing away from the centre of the town, the City Council had, over the years, been involved in several border feuds concerning the acquisition of land on the edges of the city. Everyone involved in local government across the county was acutely aware that within a very short time there was to be a merging of town and county authorities, in the interests of efficiency. Hence Chamberlin's assertions that they would build 'a seat worthy of government'. Leicester's aspirations were to create a City Hall capable of housing the administration for both authorities.

Late in November 1966 matters for the City Council were pressing. A Royal Commission on local government was on the point of recommending sweeping reorganisation nationally, and had already stated that approval for major schemes would not be given unless they were likely to be essential to whatever pattern of government might emerge from its findings. Two major and potentially expensive decisions needed to be taken. The first of these was the most basic. Should Messrs Chamberlin, Powell & Bon be authorised to continue with the planning process? Second, if the answer to the initial question was 'yes', it would be necessary to appoint four specialist companies for further consultancy work, and that would be expensive. The projected cost of fees for this aspect of the planning amounted to £332,000. Because the Ministry of Housing and Local Government had already indicated that it was not prepared even to consider an application for a loan from central funds, the money would have to be found from the Council's own resources. This became a highly relevant factor later on when it became necessary to find the finances needed to purchase New Walk Centre.

In support of its aspirations, the General Purposes Committee put forward a report stating that

> the most extreme reorganisation of local government might be a combination of responsibilities necessitating the doubling of the amount of accommodation required to meet the present needs of the Corporation . . . the consultants have therefore given special consideration to meeting this hypothetical requirement . . . the Council Chamber now proposed would accommodate a much larger Council than at present [a reference to the existing Chamber in the Town Hall] and the civic facilities generally are likely to be more than adequate for a new Authority whatever its size . . .

In essence, a clear statement that the race was on.

With central government refusing to make any contribution towards paying the mounting project fees, a decision had to be taken as to whether or not the ratepayers should be made to foot the bill.

There were several points to consider. Should the Royal Commission decide that no new local authorities were to be formed in the foreseeable future, then the spending could not be justified. If this were the case, there would be adverse financial and practical consequences. Should work be put on hold for a period of possibly four years while the government debated its position, and then resumed, time scales would be put back by an additional six years and costs would rise accordingly. In this – the worst-case scenario – the actual occupation of any new premises could be put back by between ten and fifteen years. Another very real consideration was that the Albion Hill location, on a main approach road into the city and immediately opposite to the Midland Railway station, was in every way a prime site and could not be allowed to stand derelict for a lengthy period; any delay now ran the risk of the site being lost to a private developer.

On the other hand, if a bold decision was taken immediately, and development pushed ahead, the site could be almost ready for occupation within five years. A further argument, so far as the General Purposes Committee was concerned, was the current fragmentation of the Council's organisation. Money was being spent on leasing offices all over the town, resulting in confusion and a lack of communication between departments. A further valid point was that at such times as the Assize Courts or Quarter Sessions were sitting at the Town Hall, working conditions in the building became intolerable.

After due discussion it was decided that the Finance Committee should make available £332,150 from capital expenditure and, despite a government freeze on local authority spending, the project was begun in earnest.

Early in 1969 the results of Chamberlin's work were endorsed by the Planning Committee and presented to the Council. Using a smaller site than originally envisaged, which covered 6½ acres (coincidentally, exactly the size mooted during the contentious Victoria Park episode), £½ million was trimmed from the estimated £7 million, bringing the costs of the scheme down to around £1 million per acre. The new site spread over the area bounded by New Walk, Waterloo Street, South Albion Street and a new link road between Calais Hill and Wellington Street. This released for private development two blocks of land hitherto earmarked for what had become known as the Chamberlin Civic Centre. The first was the block between London Road, Waterloo Street, South Albion Street and East Street. The second was East Street, South Albion Street and Calais Hill. Essentially, what would have been the front of the complex was now moved back, away from London Road, and talk of a new concourse for the Midland Railway was abandoned. In the interim, responsibility for the scheme had been passed around. First it had been under the Administrative Offices and Civic Buildings (Special) Committee, then the General Purposes Committee, and finally the Leicester Town Planning Committee. At this juncture the Town Planning Committee made what was to become a very prescient observation, stating that

only when the Royal Commission's Report has been published will the changes be clear and this could take some four to six years . . . this could cause some considerable financial hardship for the City Council . . . the construction of the new County Hall at Glenfield cannot be ignored . . . in the case of the amalgamation of the City and County Councils as an administrative unit, a dual civic centre would become a reality . . .

In this pronouncement lay the seeds of doom for the Albion Hill Civic Centre Project.

So far as the long-standing argument involving the dispersal of the various departments throughout the city was concerned, the situation, although not insurmountable, was an inconvenience which to a degree impeded the efficiency with which the Council machine functioned. The City Engineer's Department was in Greyfriars at the old headquarters of the County Council, while the Estates Department was housed in Bishop Street. The City Attorney was located in New Walk and the Treasurer in Charles Street at the Municipal Buildings, along with Personnel and Management Services. Other departments were similarly dispersed around the town.

The decisions made in January 1969 were crucial to the finished design of the complex. After nine years Peter Chamberlin's final recommendations were on the table, and it was time to move on to the laying of bricks and mortar. At this, the final stage, the city's Chief Planning Officer, Konrad Smigielski, having reviewed the Chamberlin Plan, became actively involved with ideas of his own.

Smigielski envisaged a flexible concept, creating the civic centre in three blocks from Waterloo Street to Dover Street along the line of New Walk. These could be built individually in separate phases, thus staggering the building work and expenditure. A departure from the Chamberlin concept (which called for the purchase of all of the properties along London Road from East Street to Waterloo Street) was to leave the land east of St John the Divine Church untouched, for development by the private sector. The savings to the Council in not purchasing this ground were £571,000 (thus clipping £½ million from the Chamberlin estimate). Smigielski put to the Council his opinion that 'maximum development of the site could give three times the accommodation envisaged by the Chamberlin Plan . . . as an initial stage the work could encompass a Council Chamber, Civic Suite with committee rooms, and Town Clerk and Treasurer's Departments, releasing the Town Hall for Law Courts . . .'.

In a revised proposal submitted to the Planning Committee on 8 January 1969, the grouping of buildings was reduced from three to two, with an increase of office

By the summer of 1971, at a cost of £600,000, the first phase of the Albion Hill Civic Centre project was begun by John Laing Construction Ltd, with the building of an administration block next to St John the Divine Church. (Courtesy: E.R. Welford)

Work on the Albion Hill project continued on schedule with the Planning, Housing and Architect's Departments moving in during August 1973. *(Courtesy: E.R. Welford)*

space from Chamberlin's 237,000sq. ft to 380,000sq. ft. This restructuring, as the Chief Planning Officer pointed out, allowed for the building line on London Road to be widened into a dual carriageway.

Given that Konrad Smigielski did not take up his post in Leicester until September 1962, by which time the Chamberlin, Powell & Bon consultancy work was well under way, the question still has to be asked, why did he not choose to contribute his own suggestions and ideas earlier, rather than wait until Chamberlin had submitted his recommendations and gone back to London?

One possibility is that the new Chief Planning Officer did not feel it appropriate to interfere in a project that was already under way, and instead decided to await the outcome (albeit several years) before adding his own contributions. This is an unlikely probability – Smigielski was certainly not a man to be overawed by an eminent London architect. A more likely supposition is that, given the circumstances and proposed siting of the project, he agreed in principle with Peter Chamberlin's ideas (unquestionably, he would have had access to any interim reports made by the consultancy) and was content to let Chamberlin do all of the hard work, while privately amending some of the findings and formulating his own revised plans. This would account for his ability to produce a 'slightly revised' proposition that not only gave vastly improved floor space but also cut a considerable amount from the expenditure.

By the summer of 1971 tenders and contracts had been dealt with and, at a cost of £600,000, work on the first phase – an administrative block next to St John the Divine Church, facing onto South Albion Street – was commenced by John Laing Construction Ltd. Eighteen months later the construction work had reached a point where commissioning of the building could begin and towards the end of the summer, in August 1973, the Planning, Housing and Architect's Departments prepared to move in.

Work on the Albion House section of the project was completed by the first week of June 1974, and a decision now had to be taken by the Council in relation to proceeding with the next phase. However, events were about to take an unexpected turn.

In common with many other cities across the country preparing for a grand new era of trade, commerce and travel, Leicester had seen an upsurge of speculative investment in the building of office blocks and hotels, most of which stood empty from the day that they were completed. In 1960 Curzon Agencies of London declared that it was going to build a multi-storey hotel on Charles Street, at the back of the Midland station. In less than twelve months the project had passed to another London development company, Grosvenor House Properties Ltd. They announced that they would on the same site invest £2.5 million to erect an eleven-storey, 200-room hotel with a 200-cover restaurant and a ballroom, together with a twenty-storey office block with underground parking for 300 cars.

Accompanied by much publicity, the scheme lasted a mere four months before being pronounced dead owing to lack of funds. Amid a flurry of unoccupied office blocks emerging across the city, in 1973 the Magnum Hotel Group opened Leicester's 240-room Magnum Hotel on the site of the old Freeman, Hardy & Willis factory at the junction of Humberstone Gate and Rutland Street. A year later, with debts estimated at £9 million, the group went into liquidation.

Thus, it was with little cause for excitement that in August 1971 the people of Leicester received the news that the ancient block of properties in Welford Place, watched over impassively by the statue of the venerable Victorian businessman, politician and erstwhile town father John Biggs, was to be demolished to make way for yet another building project. The 2-acre site was being cleared in order to build a twin-block office complex, one of fourteen storeys at the front, overlooking Welford Place, the other a nine-storey building to the rear, butting onto New Walk.

This particular venture had taken longer than most to come to fruition. Nine years earlier, in May 1962, Wolsey Ltd, which owned most of the land affected, had submitted plans for the building of a ten-storey, 200-room hotel on the site. Doubtless, the subsequent failure of other hotel projects in the city dissuaded them from the idea, and nothing was done, with the result that the site was passed on for later development, culminating in the decision to erect the present office blocks. Overall costs of the work, including the demolition of two public houses in Welford Road (the Prince Leopold, known locally as the Big Window, and the Royal Arms) and several business premises, a projected £8 million, were undertaken by Geo. Wimpey & Co.

With the Albion Hill Civic Centre programme well under way and Council departments already in the process of taking up occupation, the Council's controlling Labour group's announcement in January 1975 of its intention to discontinue work on the agreed project and purchase the newly built office block at Welford Place came as a stunning blow.

On Wednesday 29 January the *Leicester Mercury* apprised the electorate of the decision taken by the City Policy and Resources Committee. The Albion Hill scheme was to be abandoned and for £5.25 million the City Council was going to buy the two office blocks, known as New Walk Centre. With an additional estimate of a further £1 million to furnish and equip the blocks, the total sum involved would be £6.5 million.

The Conservative group on the Council were appalled. This latest development by the Policy and Resources Committee under the chairmanship of the Revd Kenneth

Middleton, leader of the controlling Labour group, had been decided under a close veil of secrecy, and they had been caught unawares. In answer to demands for an explanation from Michael Cufflin, the chairman of the Conservative group, the Council's Executive Officer, John Phipps, revealed that while negotiations for the purchase of the office blocks had been going on for some time, actual financial arrangements had only been put in place in January. In a statement issued by the Labour leader, he cited a list of reasons as to why the original plans were being ditched. The Council departments were presently housed in nine separate locations across the city and telephone communications were not good because of the absence of a central switchboard, so calls could not be transferred. Travelling between buildings was an incon-venience to council workers and was counter-productive. The full Albion House development would take

The Revd Kenneth Middleton, leader of the Labour group on the City Council, who was responsible for the abandonment of the Albion Hill project and the subsequent puchase of the New Walk Centre. *(Courtesy: Urban Design Group, Leicester City Council)*

five years to complete and eventually add up to £9 million. To provide office accommodation at that site only would cost between £6.4 and £7 million. Finally, by taking possession of the New Walk Centre the Council would be occupying an otherwise empty office block in the city, and relinquishing the site on Albion Hill would free up land for commercial development.

The arguments were, at best, weak and the opponents of the scheme were having none of it. Once again, as with the Victoria Park scheme nearly twenty years before, the Labour group had in total secrecy negotiated the spending of a vast amount of public money and was about to reap a whirlwind.

The Conservatives brought in counter-arguments. Albion House, in the process of being occupied by Council departments, was already beginning to answer the logistical problems. No account was taken, in the new projections, of monies already spent; and with offices and premises built by speculators in recent years still standing empty, who was going to buy Albion Hill? In answer to a further argument that, with a capacity for 200 or 300 more staff than the local authority actually employed, the New Walk Centre buildings were actually too big, the reply was given that letting out space was not an option and that more staff would eventually be employed to fill the empty offices.

A further point made by opponents of the purchase was that with absolutely no prospect of any new money coming from central government, the asking price would have to be paid by the ratepayers. The purchase, if it went ahead, would have an adverse effect on the city rates until 1982–3. Taking a stand with the scheme's opponents, in February the *Leicester Mercury* conducted a straw poll through its pages, and showed that of the 29,553 people surveyed, 860 were in favour of the new centre, while 28,693 were against.

Meanwhile, Kenneth Middleton continued to push things forward, stating that this was an opportunity not to be missed and that cash would be saved by not having to spend money on buildings that could be relinquished and disposed of as assets.

A few weeks later, in April 1975, events took another turn when local businessman Hugh Murphy stepped into the dispute. Hugh Murphy owned Charles Street Buildings Ltd, a construction company with experience of large building projects. He made an offer to build a civic centre on the Albion Hill site for £3.5 million. The proposal included his putting up a Performance Bond in any sum that an arbitrator might require to guarantee completion within the stated price, his only stipulation being that his company must start work within the next six months. The offer, strongly supported by the Conservatives, was rejected out of hand by the Labour group as a red herring.

The day after the refusal of Hugh Murphy's proposal, Michael Cufflin issued a challenge to Kenneth Middleton. They would both resign their seats and fight the ensuing by-election on the issue of whether the voters of Leicester wished the purchase of the New Walk Centre to go through. Middleton refused to accept the challenge.

Because no government funding was forthcoming a deal had been made with Morgan Grenfell (Local Authority Services) Ltd, a subsidiary of Morgan Grenfell Merchant Bank, to borrow the money – and the matter had to be completed within days, by 30 April.

Now it was the turn of the Leicester Chamber of Commerce to become involved. They decided to take legal action against the City Council under the General Rate Act 1967, on the basis that to impose the cost of purchasing the buildings on the rates was unlawful. On Tuesday 10 June Messrs Gardiner & Millhouse, acting on behalf of the thirty member companies of the Chamber of Commerce, served a Notice of Appeal under the General Rate Act on the City Attorney.

Unperturbed by the furore going on around them, the Labour group put the matter to a vote at a meeting of the Council on 24 April. A motion to continue with the purchase was passed by a vote of twenty-nine to thirteen (five Labour members contrived to be absent from the vote, and a further member abstained).

Despite the acrimony and controversy surrounding the New Walk Centre project, its protagonists eventually won the day. On 19 June 1975 the City Attorney, David Mellor, announced that the Council had acquired the freehold of the 214,00sq. ft site as civic offices from the developers, Land and House Property Corporation, and the British Steel Corporation Pension Fund for £5.2 million, and that contracts had been exchanged.

The Appeal against the Council's proposed levy of 2.3p in the pound in order to fund the scheme was dismissed in the High Court on 28 January 1976 by Judge Harry Skinner, with a summing up that 'the City Council had acted in a businesslike way and used skill and caution in deciding to buy the premises . . .'. Seven months later, in the middle of August 1976, the *Leicester Mercury*, a staunch opponent of the project, carried an aerial photograph of the twin blocks with the caption, 'New Walk Centre, now being occupied by Leicester City Council departments. Leicester City's giant computer being moved into New Walk Centre from Municipal buildings'.

CHAPTER NINE

Economic Decline in the 1960s and 1970s

The 1960s are remembered by all who lived through them as a golden decade. For the teenager leaving school at 15 or 16 there was an abundance of opportunities in almost every field of endeavour. For those who were older and had struggled through the austerity of the 1950s, with an influx of consumer goods in the shops, plenty of work and an increasing pay packet, the future was suddenly looking much brighter.

Based upon what appeared to be a now stable economy, the man in the street could not be blamed for assuming that all was well and would continue to be so. In Leicester, because of the imbalance between 'jobs available and job applicants', a situation existed where anyone could apply for three jobs: attend an interview for the first, decline it, accept the second, and not bother to go to the interview for the third. So dire were the employers' needs for labour that it was most likely that the prospective third employer would later contact the applicant asking whether, despite the missed interview, they were still interested. The result was that while giving an illusion of prosperity, a very fragile situation existed which, combined with other factors, would eventually cause huge cracks to appear in some of the city's main industries.

In 1960 an unfortunate circumstance created a major problem for the City Council. As part of its plans for slum clearance and the restructuring of the road systems serving the town, Leicester City Council secured a compulsory purchase order on the factory belonging to Fox's Confectionery in Oxford Street.

Since the turn of the century Fox's, run as a family business, had been a substantial employer in the city. By the end of the First World War Eric, the son of founder Walter Fox, had developed the Fox's Glacier Mint, a clear peppermint sweet which, advertised by the cartoon figure Peppy the Polar Bear, shot the company to international fame. In January 1960 Fox's, employing 200 people, under the threat of the compulsory purchase order, entered into negotiations to purchase land on the opposite side of Oxford Street in order to relocate and continue the business.

However, central government, with its own agenda of moving industry out of city centres into green-field areas, stepped in with an unexpected prohibition. Before the Council could grant planning permission to Fox's for rebuilding its factory it became a prerequisite that an Industrial Development Certificate be granted by the Board of Trade. On the grounds that it was only prepared to grant certificates in areas of low employment the Board of Trade did not consider the relocation of Fox's a suitable case and refused to grant the permit.

In 1960, as part of plans to build a new road system through the city centre, a compulsory purchase order was obtained by the City Council on the premises of Fox's Confectionery in Oxford Street. Prevented by central government from building new premises nearby, Fox's relocated in 1967 to the old Braunstone Aerodrome site, which was being developed as an industrial estate. *(Courtesy: Fox's Confectionery)*

Protests that this was not a new development but a relocation of an existing company were in vain. Displaying monumental inflexibility, the Birmingham-based Deputy Regional Controller for the Board of Trade, J. Wardle, announced that the department would not reconsider its decision and that '[relocation] affected most Midlands centres wherever there were plans for a new factory or extension, or even the re-siting of an existing factory if the industry concerned could operate equally well in one of the under-employed areas . . .'.

Fox's thus became one of the first major employers to move out of the town. It took up an option on a site at Sunningdale Road, part of the redevelopment of the old Braunstone airfield, and by April 1967 had relocated and was in full production. Shortly after, in 1969, providing an early example of a successful local family business becoming a prime target for a takeover bid, the company was absorbed into the Rowntree Mackintosh Group.

The refusal to allow a local government initiative to permit a manufacturer to move to another part of the city presented both the Council and local industrialists with a major dilemma. With planning applications pending from a further 272 firms, the government policy had the potential to affect the future of over 4,000 workers in the city. Unlike the giant AEI organisation, which had secured 600,000sq. ft of premises at Braunstone, small and medium-sized city firms employing less than fifty staff that found themselves subject to compulsory purchase orders would be unable to afford the move to green-field sites. The brewing firm of Whitbread's did not even bother to test the system. With its warehousing facility in Willow Street being demolished as part of the proposed development of the St Matthew's estate, it simply declared that it was closing down the delivery department and moving to Loughborough. Suggestions were made to the Chairman of the Planning Committee that, with 300 industrial concerns being displaced in the next five years by the Council's renewal schemes, 16 acres of the new St Matthew's estate should be earmarked for industrial use.

With the start of a new decade, pressure was already being felt by some companies. In 1960 the estimated population of Leicester was 280,000 and the unemployment figures for the city were still relatively low – during the period April to July that year, with the constant thread that there were more people available than jobs, it fluctuated between 1,023 and 764.

Some problems had begun to appear during the late 1950s as firms, unable to compete, either laid off workers or closed down altogether. In January and February 1958 there was a dip in the fortunes of many engineering shops. Orders for machine tools dropped, causing many Midlands firms to start working short time. During February 1958, owing to a shortage of orders, the shoe firm of R.H. Bolley Ltd, having already trimmed its workforce from 300 to 220, closed its factory in Norton Street. As a direct consequence of the closure of Bolley's, the Blindell Group of shoe manufacturers at South Wigston moved its workers from piece-work to time rates. Adcock & Shipley announced that it had 'sufficient orders for the present, but future work is in the balance'. From the employers' standpoint, the blip was not helped when, in October, female engineers received a pay increase of 5s 6d a week, bringing the wages of a woman over 18 years of age to £6 6s 6d. (A man doing the same job received £7 17s 4d.)

It was at this time that a change in working practices was implemented in the hosiery trade. In the early summer of 1958, the 4,000-strong National Union of Hosiery Workers voted to accept the principle already implemented in the United States and continental Europe, that in the fine-gauge section of the industry one operative should work two machines, the agreement being that there would be an increase in pay and no redundancies. In the short term, the arrangement was to the advantage of the shop-floor workers; however, in the long

Fox's Confectionery was most popular in postwar years for its leading line, Fox's Glacier Mints, epitomised by the famous polar bear advert. This is the original mock-up of the advert dating to 1943, made up of the proposed design work cut out and pasted onto a board. While a price and the main bullet points have been arrived at, the centre area for text is as yet undecided and represented as a series of lines. *(Courtesy: Fox's Confectionery)*

term it was inevitable that industry would reduce its workforce. Technology was already beginning to influence working practices in the trade – examining machines had moved from checking 250 items a week to 600.

Closures in both the hosiery and the shoe trades now began. Established in 1930, Fosse Dyeworks Ltd, at Syston, specialists in dyeing and finishing hosiery and fully fashioned knitted outerwear, closed down in February 1961 with eighty job losses. They were soon followed by Liberty Shoes. Founded in 1900 by Disney Charles Barlow and Sir Samuel Briers, in July 1962 Liberty Shoes served redundancy notices on its 200 employees (in better times Liberty had employed 650 people). The company's extensive premises on Eastern Boulevard, which it had occupied since moving from Asylum Street in 1921, were taken over by the printing firm of Lowe & Carr Ltd.

Despite individual difficulties, industry generally was still reasonably robust at the beginning of the decade. Over sixty shoe firms operating in the city and county were turning out a total of 21 million pairs of shoes at the end of 1959. However, the situation was beginning to slip and by the end of 1964 the shoe trade was declining, with warehouses becoming clogged with unsold stocks.

In January 1965 Leslie Toft, speaking on behalf of the Leicester Footwear Manufacturers' Association, commented that Leicester manufacturers were experiencing the worst trading period for some years. One of the reasons put forward by the Association was that retailers were not clearing their stocks because of an unusually mild winter. While there was a degree of truth in this rather weak assertion it was by no means the whole story. The British shoe industry overall was failing to embrace the new techniques that were crucial to its survival, and was consequently locked into the production of styles that were no longer fashionable. Several years earlier, in October 1953, J.H. Stafford of the British United Shoe Machinery Co. in Leicester, pointed out to the industry that 'there is a craze for new styles – for which the public are prepared to pay. Immediately following the war females began to demand a return to soft and light shoes, many based on American designs. Standard shoes [made on existing machines], welted and machine sewn, are diminishing in popularity – new manufacturing methods are needed to accommodate the new marketplace. . . .'

By May 1965 the situation had deteriorated badly. In the preceding twelve months, nationally, while £21 million worth of footwear had been imported, production of shoes exceeded that figure by about 11 million pairs – and in Leicestershire production was above the national average.

As with any other industry, some firms held on to their order books. In the summer of 1966, when production in the county had, as a result of high production costs and a tight market, dropped by 6 per cent, the Co-operative Wholesale Society, with its Wheatsheaf factory at Knighton Fields Road East (established in 1891, the Wheatsheaf had been one of the largest shoe factories in Europe), signalled an improvement in sales. Five of the Society's six factories were working overtime to service increasing markets in America and the Soviet Union.

By the mid-1960s the decline of the shoe trade was virtually unstoppable. Employment by city firms engaged in the boot and shoe industry had fallen to 12,500. A trade that in 1948 employed 28 per cent of the city's workforce had, by the 1970s, dropped to well below half that figure.

Away from the hosiery and shoe trades there were areas of business that, through a combination of diversity and good management, prospered after the war and continued to be highly successful throughout the subsequent years of financial crises.

A prime example is that of Murphy Brothers Ltd. During the early 1930s three brothers, Hugh, Patrick and Paul Murphy, arrived in Leicester from Newry in County Armagh, and set up a business in Bedford Street trading as scrap-metal and general dealers. After the war they diversified by buying ex-army lorries, refurbishing them and selling them on – many for export overseas, primarily to Australia. By 1954 the brothers owned a 17-acre site on Loughborough Road, which they sold to the Metal Box Co. for £237,000 before moving to the disused Ministry of Works vehicle repair site on Melton Road, Syston. Metal Box was itself a prosperous group, valued at the time at £25 million, with thirty-four factories across the United Kingdom. Having invested £500,000 in setting up a new plant on the old Murphy site, the company embarked on an operation employing 250 workers, 170 of them women, to produce 25,000 tin boxes a week for the confectionery trade. Continuing to expand, fourteen years later the company formed a multi-million-pound alliance with British Traction.

Businesses in the services sector, such as cafés and restaurants, prospered despite difficult times after the war. One specialist group was that of the ice-cream parlours and coffee houses opened and run by Italian families such as the Bruccianis, Massarellas, Rossas and Espositos who had for many years been settled in the city. Some specialised in producing and selling ice-cream, others diversified.

Three brothers, Dominic, Anthony and John Masserella had come to England from Italy at the turn of the century. Dominic and Anthony set up an ice-cream business in Leicester, while John moved to Doncaster. By the 1950s the Masserella Group, with interests in Leicester and Yorkshire, was attracting the attention of larger national firms and in 1954 it was absorbed into the J. Lyons group of companies.

The Brucciani family is another example of how, away from the mainstream industries upon which Leicester's economy was based, it was possible to create and sustain a successful enterprise. Born in Carlisle in 1900, Luigi Brucciani was the youngest of four children. His father (also Luigi) originally came to Scotland from Italy in the late nineteenth century and, having first moved to Carlisle, later established a business selling ice-cream and coffee in Barrow-in-Furness. The younger Luigi, after working first in the family undertaking, opened a grocery shop (Rashers) in the same town. During the difficult years of the 1930s he discovered that women eking out their meagre housekeeping funds in his shop, while grumbling and haggling over the price of such essentials as a pound of potatoes, would not question the asking price of a cup of coffee and an opportunity to relax away from the pressures of life for a short time in his father's coffee house. Selling his grocer's shop, Luigi moved away from the north-west, down to Leicester, bought the lease on premises in Horsefair Street, and in late 1937 opened what was, for the next fifty-four years, to be Leicester's most famous ice-cream parlour and coffee house. An ambitious businessman, Luigi Brucciani's interests also took him to the United States where, during the 1950s, he saw an opportunity in the American practice of workers in the food industry using disposable paper hats for hygiene purposes. Unable to find an American company prepared to sell him the

equipment to produce such items, on his return to England Luigi Brucciani had a purpose-built machine made by Bakewell Engineering in Parker Drive. As he had only a sketchy idea of how to produce the hats, manufacturing was problematic, and the experimentation required 1 ton of paper to provide the first satisfactory prototype. From that point on, however, the venture never looked back and was soon in full production. By the turn of the century, based at Oadby, the family company of Pal International Ltd became one of the country's biggest suppliers of chefs' headgear, hygienic work-wear and disinfectant wipes.

In 1963 Brucciani's bought out the long-established Leicester firm of J.S. Winn & Co. which, apart from its three city-centre cafés, also gave them a bakery in Bath Lane from which to service their coffee and ice-cream houses. When Luigi retired and his son Michael took over in 1965 Brucciani's had premises in Horsefair Street and Fox Lane, plus the Sunset Café near to the entrance of what was to become the Haymarket Centre, the Turkey Café in Granby Street and the Royal Café on London Road, near to the railway station. In 1976–7 Michael Brucciani bought the premises of Excel Hairdressing Suppliers in Churchgate (originally the old tramways stables and garage), along with an empty premises at the rear which, in recent times, had been a coffee bar and was in the process of being converted into offices. By combining the two premises he created another coffee and ice-cream parlour with entrances in both streets.

Regrettably, the town's most popular meeting place, Brucciani's in Horsefair Street (opposite to Kemp's the jewellers, famous for the clock over the shop that made it a favourite rendezvous for couples on a first date), closed in 1991 when the lease expired.

The postwar years also presented golden opportunities for the entrepreneur in the retail trade. As a forerunner of national and multinational supermarkets, two men with a fresh approach to selling to the public now appeared independently on the Leicester scene.

In 1958, starting out with small premises in Vaughan Street, Anthony Roger Bramley began a group of corner shops offering cut-price groceries. Based on selling for cash only (in itself a major departure from the time-honoured practice of corner shops running a 'slate', enabling housewives to buy goods on credit throughout the week and pay their bill on Friday when the husband drew his wage packet), Tony's Cut-Price Stores 'piled it high and sold it cheap'. It was a winning

Opposite page and right: Despite the economic depression sweeping the country, people still needed somewhere to relax and have a quiet cup of coffee. During the mid-1960s Brucciani's acquired the city-centre chain of cafés owned by J.S. Winn, which included the historic Turkey Café site in Granby Street. *(Courtesy: M. Brucciani)*

Above and right: Begun in Horsefair Street in 1937 by Luigi Brucciani, by the late 1960s, under the stewardship of his son Michael, Brucciani's owned a chain of premises which included the Winn's group of cafés, along with parlours in Fox Lane and Churchgate. *(Courtesy: M. Brucciani)*

format and by the early 1960s Bramley owned eleven shops across the city and a wholesale outlet, trading as Four Counties, in Thornton Lane. Sadly, although the company continued to trade for several years afterwards, following a long illness Tony Bramley died in September 1962 at the age of 29.

Frank Brierley was a more flamboyant character. A middle-aged market trader, by the mid-1960s he had established a supermarket chain with stores in Leicester, Northampton and Peterborough. The Leicester shop in Belgrave Gate, identifiable by the large American Confederate flag flying over the store, flourished under Brierley's motto: 'If I can't sell it cheaper, I don't stock it'. Brierley was well on the way to creating what could have been one of the largest UK supermarket chains in private hands when things turned sour in October 1973. Along with some associates he was charged with fraud offences relating to their business dealings in London. The ensuing legal proceedings, involving a trial and a retrial at the Old Bailey, took over one and a half years to come to a conclusion, and although Brierley was found not guilty of the charges, his supermarket interests had in the meantime suffered badly. It was announced in April 1974 that the Northampton-based firm had ceased share trading at the request of its directors, following the disclosure of problems in the audit of its last year's accounts. Six weeks later the receiver was called in and the first of Leicester's major supermarkets closed its doors.

While new and diverse enterprises generally did well, the biggest employers in the city were still based either directly or indirectly around the two main industries.

By the early 1970s the shoe trade was beginning to lose ground rapidly. On the one hand, foreign competition was putting more and more pressure on declining sales, while on the other, high labour costs militated against firms being able to produce goods at attractive prices. One avenue that manufacturers were obliged to explore was the reduction of labour costs through the use of improved technology. By retooling during the late 1950s and throughout the 1960s it became possible to make the production of a pair of shoes less labour intensive. The number of stages required to turn out a pair of ladies' shoes was reduced from 100 to 62. By using man-made materials in the production of women's and children's shoes it was possible not only to reduce the cost of materials but also to eliminate twelve of the fifteen operations previously required for the preparation of soling materials. Technological advances were achieved in a three-way marriage of engineering, tradesmen and chemistry. It was probably in the latter field that some of the greatest advances were made in the 1960s.

By the beginning of the 1970s leather was being supplanted by PVC and by synthetic leathers for uppers and linings, and newer and better adhesives were replacing traditional stitching methods. One of the prime innovations was the use of polyurethane. Weighing half as much as conventional soling materials, and with improved non-slip properties, polyurethane enabled manufacturers to produce an improved lightweight shoe that was cool in the summer and warm in the winter. The problem was that firms in other countries were also taking advantage of the new technology, and the struggle for manufacturers in the home market (nationally, in 1971 the British industry was producing in the region of ¾ million pairs of shoes a day – sufficient to supply the needs of the combined populations of Leicester, Northampton and Norwich) was to keep up with the competition.

In 1971 the Leicester Footwear Manufacturers' Association reported that 'most firms in the county, last year began poorly as the dull footwear trading conditions and short order books of the previous year [1969] carried forward into 1970. The situation gradually picked up and by the middle of the summer factories became busier and attempted to regain the productive momentum which they sacrificed during the long slack period. . . .'

In Leicester city during early 1970 a hard winter retarded the sales of spring shoes, with the consequence that for some smaller manufacturers short-time working was inevitable. The setback was not helped by the fact that during the year imports from overseas into the UK amounted to a formidable 65 million pairs of shoes, the majority of them from Italy, France, eastern Europe and the Far East. In real terms these imports represented one in four of every pair of shoes bought in the shops. Inflation made the situation worse by pushing up the prices of materials. With an uncertain financial climate looming, many manufacturers viewed the future with trepidation. In an attempt to diversify, some local firms invested money by producing fashion boots to meet one of the latest demands for new styles. Set against the competition posed by foreign imports, these locally produced boots were one of the goods that still sold well. During the twelve months between January 1970 and 1971 the shoe trade lost 664 operatives, reducing the city's labour force from 6,813 to 6,149. In March 1970 the President of the Leicester Branch of the British Boot and Shoe Institution, R.M. James, while denying that the boot and shoe industry was dying, commented that 'it is true that some smaller units are going to fall by the wayside . . . if [the shoe] industry is to survive a lot more technological research will be required, especially in the closing department, which is still very labour intensive'.

These prophecies – which as time passed proved to be inaccurate only inasmuch as it was not only 'small units' that fell by the wayside – were soon being fulfilled. In January 1972 Airborne Shoes at Anstey went into receivership with a loss of 200 jobs and was followed in October that year by the closure of the Leicester factory of Brevitt Shoes, putting a further 200 people out of work. (Brevitt, in an effort to consolidate its operations, continued to manufacture at its Northampton site.)

At the end of the third week of February 1973 the shoe firm of Stead & Simpson, established first in Northampton in 1844, and twelve years later in Leicester, announced the closure of its manufacturing plants in both towns, with a loss of 400 jobs, along with the rider that its retail shop trade was also suffering badly.

In 1975 Harry Levison, Chairman of Charles Clore's British Shoe Corporation, took a different view: 'when things are going well British manufacturers price themselves out of the market, when they are going badly they blame unfair foreign competition . . . manufacturers have neglected to build up foreign export business because they say we have the best retail set-up in Europe, which has made them complacent . . .'.

Nationally, the 1960s heralded the beginning of a long period of economic woes and political strife. When the Labour Party under Harold Wilson won the October 1964 general election it was by a mere five seats, which was in itself going to make strong government difficult. Wilson inherited considerable problems with the balance of payments and the strength of the domestic economy. In November 1967 the government was forced, in an attempt to turn the economy around, to devalue the pound by 14.3 per cent. Britain was not alone in its problems – among others, Cyprus devalued in line with sterling, and New Zealand devalued by 19.45 per cent. The move did mean that certain imports, especially from New Zealand, became cheaper than their European rivals, but the trade-off was huge stock market losses for many prominent companies trading in the UK (the value of Debenhams, for instance, fell by £11 million overnight). Another serious consequence was that the British worker's pay packet also became worth 14 per cent less. (The government's economic policies at this time were in tatters; for higher earners increased taxation was becoming crippling, and the situation was not improved by a particularly inept television appearance by the Prime Minister who tried to assure people that the pound in their pocket was not affected by recent events.)

Devaluation did not stop the slide, and three months later the balance of trade figures for February 1968 showed that imports had soared to a record high of £655 million, plunging Britain's balance of payments a further £70 million into the red. The value of the pound sterling fell to $2.40. On Friday 15 March 1968, in a state of crisis, the London gold market and all British stock exchanges closed temporarily, resulting in the Governor of the Bank of England, Sir Leslie O'Brien, flying to Washington for urgent talks with the Johnson administration.

The dire economic situation was viewed by many industrialists with a high degree of trepidation, and there were those who, when made a tempting offer, could not be blamed for taking it. At the beginning of 1970 D. Byford & Co., whose profits had fallen from £240,342 in 1968 to £174,503 for the year ending December 1969, accepted a merger offer from the Coats Paton Group for £2 million. A major employer in the city, Byford's had factories at Leicester, Immingham and Maltby. The move came after Coats Paton, which employed between 70,000 and 80,000 people worldwide, as part of a £1.5 million takeover deal, acquired the firm of H.L. Driver at Barrow-on-Soar, giving Coats control of fourteen other companies employing 1,300 workers.

A cause of concern to some of the more perceptive hosiery industrialists was control of production (and, consequently, competitive capabilities) by major retailers – or, more colloquially, 'the tail wagging the dog'. Speaking at a conference in Harrogate in October 1970, L.Van Praag, the Managing Director of Sabre Sportswear Ltd, told the delegates

if the knitwear industry does not make the right decisions now it will become as bankrupt as the old Lancashire cotton industry . . . in the Midlands aestheticism has been sacrificed for more dozens per operative . . . in Scotland the industry has become locked into stylized designs that have not changed for years . . . in the Midlands it is one big chain store that is holding the Midlands knitwear industry together . . . industry has concentrated too much on technology to aid production and has failed to keep up with fashion aspects . . . the manufacturers lock themselves into contracts with retail stores thus becoming at the mercy of those retailers . . . where a manufacturer locks himself into a system of 'specification buying' dictated by the large retailer he loses the marketing initiative . . . the retailer takes over the role of designer and the function of marketing . . .'.

The speaker was correct in many respects. Certain chain stores, such as Marks & Spencer, were already tying hosiery manufacturers closely to themselves, first by offering lucrative contracts for goods supplied to their exact specifications, then, when the supplier had given over the larger part of his production capability to them, tightening contractual terms to a point where the manufacturer was in a virtual stranglehold.

One example of this was Welsmer (Manufacturing) Ltd, in Percy Road. Starting out in the 1930s as Fine Gauge Hosiery, producing stockings, the company was taken over in 1955 by Debenhams. For several years the firm continued to trade, exporting goods to the Soviet Union, before Debenhams took a decision that all of Welsmer's production should be directly supplied to its own company. In November 1975 Debenhams declared that the firm was no longer profitable, closing it down at the beginning of 1976 with the loss of fifty-nine jobs. Initially peculiar to the hosiery trade, in later years this was to become a widely practised business strategy, employed particularly by supermarkets in relation to food suppliers.

In Leicester and the surrounding district 1970 was generally a bad year for the hosiery manufacturing industry, resulting in widespread short-time working being implemented by many firms. Depending upon the individual enterprise, the following years were either full of opportunity or fraught with difficulties, when, under the leadership of Edward Heath in 1973, Britain became a member of the European Economic Community.

A major problem for the declining fortunes of Leicester's economy was that both of its traditional industries were hit at the same time, and in the case of hosiery production it was not simply down to the economic problems besetting the country. Fashions changed, making the plant installed in many factories virtually redundant, and equally importantly for Leicester causing loss of sales of the hosiery machines manufactured by local engineers.

At the end of the 1960s there was a worldwide upsurge in the sales of double jersey fabrics. Produced on circular knitting machines, they created one of the biggest textile booms of the century. Knitting-machine manufacturers from Leicester to Tokyo jumped on the bandwagon, with new machine manufacturing companies springing up in the United States, Germany and the Far East – and consequently a vast over-investment in the production of circular knitting machines. Before the boom, circular knitting machine manufacture had been restricted to a relatively specialised group of manufacturers. The new demand was for one standardised device designed to knit 18-gauge polyester for women's clothing. At its height, worldwide there were an estimated 75,000 circular knitting machines in operation (in the US alone there were over 24,000). To compound the problem, bigger and better machines were quickly developed, with the inevitable consequence that manufacturers of knitting machines, in an incredibly short period of time, locked themselves into this type of unit, with all the financial commitments that went with the technology. In hindsight it is difficult to believe that astute businessmen across the world allowed themselves to be swept along by what was, after all, a fashion statement. Women's dresses and coats in polyester, men's suits, slacks, trousers and sportswear – all manner of clothing was made from the fabric. The bubble burst after a few years, and by 1973 the craze for polyester was declining, leaving in its wake hundreds of hosiery firms in desperate straits.

Leicester's most high-profile casualty was G. Stibbe & Co. Ltd. Stibbe's, one of the city's oldest-established knitting-machine manufacturers, was one of the first to feel the cold wind of change when the need for machines to knit fully fashioned textiles took a sudden dip in favour of circular machines for turning out polyester; 1970 was a particularly bad year for the company. The downturn in sales figures caught Stibbe's wrong-footed, as it had during that financial year, reconstructed the company's site in Newarke Street to form a group head office, while at the same time establishing an engineering works at Consett in the north-east and opened a sales subsidiary in North Carolina to handle the group's American business. Taking a leap of faith, Stibbe's invested heavily in the industry's swing towards producing the new wonder fabric and, along with so many other knitting-machine manufacturers, ultimately paid the price. Compounding its problems in relation to cash flow commitments, the management also invested in further premises on the development site of the old Braunstone airfield at Scudamore Road, which it moved into in July 1973.

In the following December the company announced its intention, in view of anticipated trading losses, to cancel any interim shareholders' dividend. The reason behind the losses was given as 'due to a move to the new factory at Braunstone and enforced acceleration of the introduction of a new range of knitting machinery a result was a drop of £500,000 in the first half of the year's pre-tax profits . . .'. The 'new range of machinery' referred to was, of course, the circular knitting machines that had been so heavily invested in. At the end of the next six months, in June 1974, through a combination of poor trade figures and high debt repayments, the company announced a loss of £220,000 in the previous year's trading. In what can only be seen as an act of desperation to try to ease cash-flow problems, Stibbe's sold its new site at Braunstone to Standard Life Assurance for £1.85 million, then leased it back at a rental of £165,000 a year, at the same time attempting unsuccessfully to sell its engineering works in Great Central Street. With liabilities in excess of £2 million it was now proposed also to sell the group's headquarters in Newarke Street. Despite the management's best efforts, the situation was not recoverable. The same month Stibbe's closed its subsidiary, Harrico Ltd (makers of textile finishing machinery) in Syston Street with sixty redundancies. In October, with the firm in the hands of the receiver, a further 300 shop-floor workers at Braunstone were given redundancy notices. The following month it was announced that the plant that the firm had moved to the Scudamore Road site in 1973 at a cost of £1.5 million was to close, with 120 job losses. The latest closure brought the number of people employed by the firm down from 1,100 to 340. Because the Braunstone site had been sold to Standard Life to generate cash and then rented back and most of the equipment also leased, the company's chief remaining assets lay in its buildings in Newarke Street, Syston Street and Great Central Street, which it sold. One positive result was that Stibbe Pressworks Ltd in Oakland Road was sold as a going concern to Cox's of Watford, saving the jobs of the 110 workers employed there. In view of the problems being experienced nationally, the government refused financial help to bail the company out, and in November 1974 the Stibbe site at Braunstone was closed down.

The other main producer of knitting machines in the city – Bentley Engineering – was also hit by the sudden collapse of the polyester boom. In June 1974 one of its

Acquired in 1950 from Clarendon Engineering Ltd, the Bentley Group's engineering plant on Parker Drive was opposite the dog track and Speedway Stadium. *(Courtesy: E. Selvidge)*

subsidiaries, Wildt Mellor Bromley at St Saviours Road, with 600 shop-floor workers and 100 staff, went onto short-time working, and at the beginning of October it announced that it was considering closing down the site altogether. Six months later, in July 1975, the firm introduced a three-day week at its factory on Aylestone Road. In September the parent company, Bentley's, with stocks piling up, introduced a four-day week at its New Bridge Street and Parker Drive plants. Redundancies in the group became inevitable, and these were made first at the Bentley subsidiary of William Cotton Ltd at Loughborough, with 663 white-collar and shop-floor workers, comprising 55 per cent of the workforce, going in February 1973. Between December 1974 and July 1975 Bentley's made 300 workers redundant at its two main sites, and put those who remained on short-time working. It was somewhat ironic that one of the group's poorest performing subsidiaries was Cotton's. The founder of the company, William Cotton, born in about 1819 at Seagrave Lodge in Leicestershire, had been a central figure in the development of powered knitting machines, his 'Cotton's Patent' fully fashioned knitting machine being responsible during the Industrial Revolution, for taking the hosiery trade from the old hand-operated knitting frames into the machine age.

Bentley's troubles deepened. During 1974 the company made a £1.5 million trading loss and had to be supported by its holding group, Sears. A series of industrial disputes – which served to aggravate the company's declining trading situation – culminated in April 1976 with the group having 2,000 workers on strike in support of 18 men at its Komet Works in New Bridge Street, who refused to accept flexible working during a four-day week. The situation was disastrous for the company and, faced with 300 job losses, it sought candidates to take voluntary redundancy at Parker Drive and also decided to transfer 250 workers from New Bridge Street to Parker Drive. At that time the company employed 1,150 workers between the two factories, Parker Drive being the larger and more modern of the two.

The eventual demise of Bentley's when, in March 1988 with debts of £7 million, the company went into receivership, gives one of the clearest snapshots of the rise and fall of the economic fortunes of Leicester during the twentieth century. Beginning life as a small engineering firm in 1910, in 1919 after the First World War the company launched onto the international market with its Komet double-cylinder sock machine. The firm was the object of a mid-1950s takeover by Charles Clore's Sears Group and its fortunes soared. During the 1960s the Bentley Group, with an overall workforce of 9,000, was supplying an estimated 90 per cent of the UK requirements for knitting machines. At the height of the double jersey boom the Wildt Mellor Bromley division was producing more than 100 knitting machines a month and making an annual profit of £7 million on a £50 million turnover, while the William Cotton subsidiary was exporting as many fully fashioned machines as it could produce to the Soviet Union. Worldwide, companies specialising in the production and maintenance of Bentley machines were developed in Japan, Germany and Italy.

Following the collapse of sales in circular knitting machines the decline was rapid. Double jersey was superseded by other products and, caught wrong-footed, the company fell behind on technological developments and began to lose sales. In 1982, with the withdrawal of the Sears Group, first a management buy-out and then the purchase of the group by the American-based Mayer Wildman Industries through their German subsidiary, Mayer Cie, temporarily secured the company. But in 1988, plagued by industrial disputes and with an estimated 1,000 creditors, the company issued redundancy notices to its remaining 300 workers.

Situated on Aylestone Road near to Granby Road School, on the far right is the Mellor Bromley subsidiary of the Bentley Engineering Group. A victim of the collapse of the double jersey knitting boom, at one point the Wildt Mellor Bromley Division of Bentley's was producing more than 100 knitting machines a month. *(Courtesy: E. Selvidge)*

Looking decidedly tired is the Cameo Cinema in High Street. Opening in 1910 as the 'High Street', it traded under several names over the years, such as Imperial Playhouse, Arcadia, until its final closure in 1975. In the scrollwork above the top storey, behind the neon signs, is the legend 'Electric Theatre'. The building to the right, at the corner of Cart's Lane, bears on its upper wall painted advertisements for Co-op pork pies, harking back to the days when the premises was a pork butcher's. *(Courtesy: Midlands Co-operative Society)*

Things did not improve as the 1970s reached its mid-point. Copying Western fashion design, foreign imports from Hong Kong, Taiwan and South Korea undercut prices across Europe. During 1974 imports from these countries totalled £50 million. In March 1975, 88 per cent of hosiery firms were working at below full production levels and, particularly hard hit, 60 per cent of underwear factories were on short time.

At the end of 1975 the Department of Employment estimated that nationally, during the previous two years, 12,000 jobs had been lost in the hosiery trade. In the six-month period up to May 1975 the labour force engaged in the industry had fallen from 124,700 to 115,900. With approximately 61 per cent of the workforce concentrated in the Midlands, the towns worst affected were Leicester, Nottingham, Loughborough, Hinckley and Mansfield.

For the many companies involved in the main industries in Leicester, the postwar years were dominated by decline, brought about by a mixture of many factors, ranging from overemployment to an inability to come to terms, and consequently compete with, the changing world markets that were overtaking them.

CHAPTER TEN

The Smigielski Years

The physical development of Leicester city during the years after 1945 was strongly influenced by two men. John Leslie Beckett, the City Engineer and Surveyor (1941–64) and Konrad Smigielski, the city's first Chief Planning Officer (1962–72). Born in 1900, John Beckett began his working life in the employ of Liverpool Corporation in 1918, immediately after the First World War, and remained there until 1927 when he moved to nearby Runcorn as the authority's Surveyor and Water Engineer. Between 1930 and 1935 Beckett was the Borough Engineer and Planning Officer at Tynemouth, before moving to Burnley in 1936. Finally, a year and a half into the war, he went to Leicester in 1941 at a salary of £1,500 a year, on the retirement of his predecessor Arthur Gooseman.

A capable engineer and a man of some vision, Beckett was in his element when, as part of the City Council's strategy for the postwar years, he was charged with preparing a 'Fifty Year Plan' for redeveloping the layout of the roads serving the city and for the revitalisation of much of the town. Beckett presented his proposals to the Council in March 1944, and it is a tribute to him that much of what he recommended was implemented within the timescales that he envisaged. The slum clearance work across the city, and the creation of New Parks housing estate, the building of St Margaret's swimming baths and the sports stadium on Saffron Lane, all were provided for in his plan, as was the demolition and relocation of the old Wholesale Fruit and Vegetable Market. (Originally, this site, once cleared, was to be the location of a new bus depot. However, the closing down of the public air-raid shelters at the pre-war Burley's Lane bus station in December 1944 facilitated the creation of St Margaret's bus depot, giving the Wholesale Market a temporary reprieve.)

Although John Beckett realised that in future years the existing Town Hall would become inadequate as an administrative centre for the city, and that in common with other municipalities Leicester would have to rethink the issue, he, along with others after him, never foresaw the form that it would eventually take. Beckett was the first to suggest using an entire block of city properties – the area bounded by Granby Street, Belvoir Street, Albion Street, the (new) central ring road, King Street and Marlborough Street – and building an inner-city complex of law courts, library, theatre and centralised local authority administration offices.

In October 1964 at the age of 64 and after twenty-three years in office, John Beckett retired from his post as City Engineer and Surveyor. Two years before his retirement a new and dynamic role – that of Chief Planning Officer – was created within the City Council.

The successful applicant for the new job, Konrad Wladyslaw Smigielski, was 53 years old when he came to Leicester city in September 1962. A Pole by birth, before the Second World War Smigielski had been Senior Planning Officer of Cracow. During Poland's short participation in the war he had served as a Lieutenant with the army in southern Poland. Following Poland's collapse,

Smigielski was interned in Hungary along with other soldiers. Escaping from Hungary he then journeyed to France, where, in Paris along with 100,000 of his fellow countrymen, he joined the Free Polish Forces under General Wladyslaw Sikorski. With the fall of France in 1940, Smigielski crossed the Channel and was based for a while in England before serving with the Polish Armoured Corps as a gunnery specialist in the Middle East and Europe. The end of the war saw Smigielski in Italy. There, for a very short time, he worked as a tutor to Polish students of architecture at the University of Rome before returning to England, where, along with a group of academics, he helped to found the

Konrad Smigielski (1908–99), pictured with a model of the proposed new retail market. *(Courtesy: Urban Design Group, Leicester City Council)*

Polish University College in London, serving there as Professor of Town Planning. Having become a naturalised British citizen in 1950, two years later in 1952 he moved to the north of England to take a job as head of the School of Town Planning at Leeds College of Art. Attracted by the high-profile prospects of the newly created position of Chief Town Planning Officer at Leicester, Konrad Smigielski decided to add another dimension to his career.

Epic House in Charles Street, for thirty-eight years home to Radio Leicester, from 1967 until the station's relocation to St Nicholas Place in 2005. *(Courtesy: Radio Leicester)*

Redevelopment had, not unreasonably, begun in an *ad hoc* manner before Smigielski's arrival, and much work was to continue afterwards that was independent of the Chief Planning Officer. For instance, in January 1959 Sir Robert McAlpine announced that he intended to develop the area at the top end of Charles Street near to the police station. A month later J. Tempest Bell, Chairman of the Horse Repository Co., declared that the Leicestershire Horse Repository (occupying the block between Kildare Street and Lower Hill Street) would be closed down and sold, as 'a city centre no longer has a place for premises selling horses'. Established in 1875, the company had set up the premises (with accommodation for ten horses) in 1930 when the main Charles Street development plan had been implemented, resulting in the loss of its original buildings. A prime site, it was quickly snapped up and in late 1961 plans were set out for the erection of a high-rise office block and shops, part of which was Epic House, the home until 2005 of Radio Leicester. Meanwhile, further along the road, near to the Standard public house, in March 1959 Martin's Bank opened the second 'drive-through bank' in the country, with an entrance in Charles Street and the exit in Free Lane.

In November 1965, following the collapse of the Grosvenor House Properties scheme to invest £2.5 million on a hotel complex at the London Road end of Charles Street, the General Post Office acquired 10,000sq. ft of land from the British Railways Board and an assortment of other small property owners. The GPO intended to build a twenty-storey office building to house an extension to the existing parcel-sorting office in Campbell Street and the Telephone Manager's Department, expecting to complete the building by 1969. (This was before the separation of the postal and telephone services, with British Telecom becoming a separate entity from the Post Office.)

Konrad Smigielski was always a controversial figure in his role as Chief Planning Officer for the city. In many ways one of the most brilliant architects of inner-city development of his time, because his ideas demanded change and on occasion portended astronomic cost, he was not always well received. The first project in which he became involved was a plan to redevelop the old Retail Market Place. Although the actual work was not commenced until much later, in 1970, around the time of Smigielski's arrival, a beginning of sorts was made with the renovation of the Corn Exchange.

A building had existed in the Market Place since the seventeenth century, when a two-storey structure known as 'the Gainsborough' was built, its ground floor occupied by shops and the upper level accommodating magistrates' courts (this was prior to the establishment in 1836 of the Guild Hall as a police station and court house) and rooms for public meetings. Demolished in 1748, it was replaced by a market hall, which stood until 1851, when it in turn was pulled down and replaced by the present Corn Exchange. Renovation of the Corn Exchange was completed in November 1962 at a cost of £13,500 (the monies to pay for the work were raised by the sale of some of the adjacent shop properties owned by the Corporation). The alterations included replacement of the roof, and construction of a new stage, along with a kitchen capable of serving 100 covers and a soft drinks lounge. Modest as this may have been, it provided the Council's new incumbent with the basis for his first project. Although in later years Konrad Smigielski claimed that he initially placed a moratorium on development work while he assessed the city's needs, this is not absolutely correct, because within six months of taking office he was, in April 1963, describing the Leicester market traders who objected to his proposals to create a 'Market Place Piazza' as 'narrow minded, selfish, barbarians'. A man of creative temperament, over the coming years he was not renowned for being overly receptive to opposition.

Basic planning work for the new-look Market Place was completed by June 1965 and the design proposals were submitted by the City Architect's Department to the

Town Planning Committee, which approved them in readiness for the final assent of the Markets Committee and the full Council. (A proposal in 1961 to completely relocate the Retail Market to a site in the area of Loseby Lane met with so much public opposition that in 1962 the Council commissioned a Consultant Architect, J.D. Trustram Eve, to examine the proposal. Along with the newly arrived Smigielski he advised that it was not practical.) At a cost of £182,000 the plan was for a new layout of standardised stalls based on a grid system, with central steel columns supporting a permanent roof structure. The stalls would be arranged around a small, 72sq. ft piazza directly in front of the Corn Exchange. New stalls, each measuring 16sq. ft, were designed by the City Architect Stephen George, assisted by Principal Architect Alistair Reed and Project Architect Robin Bellamy. Gangways 6ft wide would separate the stalls, with a 14ft wide service aisle running across the market directly in front of the Corn Exchange.

Although planning was agreed, matters did not progress particularly swiftly. Financial constraints on local authority spending were being imposed by central government, and those market traders whom Smigielski had injudiciously referred to as narrow-minded and selfish, realising that the improvement scheme would materially affect the rents charged for their sites, mounted a fierce opposition to the whole affair.

Acutely aware of the cash implications, in January 1968 the Finance Committee unsuccessfully put forward a motion that, in view of the national economic situation, both work on the Corn Exchange (which was being treated to yet another facelift) and the plans for the development of the Market should for the time being be deferred. At this point the Estates Committee under the Chairmanship of Councillor Bernard Peach was engaged in granting a 99-year lease on the Corn Exchange to Chef & Brewer Ltd (owned by Maxwell Joseph's Grand Metropolitan Group). The agreement was that for an annual rental of £12,500 (reviewable every seven years) the company would convert the Corn Exchange building (at a cost of £200,000) into a restaurant complex with licensed bars. This negotiation was a primary factor in the failure of the Finance Committee's plea to put any alterations on hold, the deal with Chef & Brewer being dependent upon the completion of the remainder of the Market Place development.

In July 1970 work began on erecting the steel central drainage columns and plastic roofing, despite the protests of some 200 market traders who claimed that rents would be doubled and trading space reduced. While this was an appreciable number, they only represented about a third of the 600 stall holders involved. (The new layout, when finished, would result in a small loss of trading area, the 409 stalls presently on the site being reduced to 390.) Work on this phase was concluded and the statue of John Henry, Duke of Rutland, was returned from the Castle Gardens to stand in the Market Place piazza, whence it had been removed in 1930. The new Retail Market, with a roof area of 36,000sq. ft, was held to be the largest covered market of its kind in Britain and was opened on 22 October 1971 by the Lord Mayor, Percy Watts.

The second and most costly phase of the scheme began during the summer of 1972 and involved the removal into a multi-storey block between the Corn Exchange and the Saracen's Head public house of the traders from the Fish Market. Two licensed premises (which had already closed down in readiness), the White

An elderly couple taking the weight off their feet for a few minutes on a trader's hand barrow, c. 1964 – before the renovations and creation of the Market Place piazza. Note the cobbled stone surface. *(Courtesy: J. Gunby)*

Prior to the advent of supermarket shopping the old fish market was one of the busiest areas in the city. Seen here during the late 1950s, this is probably just before Christmas – the peak trading time for the stall holders, such as butcher K.J. Percival. *(Courtesy: E. & T. Howe)*

With façades looking out onto both Gallowtree Gate and the Market Place, the Marshall & Snelgrove building (formerly Adderley's) was one of Konrad Smigielski's triumph's inasmuch as he succeeded in preventing the developers from altering the façade that overlooked the Market Place. The other side of the building in Gallowtree Gate was not so fortunate and was replaced by the concrete frontage of W.H. Smith.

Pictured in 1970, before moving into the new fish and meat market, is the family group of A. & B. Peet, at their stall. Front row, left to right: Evelyn Andrews, Evelyn Howe, Brenda Peet (née Howe). Back row: Nigel Williamson, Alan Peet. In 1994–5 Nigel Williamson bought the business from Alan and Brenda Peet and continued to run it as a family concern with his son Ryan. *(Courtesy: A. & B. Peet)*

Swan and the Bull's Head, were demolished to make room for the building work. During this part of the project Smigielski became involved in one of his famous battles over the preservation of existing architecture (here he differed from John Beckett who, in the name of progress, removed some of the oldest buildings in the city) when he refused to allow the developers of the Link Complex to take down the façade of the old Marshall & Snelgrove building that faced onto the Market Place.

Once more, the Council's modernisation proposals were met, by the traders involved, with less than enthusiasm. By July 1973 the estimates for the new meat and fish hall had doubled from £1 million to £2 million, and the fishmongers and butchers who were eventually going to have to pay for it were expressing grave concern over the fact that, at around £40 a week each, stalls were going to cost several times the price of their existing locations in the old market. Irrespective, the Council was committed to the move and the work continued, and at the beginning of November 1975 the indoor fish and meat market was opened.

As work on the indoor market came to an end, in September 1975 the Planning and Improvement Committee announced that the Leicester Rotary Club, in order to mark its sixtieth anniversary, had donated sufficient funds for Cheapside to be landscaped, the ancient 'high cross' to be brought from the Newarke houses for erection in the roadway, and the area between High Street and the Market Place designated a pedestrian precinct.

In September 1963 City Treasurer S.J. Kent published a pamphlet entitled *The City Ratepayer and His Money*, which seemed to give a mixed message. On the one

The old fish and meat market was eventually closed in late 1975 when it moved across into the new purpose-built premises at the rear of the Corn Exchange. *(Courtesy: Leicester Retail Market Management)*

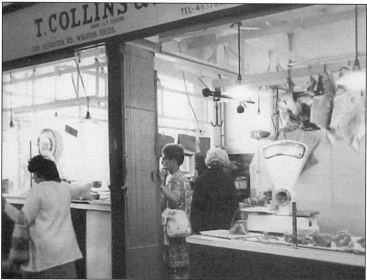

Middle and left: Many of the stallholders were quite content with their pitches in the old premises, which were clean and smart – and the rentals were considerably less than in the new building. *(Courtesy: Leicester Retail Market Management)*

hand he pointed out gloomily that, with a present population of 272,000 people, the city was £41 million in the red. Of this debt, £26 million was attributable to housing, £5 million to education, and £2.5 million to public health spending. A large part of the monies spent on maintaining essential services went on salaries for the Corporation's 12,240 employees, about half of whom worked for the Education Department. On the other hand, despite its debts, the rateable value of the city stood at £13.25 million, with assets to the value of £67 million. To put things into perspective, the City Treasurer pointed out that 'for the 2½d cost of a cigarette, the rate payer gets baths and Council Housing . . . for the 3d cost of a *Leicester Mercury* the streets are cleaned . . . and a pint of milk at 8½d is the equivalent of the combined cost of the police, cemeteries, and child care'.

Meanwhile, the head of the Town Planning Department was laying out his ideas for the future. With work on the Market Place Development Scheme under way, his other proposals included a redevelopment of the traffic-clogged Clock Tower area, along with the pedestrianisation of Gallowtree Gate; the Rowlatt's Hill Plan, to turn 20 acres of land between Wicklow Drive and Coleman Road into a new housing estate; and a project to demolish a 30-acre plot of terraced housing in the Upper Conduit Street area in order to erect a series of three- and four-storey maisonettes separated by traffic-free squares and linked together by balconies and overhead walkways.

In November 1964 Smigielski put forward his most ambitious (and least likely to succeed) grand strategy – a futuristic, inner-city monorail, the function of which – in a similar fashion to the London Underground and the Paris Metro – would be to provide a high-speed, bulk carrier form of inner-city transport.

The Chief Planning Officer wanted to build the monorail system, incorporating express buses, electric 'rickshaw' taxis and moving pavements, at a cost of £135 million, to service Leicester's traffic needs in the mid-1990s. Replacing Beckett's concentric ring roads plan, the monorail scheme would be supported by an inner-city motorway with a radial network of roads linking into it. These roads in turn would originate from a series of interchange car parks situated at the outer edge of what was described as a perimeter cordon, defining what would then

The concept of an urban monorail, proposed in 1964 by Konrad Smigielski, was not new. The first to be seen in England ran at Cheshunt in 1825. The model favoured for the Leicester project was the French SAFEGE. *(Courtesy: Urban Design Group, Leicester City Council)*

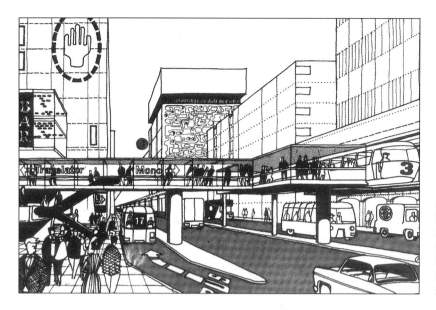

An artist's impression of the monorail station to be built in Charles Street. *(Courtesy: Urban Design Group, Leicester City Council)*

become the 'Greater Leicester Area', where motorists would be obliged to forsake their cars for public transport.

Impressive traffic figures were produced in support of the scheme. In the area within the 'cordon', the Planning Department estimated that there were 58,632 vehicles, which would have grown to more than 257,000 by 1995; and during the same period the existing number of 14,332 commercial vehicles would increase to 51,200. In relation to daily road usage in the designated area, the amount of traffic entering the city in the morning peak period was 27,000, and exiting in the evening 30,000 – figures that by 1995 would have reached 148,800, and 160,150 respectively.

The scheme for making the monorail system feasible centred around the proposed inner-city motorway. Just over 7 miles long, this was to replace the three planned ring roads and to link up with the seven radial feeder roads. The interchange car parks would accommodate shopping areas, entertainment and sports facilities, thus helping to deflect people away from the city centre. For those obliged to continue into town, their onward journey would be by means of an upgraded city transport system using different types of buses (one of which would be a small 'crush bus', with standing room only), the monorail, and electrically powered 'rickshaw-style taxis'. Presuming the virtual exclusion of traffic from the centre of the city, vehicular access would be restricted to delivery vehicles and essential users. Pedestrian conveyors would be built along the town's main routes, either as overhead bridges or moving walkways.

Acknowledging that the volume of 'essential users' vehicles entering the city was still going to be relatively high, short-term car parking facilities could be provided within the central area for an estimated 22,500 cars. Traffic circulation would be assisted by the creation of one-way streets, the flow managed by a system of computer-controlled traffic lights.

The concept of the monorail as a form of transport was not in itself a new one. The first passenger-carrying monorail in Britain, with a one-horsepower engine, ran at Cheshunt in Hertfordshire in 1825, and by the 1950s they were in regular use throughout the world. Beginning in 1956 the Skyway Monorail operated in the United States for many years at the Texas State Fair, and the first Japanese monorail began working at Tokyo's Ueno Zoo in 1957. In 1959 the ALWEG system, designed after the Second World War by the Swede Dr Axel Wenner-Grunn, was used by the Walt Disney Corporation at its American Disneyland theme park.

The model favoured for the Leicester project was the French-made SAFEGE. Deriving from a combination of the Bennie Railplane experimental system and the Paris Metro (which used rubber wheels), the suspended monorail was developed in 1947 by a French bridge builder, Lucien Chadenson. Although the French were relatively uninterested in Chadenson's work, others in later years took up his designs; the Japanese built two SAFEGE-based lines, as did Siemens in Germany, Aerorail in Texas, and Skytrain in Florida.

The SAFEGE system, with its pneumatic tyres, offered a high-speed, rapid acceleration and deceleration system (top speed 75mph, cruising speed 37.5mph), along with carriages designed for 48 seated passengers and 100 standing. Probably the major factor in its favour, so far as Leicester Corporation was concerned, was the fact that the construction company of Taylor Woodrow Ltd had acquired the UK licence in respect of SAFEGE which, if approved, would make the building of the system relatively easy.

If adopted, it was planned initially to run two double-track routes for the monorail. The first would run from Beaumont Leys shopping centre to the Clock Tower, with two intermediate stations. The track length would be 2.9 miles, and the journey time 5 minutes. The second route, from the Tower to Wigston, was the longer of the two at 4.3 miles, with stopping points at London Road railway station, Stoneygate and Oadby. It was anticipated that the combined routes would handle 12,000 passengers an hour at peak periods. Smigielski's projections were that if the SAFEGE system were installed by Taylor Woodrow, it could be completed within fifteen months of commencement, because all constituent parts were made of precast concrete. The stations would all have to be raised to the same elevation as the track and be accessed by escalators, ramps and stairs.

Despite the surveys and the production of a series of highly imaginative artists' impressions, the Council members and the ratepayers were not impressed. With the Council already deeply involved with Peter Chamberlin's plans for a new civic centre, which in itself was a major long-term project, and alarm at the costings for the monorail scheme (starting out at £135 million over the next thirty-five years, anyone who did not realise that this figure would undoubtedly escalate was rather naïve), Smigielski's flagship project never got off the drawing board.

Independently of the City Council, development work on two ventures in the Abbey Street area was begun in April 1965, one on a grand scale, the other an innovation for the city.

Plans for one of the three ring roads to carry traffic along the line of Burley's Lane, past the main city bus station towards Belgrave Road made the building of a high-rise car park and hotel in nearby Abbey Street an attractive development opportunity, and in April 1965, Thistle Hotels Ltd (a subsidiary of Scottish & Newcastle Breweries) decided to take up the option. Towering 70ft above ground level, with a multi-storey car park beneath it, the Abbey Motor Hotel opened on

A view of a
pedestrianised
Charles Street,
looking from the top
end towards London
Road railway station.
The foot bridge in the
background (centre)
carries the word
'TRAVELATOR'.
*(Courtesy: Urban
Design Group,
Leicester City Council)*

Tuesday 18 April 1967. The hotel section of the new building, looking out across the city, occupied two floors at the top of the structure. Costing £220,000 to build and a further £90,000 to equip, the Abbey had a relatively small number of rooms – 31 single and 23 double – and its main feature was its two restaurants and a cocktail bar to attract city-centre diners, along with conference and banqueting facilities for corporate entertainment.

Immediately opposite the Abbey Motor Hotel, at ground and first-floor levels, in April 1967 Leicester's first night club, the Penny Farthing, was opened by Direct Caterers Ltd, a subsidiary of Star Associated Holdings. Already owning similar clubs in Sheffield, Doncaster, Bradford, Hanley and Southend, the proprietors declared that their philosophy was 'to bring to Leicester a unique late night entertainment facility where members may eat, drink, dance, and socialise, or merely sit back in modern comfort and enjoy the extensive range of music . . .'.

For many years the Clock Tower area of the city had been the bane of planners' lives. Built of Ketton stone and erected in 1868 by public subscription, the structure was intended to have a dual function, first as a memorial to four benefactors of the town, Simon de Montfort, William Wyggeston, Sir Thomas White and Gabriel Newton, whose statues adorned the corners of its base, and second as a means of regulating the flow of vehicles across its five-way junction. With the increase in motor traffic after the turn of the century, the Clock Tower became a focal point, motorcars now mingled with tramcars and pedestrians to create one of the busiest areas of the town. In 1922 the Chief Constable, Herbert Allen, among other things, advocated that 'the footways around the Clock Tower should be reduced in favour of road widening as in his opinion the wide footways were mostly used by idlers . . .'. In 1926 a rotary system to improve vehicular flow was introduced, and police 'pointsmen' (usually two throughout the day, although at busy times this was increased to three) were strategically positioned to regulate the traffic. Allen's comments about the number of people using the footways around the Clock Tower was not unfounded, and in 1948 an ill-conceived idea was tried whereby safety barriers – quickly dubbed as 'pens' by those frequenting the city centre – were erected along the surrounding footways during the pre-Christmas period of November and December. The experiment was short-lived. Sheer volume of people forced the removal of some of the barriers after injuries were caused to pedestrians who were trapped in the crowds of Christmas shoppers, and it was found necessary to deploy eight policemen during the day to manage the scheme. On the Wednesday of Christmas week the Watch Committee met and, based upon the (apparently newly realised) fact that people working a five-day week from Monday to Friday created an unmanageable volume of pedestrian traffic on a Saturday, decided to remove the barriers.

The situation in relation to the Clock Tower and its environs was reviewed in July 1961, when the Town Planning Committee under Alderman Kenneth Bowder began to examine the possibility of undertaking a major new development. With a slum clearance and redevelopment programme already under way in the nearby Wharf Street district, the idea of demolishing an adjacent city-centre block of properties bounded by Humberstone Gate, Charles Street and the Haymarket to allow for the construction of a new, purpose-built shopping centre, was very attractive. To be called the Haymarket Centre, the project (as envisaged at that point) was to include a shopping centre, offices and a hotel.

Gaining possession of the land required was not a particular problem. Seven-tenths of the site was already owned by interested parties – Littlewood's Mail Order Stores Ltd, Trust House Forte (the Bell Hotel) and Leicester City Corporation. Once accepted as a viable option, planning for the project, which was costed at around £10 million, took time, and while some of the proposals eventually came to fruition others did not. In September 1963 a piazza-style layout for the Clock Tower area was decided upon (Konrad Smigielski seems to have particularly favoured this approach, which coincided with his design for the Market Place). Just under a year later, in August 1964, a plan for a civic theatre was added, and the Council entered into talks with Bearwood Ice Rink Ltd of Birmingham, with a view to having an ice rink on the top floor of the Littlewood's section of the complex. (Bearwood had already been refused permission to open a rink at Granby Halls on the grounds that it would close the venue to other users.)

The Clock Tower area from Lewiss's tower in 1962. Demolition work is evident in Humberstone Gate near to the Yorkshire Bank and The House of Bewlay tobacconist shop. On the far side the famous Bovril sign still dominates the skyline above Timothy White's chemist shop. In the background is the massive Fielding Johnson factory, later pulled down as part of the redevelopment which involved the building of St Peter's car park and the Shires shopping centre. *(Courtesy: Urban Design Group, Leicester City Council)*

Viewed from Humberstone Gate between late 1969 and August 1970, a gap in the property line has been cut between the newly created Top Rank Suite development (the first part of the Haymarket Centre to go up) and the Bell Hotel (right), which is empty and derelict, awaiting demolition. *(Courtesy: Urban Design Group, Leicester City Council)*

Following extensive demolition work in April 1965, tenders for the Haymarket Comprehensive Development Scheme were submitted by Laing/Mecca Partnership, Ravenscroft Properties, Taylor Woodrow Property Co. Ltd, and Town & City Properties Ltd. The long-term lease on the site, which went to the successful bidder, made the development a sound proposition. However, the downside was that whoever obtained the contract also had to offer 'alternative accommodation, so far as may be practicable to persons and firms carrying on business within the area to be leased . . . the alternative accommodation to be suitable to their reasonable requirements in size, situation, and value . . .'.

Negotiations concluded, the contract was finally awarded in April 1966 to the Taylor Woodrow Property Co., with a 99-year lease carrying an initial £101,000 annual basic ground rent (this was to be renegotiable, dependent upon the amount by which the rental of the complex's properties increased). The original specifications for the development were that it would provide 222,000sq. ft of space for shops, including licensed premises and ancillary storage accommodation at ground and first-floor levels. Within the complex there would be a cinema on the first floor with a 450–500 seating capacity; an ice rink with a skating area 100ft in diameter and seating for 800 people; a motel above the Haymarket shopping frontage with provision for 32 double and 32 single bedrooms, and 7 suites; a night club with 13,000sq. ft of floor space; a tower block with 59,000sq. ft of office space; and a civic centre (theatre) with seating for 600–650 people, which was either to be financed by the Corporation or leased by them from the developers. Additionally, suitable car parking was to be provided.

In July 1967 final approval was given by the Ministry of Housing and Local Development for work on the scheme to commence on the 5½-acre site. Progress in the early stages was fairly swift, and by November 1967 work was completed on the corner block of the development at Humberstone Gate and the Haymarket, allowing the Top Rank Leicester Suite, boasting a dance floor and five bars, to open on the 25th with its 'Saturday Night Out' programme. The company's tenure was short-lived. On Saturday 14 August 1971, after only four years, the owners, Rank Leisure Services, issued a statement that the premises had been running at a loss for some time and was to close. The facility was later reopened by Bailey's as a night club.

One of the last remaining old buildings (landmarks such as the Tower Vaults, the Stag and Pheasant, the Admiral Nelson, and the Plough public houses were already gone), the Bell Hotel in Humberstone Gate, closed during the late summer of 1969 and the premises were pulled down in August 1970 to be relocated to a new site as the Post House, on Narborough Road, which opened in September 1970. The move prompted a change in the overall design of the complex inasmuch as, in the words of the contractors, 'the original concept of the development with the civic theatre at the north end of a mall remains unchanged, but there will be a continuous shopping frontage to Humberstone Gate . . . the loss of a central hotel with 103 rooms is a matter to be regretted'. Other aspects of the project that never materialised included the ice rink, cinema and office block.

The Haymarket Centre Project was officially unveiled on 5 June 1973. The opening of the Haymarket Theatre a few months later, on Friday 30 November, with Sir Ralph Richardson as guest of honour, saw the final phase completed.

The early 1970s were Konrad Smigielski's final years as Chief Planning officer. At the beginning of 1970, at a meeting of the Traffic Committee under the Chairmanship of Sir Ernest Oliver, it was agreed that Gallowtree Gate should become a pedestrianised thoroughfare. This had been one of Smigielski's early proposals, mooted in 1963 soon after his arrival. The plan was adopted in late 1971, although for several years afterwards the dilution of the scheme, caused by the continued presence of double-decker buses threading their way through crowds of pedestrians, gave cause for criticism and complaints.

The Chief Planning Officer's grandiose strategies had inevitably, over the years, brought him into conflict with those in the city whose interests were affected, and things now started to come to a head. There was a perception that despite the public money being spent, the city was suffering badly from a malaise caused by empty shops and ugly, rubble-strewn demolition sites. There were mitigating circumstances. The country as a whole was going through a period of extreme financial constraints, which affected Leicester as much as every other major city. Businesses closing down or relocating to cheaper sites away from the town centre resulted in office blocks and shop premises standing vacant. In August 1970 Smigielski, in defence of the current trough through which his department's fortunes were passing, made the statement that 'empty shops in the city centre are not the responsibility of town planners . . . the reason for each shop's closure was that it was an individual commercial failure, the liquidation of Marshall and Snelgrove was not just a local phenomenon, [the company] closed other stores elsewhere because they were doing badly . . . competition and big new department stores are forcing smaller traders out of business'.

With the demolition of the Bell Hotel in August 1970 (the premises originally to be rebuilt as part of the Haymarket complex, in fact reopened as the newly built Post House on Narborough Road), the final stage of levelling the 5½ acres was completed and building could begin. *(Courtesy: Urban Design Group, Leicester City Council)*

The Haymarket shopping centre, the first of its kind in Leicester, opened on 5 June 1973. *(Courtesy: Urban Design Group, Leicester City Council)*

The Haymarket Theatre was opened on 30 November 1973 by Sir Ralph Richardson. *(Courtesy: Urban Design Group, Leicester City Council)*

Whereas a few years previously Smigielski's proposals were almost universally viewed sympathetically (even the monorail scheme was given decent consideration), now his credibility was in decline. A proposal by the Chief Planning Officer to build – at forty-four storeys high – the tallest office block in Britain on the Fielding Johnson factory site off East Bond Street was given a lukewarm reception.

For each of his arguments in support of the building, a counter-argument was put forward. Such a building, incorporating 387,000sq. ft of floor space, would provide accommodation for 2,000 office workers, bringing an extra 2,000 potential shoppers into the city centre and revitalising the ailing businesses, he suggested. The response was: who were the employers of this mass of people going to be? Certainly not local firms, and if an outside enterprise could be persuaded to move its workforce to the city, where were they going to live? An influx of this proportion could only generate a housing shortage, while not creating a significant increase in local employment. To this particular point the Chief Planning Officer's petulant – and so far as his cause was concerned, decidedly counterproductive – reply was that 'it was not the city planners' responsibility to control demand and supply, that was not a planning problem'. The assertion seemed to completely destroy his basic argument for the need of the office block in the first place.

Smigielski also postulated that his new building would alleviate traffic congestion in the town. Despite the already negative responses, he persisted with the unpopular if not arrogant stance that 'we want people in the city centre, we do not want their cars, so we have a strict parking policy . . . this scheme will benefit the nearby multi-storey car parks'. Once more, the obvious flaw in the argument was that if 2,000 new arrivals were vying on a daily basis for parking spaces, where did this leave the city's existing commuters?

Smigielski's problems became intolerable when, at the end of March 1972, plans to demolish the old Wholesale Fruit and Vegetable Market in Halford Street (part of Beckett's original 'Fifty Year Plan') received an unexpected setback. Unbeknown to the City Council, and posing a direct insult to Smigielski and his department, an unidentified person or group had made a successful application to the Department of the Environment for the Wholesale Market to become a listed building, thus preventing – for the time being at least – the destruction of the site. It was not what the Chief Planning Officer wanted.

Four weeks later a second incident delivered what Smigielski considered to be an unacceptable blow to his prestige. He had for some time been engaged in preventing, as part of a redevelopment scheme, the demolition of the Victorian Sun Alliance Building in Horsefair Street, and had recently had the satisfaction of seeing it awarded the protective status of 'listed building'. Hours before a meeting of the Town Planning Committee was to take place to discuss the future of the building, he was informed that the Sun Alliance had been granted, by the Department of the Environment, 'listed building consent', which effectively removed the building's protection and gave the developers a free hand to do as they wished.

Smigielski was furious, and a visit to his office by the Chairman of the Planning Committee, Kenneth Bowder, and his deputy resulted in a stormy exchange. It was apparent to the Chief Planning Officer that the same hand that had thwarted him over the Wholesale Market Project was also guiding the Sun Alliance in its manoeuvring, and he was not prepared to tolerate such interference. The result of the row with the two Council members was that Smigielski's early retirement, 'with immediate effect', was swiftly announced by the Chairman of the Planning Committee, and he was granted a hurriedly arranged leave of absence to 'pursue his researches into the problem of urban design' until his effective retirement date in the early autumn. In the meantime, the Deputy Planning Officer, D.L. Sabey, became Acting Planning Officer.

Konrad Smigielski served as Chief Planning Officer for Leicester City Corporation for a period of just under ten years, from September 1962 until April 1972. He was an ambitious and talented man who secured much for the city's future, and he was, undoubtedly, politically shrewd; in the matter of the new civic centre to be built at Albion Hill, he maintained a low profile during the years when Peter Chamberlin was conducting his researches, before, at the eleventh hour, when Chamberlin had submitted his work and returned to London, producing a better plan of his own. What his attitude would have been to the eventual abandonment of the entire project in favour of the New Walk Centre is a matter for speculation. Other than an initial proposal to develop the 30-acre site along Upper Conduit Street with a series of three- and four-storey maisonettes, exhibiting a consummate display of footwork, he successfully distanced himself from the eventual problems surrounding the St Peter's housing estate débâcle, which involved the downfall of the City Architect Stephen George.

So, what was the sum of Smigielski efforts during the decade in which he was responsible for town planning? The 1960s and '70s were the years when a 'new look' Leicester was to be created, a prospect that was not quite achieved. Although areas of ground were cleared of slums in readiness for better things, circumstances militated to detract from the planners' aspirations. Empty shop fronts appeared on main thoroughfares where financial and trading problems had forced closures – it was estimated that 10 per cent of the city centre's 590 shops were standing vacant in 1970. Office blocks, built and abandoned by entrepreneurs, stood unoccupied. Although the new City Planning Department was set up in 1962, essentially it was not until late 1964 that a blueprint for the future began to emerge, with the financially prohibitive monorail proposals. The timing was particularly unfortunate, as 1964 heralded the economic difficulties experienced under Harold Wilson's newly elected Labour government, which had a particular effect on local authorities. A Royal Commission into local government spending resulted in a further slow-down of the redevelopment of cleared sites, and their interim use as unsightly off-street car parks did little to improve the overall appearance of the city. Large sums of money were ploughed into the research by Peter Chamberlin, the London-based architect, and on the initial construction work for the purpose-built civic centre on the land at Albion Hill before, in a complete *volte face* in 1975, it was decided to move into the New Walk Centre.

Some things were definitely achieved during the Smigielski years. Large blocks of slum dwellings were removed; the whole aspect of the Retail Market Place was redesigned; the Clock Tower area and Gallowtree Gate were pedestrianised; and the Haymarket Centre was completed. It was unfortunate that a downturn in the economy prevented the Chief Planning Officer's strategies from achieving their full potential, and that eventually he was to leave office in circumstances that were less than desirable.

CHAPTER ELEVEN

The Swinging Sixties: The Early Years

Life in Leicester during the 1960s has to be taken in the context of what was happening not only nationally but also globally. As early as 1960 a landmark legal decision in a case taken by the Director of Public Prosecutions against Penguin Books ruled that the novel *Lady Chatterley's Lover* was not obscene. This was one of the first indications that the 'Swinging Sixties' would be different to any previous decade – a new generation was coming of age that had its own standards and wanted a different lifestyle. In October 1962, in the aftermath of the Korean War, an escalation in the Cold War took the world to the brink yet again, with what became known as the Cuban Missile Crisis, the result of a dispute between the United States and the Russian-backed Cuban régime of Fidel Castro. Rock and roll music, inspired by Bill Haley, the Beatles and Elvis Presley, signalled the coming of an era dominated for the first time by a previously unnoticed element of society – the teenager. In 1963 a British government minister, John Profumo, became the first in a long line of public figures to be involved in a high-profile sex scandal; and American President John F. Kennedy was assassinated. A second major conflict erupted in the Far East, this time in Vietnam, and man made his first journey into space with a landing on the moon.

Climate change was still a thing of the future and the winter of 1961/2 began during November and December with a series of biting frosts accompanied by what were described at the time as dense 'black fogs', which later became known as smog, followed a few days after Christmas on 29 December by heavy snow falls which blanketed the city and county. Five days later, on 3 January, the weather station at the Towers Hospital, which had been recording the city's weather since 1890, recorded the coldest night of the century with 23 degrees of frost (-13°C). The conditions continued through to the end of February, with snow lying to a depth of 5in.

The following year, the winter of 1962/3 was the hardest since 1947. At the beginning of Christmas week icy weather conditions were reported to be affecting the Midlands, and smog was blacking out London, with reports of fatalities for the first time. Three weeks after Christmas, on 14 January 1963, building work on sites across Leicester came to a halt and it was generally acknowledged that this was the coldest winter for fifteen years. County roads were closed by snowdrifts and persistent blizzards brought down power lines, causing electricity cuts. Once more coal was in short supply. As in previous years, gangs of Council workers laboured seven days a week in an attempt to keep the city streets open to traffic, until conditions improved at the end of February.

Although winters continued for the next few years to be traditional, 1962/3 was the last of the exceptionally hard ones. Each year snow would be an annual event, although lessening in severity and duration – the new winter hazard, until banished by the creation of smokeless zones, was fog. The heavy falls of winter snow (but without the attendant plunges in temperature) that caused so many problems continued

Many Leicester firms operating outside the mainstream industries continued to prosper during the 1960s. One such was 'Quorn Specialities' (Leicester). Operating from its base at Knighton Junction, off Welford Road, and employing between sixty and seventy workers, the firm was bought out in August 1962 by F.W. Hampshire & Co. of Derby. The new owners carried on producing sauces, jams, stuffings, jellies and custard powder, and retained the 'Quorn Specialities', trade mark. *(Courtesy: C. Chesterman)*

Viewed from the south, with the M1 motorway running along the bottom of the picture, Charles Clore's British Shoe Corporation warehouse, which opened in 1964, was the largest of its kind in Europe. *(Courtesy: E. Selvidge)*

The old Leicester aerodrome at Braunstone, taken sometime after the opening of the M1 motorway between Leicester Forest East and Markfield in January 1965, and the development of the Fox's Confectionery site in 1967. Next to the road between the motorway and the runways is the Airman's Rest public house, later demolished. *(Courtesy: E. Selvidge)*

throughout the decade, with the Director of Public Cleansing, E.E. Cochrane, bemoaning the fact that in one week alone in January 1968 he had expended £6,000 on 1,000 tons of materials, vehicles and man hours to clear the streets.

In October 1960 Charles Clore, the ubiquitous entrepreneur who so influenced Leicester's business world at this time, came up with a proposal to buy 67 acres of land near the university, between Welford Road and Aylestone Road, from the Freemen's Common Board of Deputies, in order to build a modern footwear distribution centre for the Sears Group. Clore already owned the eight-storey warehouse and office block at the junction of Rutland Street and Humberstone Gate; however, the prime site presented by Freemen's Common, less than a mile from the city centre and 5 miles from the proposed new motorway, was too good to pass up. He proposed was to buy the land for between £300,000 and £400,000. Planning permission was already in place for the erection of a 700,000sq. ft single-storey warehousing facility, with a road cutting through and linking Welford and Aylestone Roads, to be built by the Corporation on land donated from the package by Clore. Due to the commercial nature of the development, the road scheme did not qualify for any central government subsidy and it was a venture that would potentially cost the Leicester ratepayers £145,000. Additionally, Clore would allow the City Council to take 10 acres of ground on the north side of his development for an extension of the cattle market.

Welford Road, however, was not the only prime site available, and Charles Clore quickly decided that his best interests lay elsewhere. A little over a year later, in February 1962, he announced that his group of companies had acquired from the Leicester City Council a 45-acre site adjoining the Municipal Golf Course on the former Leicester aerodrome at Braunstone. Work was completed by September of the following year, and in readiness for opening in January 1964, Clore's British Shoe Corporation warehousing complex was already hiring administrative and warehouse staff. Knighted in June 1971 for his services to industry, Charles Clore retired as chairman of Sears in 1976, to become a tax exile in Monte Carlo. Suffering from cancer, he later returned to England, where he died on 26 July 1979 aged 75.

Having disposed of the Leicester aerodrome site, in August 1962 the City Council purchased, for £325,000, 54 acres of Freemen's Common for its own development purposes. It allocated 16 acres for an extension of the cattle market, a further 6 acres for the construction of the road cutting through to Aylestone Road, and 32 acres for business development. One piece of ground retained by the Freemen was an area of 6 acres facing onto Welford Road. This they disposed of for £57,000 in 1967 to Whitby's Garage Ltd, for the construction of a large garage complex. Meanwhile, on the Aylestone Road side, work had begun in June 1967 on the building of a new wholesale fruit and vegetable market to replace the one in Halford Street, which had become outdated and contributed greatly to traffic congestion. Covering 105,000sq. yd of land and costing £400,000, the new market took just over a year to complete, and the old one ceased trading on Saturday 5 October 1968.

One major government initiative at this time had a distinct effect on the lives of many in both the city of Leicester and the county district. In 1945 one of Clement Attlee's manifesto promises was to nationalise British road and rail transport

Founded in 1948, the British Transport Commission, divided into four Executives, was responsible for, among other things, the nationalisation of road haulage. Control of Britain's road transport system was handed back to the private sector in the early 1950s; however, in the meantime a huge number of lorries each bearing the Commission's badge and fleet number were a common sight on highways all over the country. *(Courtesy: C. Chesterman)*

services. Consequently, in January 1948 the British Transport Commission with four 'Executives' came into being. These Executives took over the management of railways, London Transport, docks, canals and road transport companies. Included in the restructuring were firms such as Thomas Cook Travel Agents and the major haulage firm of Pickford's; also created from the amalgamation of small enterprises was the massive fleet of British Road Services lorries.

The venture was short-lived and control of road haulage was dismantled by the mid-1950s under Winston Churchill's newly returned Conservative government, allowing local transport firms to resume independent trading. Locally, one such was Clayton's Transport of St Michael's Avenue which, in December 1953, submitted tenders to the Road Haulage Disposal Board in order to build up its fleet to between fifty and sixty vehicles, doubling the pre-nationalisation size of the company.

It was not only the Labour Party that sought to restructure the nation's transport networks. Although road transport and haulage was, for economic reasons, very quickly returned to the private sector, with operators being left once more to their own devices, the same was not to apply to the railway system.

During the late 1940s and early '50s road haulage became part of the British Transport Commission, which effectively nationalised the haulage industry. The lorries seen here, belonging to SS Haulage (Solomon Silk), are typical of the vehicles seen on the roads at that time. From left to right the makes (all powered by Perkins engines) are Proctor, Dennis, Dennis and Vulcan. *(Courtesy: C. Chesterman)*

In March 1960, with a Conservative government now in power, the Stedeford Committee was appointed to conduct a review of the transport situation in Britain. One of its members was Dr Richard Beeching, technical director of ICI, who in 1961 was appointed Chairman of the newly formed British Railways Board. Richard Beeching initiated a series of studies into the economics of the country's existing railway system. The resulting document entitled *The Reshaping of British Railways* was devastating for many. More commonly known to history as the Beeching Report, the document foreshadowed sweeping and controversial cuts in the nation's rail transport system.

Between 1962 and 1968 the staff of British Railways was reduced by 40 per cent; 9,000 locomotives were disposed of; route miles were reduced by 50 per cent; and, most relevant for passengers, just under half of the country's local stations were closed. A further change was the loss of the traditional steam engine in favour of modern diesel-powered locomotives.

Rail cuts in Leicester city and county began early. At the end of December 1961 the last train on the Rugby to Leicester London Road line ran through Countesthorpe. This closure pre-dated the publication of the Beeching Report on 27 March 1963, which disclosed that in future only four railway stations would remain in Leicestershire – London Road in the city, Loughborough to the north, and Market Harborough and Hinckley in the south. Throughout the county thirty-two rural stations were closed.

The reasoning behind the cuts was that they would save the government between £115 million and £140 million on a service that was haemorrhaging cash. For the residents of Leicester, many of whom did not have motorcars and still relied on public transport, the impact was serious. The loss of services to the east coast constituted a body-blow to the holiday trade in places such as Skegness and Mablethorpe, which relied on a large percentage of their 400,000 yearly visitors arriving by train. Local bus services between places such as Lutterworth, Rugby and Leicester, along with a host of small villages that had benefited from local railway stops, were now unable to cope with the increased volume of passengers. A substantial number of commuters who relied on train services into Leicester in order to make connections to workplaces such as Loughborough, Nottingham and Derby were suddenly bereft of transport. The Leicester to Wellingborough line closed on 4 January 1965, and with the loss of Wigston station, services to Wigston Magna, Kibworth, East Langton, Desborough and Rothwell were also terminated. The decision in October 1964 to close the Great Central line meant redundancy for between 1,100 and 1,400 railway men – a figure that included 200 staff in Leicester.

As part of cuts aimed at reducing the Midland Region Traffic Centres from eleven to seven, Leicester Divisional Traffic Headquarters in Granby Street (which had only been occupied since February 1963) fell under the axe. Its workload, which included timetabling, was shifted to Nottingham. The company's fourteen civil engineering divisions were also reduced to seven, meaning that the entire Leicester signalling area was subsequently covered by only four engineers.

The measures imposed by the Beeching Report affected the lives of many in the city and resulted eventually in the demise of such historical landmarks as Great Central and Great Northern stations, and the consequent redevelopment in later years of Swan Lake Mills and Western Boulevard.

Before the cuts imposed by Richard Beeching, Leicester was at the centre of a busy railway network. The very large brick building at the top of the picture with two large and one smaller entrances was the Great Central Railway Goods Warehouse. The rails that lead into the warehouse were used to push the wagons in to discharge their cargos at the loading docks inside. The long sheds to the left of the warehouse are carriage sheds. *(Courtesy: G. Fenn)*

Western Boulevard in later years. Although traces of the disused lines remain, the carriages, heaped up for scrap are part of the sad legacy of the Beeching Report. *(Courtesy: D. Simpson, information: D. Simpson)*

Among those who came to England as immigrants after the war were a large number of workers from eastern Europe and the Baltic States. Camp 756 at Enderby was home to such a group, seen here demolishing air-raid shelters at the nearby Grove Farm Park, which was in later years to become part of the retail trading estate near to Junction 21 of the M1 motorway. *(Courtesy: H. Raak)*

A major influence on life in Leicester from the 1960s onwards was the fact that the city became a focus for Asian immigration. During the 1960s people came to Leicester from India and Pakistan; in the 1970s the emphasis changed to a migration of East African Asians from Kenya and Uganda.

Historically, Leicester had long been home to immigrants from many countries. Records of a Jewish community in the modern town begin in about 1849, and there is no doubt that individuals from a range of European countries arrived throughout the years following the turn of the century and up to the Second World War. In August 1914, under the hurriedly instituted Aliens Act, which required local police forces to detain foreign nationals for internment, fifty Germans living in Leicester borough were immediately arrested and held at the Corn Exchange, before being sent under military escort to York. They were followed by twenty Austrians and Hungarians living in the town when the Act was extended to include them. Following the Second World War, desperately short of labour, the government operated a scheme for European Volunteer Workers, drawn from the displaced persons camps across western Europe, to come to Britain to take up employment. Locally, one such centre was Camp 756 at Enderby. Formerly a German POW camp, in the summer of 1947 it was home to ninety Estonians, ten Latvians, and one Lithuanian who were engaged in agricultural work in the area, including the removal of wartime air-raid shelters from the nearby Grove Farm, which in later years, with the advent of the nearby motorway, became the Grove Farm Triangle shopping complex.

In the immediate postwar years, and through to the 1970s, a steady flow of immigrants arrived in the city from the Caribbean islands, including Antigua, Barbuda and Trinidad. One of the main differences between this pattern of immigration and that of people arriving from the Indian subcontinent was that the Afro-Caribbeans – coming mainly to take jobs in service industries such as transport, nursing and catering – were both men and women, whereas Indian immigration was initially almost exclusively male.

Figures for 1951 show the Asian population of Leicester as 624 (mostly Sikhs from the Jullandur and Houshiarpur areas of India). Ten years later the number was 4,624, and by 1971 it was 20,190, rising to 59,709 by 1981. A census taken in 1991 gives a clear snapshot of the overall distribution of people who had migrated to the city. From a total population of 283,000, those originating from ethnic groups born outside the UK totalled 28.5 per cent, made up of 6,600 of Afro-Caribbean extraction; 9,600 from Pakistan and Bangladesh; and 60,600 of Indian origins. These figures do not take into account the large numbers of Poles, Ukrainians, Estonians and others who had lived in the city both during and after the war. (In October 1963 Father Murat, the parish priest of the community's newly acquired St Paul's Church in Dale Street, estimated that the Poles living in Leicester numbered some 3,000.)

A large number of immigrants were attracted to settle in Leicester by the plentiful work in the city's traditional industries, and with the local authority's redevelopment plans, cheap properties suitable for multiple occupancy came onto the market in the Highfields and Belgrave districts (the average price for a terraced house in the 1950s was still under £1,000).

Three pieces of legislation, combined with a shift in East African politics, influenced the continuing pattern of immigration into Leicester during the 1960s and after. The British Nationality Act 1948 divided British citizenship into two categories – citizens of the Commonwealth, and citizens of the United Kingdom and colonies. It meant that the two groups were both British, and the citizenship thus conferred gave them a right to enter and remain in the UK. Consequently, the stage was set for the first of Leicester's immigrants to arrive – predominantly men who intended to find a job and somewhere to live and, having saved sufficient money, to bring their families over from the Indian subcontinent. Next came the Commonwealth and Immigration Act 1962, which effectively restricted rights of entry inasmuch as Commonwealth and UK citizens whose passport had not been issued in the United Kingdom now required an entry visa. The legislation prompted a rush of relatives and dependants coming into the country before the doors closed to them. Finally, in March 1968, with the winds of change blowing abroad, the Commonwealth Immigrants Act was aimed at restricting the numbers of people coming into Great Britain from East Africa. This piece of legislation proved fairly ineffective, and Leicester in particular saw a steady stream of arrivals, first in 1968 from Kenya and then in 1972 from Uganda.

Almost from the beginning of the decade concern was being felt by the city elders over the capacity for coping with the numbers of new arrivals and discussion was taking place as to how the pressures – primarily on accommodation and education – could be met. In a backlash against the influx, prejudice quickly became manifest. In June 1961 the Leicester Students Welfare Committee began to keep records of landladies in the city who refused to let accommodation to black and coloured students. Later that year, on 9 October, a colour bar was instituted at the Brickmakers Arms in St George Street near to the City Police Headquarters, with the licensee declaring that 'Negros and other Coloureds' would only be served in the bar, and would not be permitted in the smoke room or lounge. This resulted in a public demonstration outside the pub by a small group of students carrying placards at lunchtime on 20 October. Soon after 1 p.m. ten of the pickets, four of whom were black, went into the pub and attempted to buy drinks. The landlord, George Claricoates, refused to serve them and summoned the police to eject the group.

Some progress was made when, just before Christmas 1962, Sohan Singh, a 34-year-old Sikh living at 18 Melbourne Street, became the city's first non-white licensee when he took over as landlord of the Durham Ox at the corner of Upper Conduit and Gordon Street. After moving from the Durham Ox in early 1964 to the Imperial Hotel on Mere Road, Sohan Singh experienced an extreme form of racism when, in August 1965, he became the target of Ku Klux Klan activity. The *Leicester Mercury* had passed information to the police during the early summer that it had received an anonymous tip-off concerning the existence of a Ku Klux Klan cell operating in the city and county. In June a 4ft-high burning cross was nailed to the door of Hinckley parish church, and in nearby Rugby a group of about a dozen white-clad figures carrying a fiery cross had been seen on a deserted hillside overlooking the Rugby Portland Cement site near to Bilton. On 11 August a 5ft-tall flaming cross was fixed to the door of the Imperial Hotel, the clientele of which was primarily Indian.

Opinions regarding who could and could not be admitted to public houses remained high-profile and newsworthy. On 12 May 1964 the *Leicester Mercury* reported that the Belgrave and District Working Men's Club, with fewer than

10 per cent of its 1,800-strong membership non-white, had decided not to accept any more coloured members 'in order to preserve a fair quota'. In the same issue the paper informed its readers that the licensee of the Uppingham Hotel on Uppingham Road had been 'summoned to the brewery', and that with immediate effect the colour bar operated in the pub would be lifted and 'coloured people would be admitted to the saloon'.

Matters came to a head a couple of months later when a group of about forty students and Young Socialists held a demonstration outside the Admiral Nelson public house in Humberstone Gate. The indignant licensee, Thomas Grant, proclaimed that 'there was no ban in the downstairs rooms . . . only upstairs'. The comment given to the *Mercury* by Everard's Brewery, which owned the Admiral Nelson, was short and non-committal, stating that 'it is up to the licensee who he lets in'. Four weeks later, on Saturday 22 August, a 100-strong group of demonstrators, including members of the Young Socialists and the Indian Workers League, marched from Dale Street School in the Highfields, to Everard's Brewery in Southgates, where they posted a notice that if the colour bar at the Admiral Nelson was not removed then affiliated organisations in other towns would organise a general ban on Everard's premises. Later that evening forty placard-waving demonstrators set up another picket in Humberstone Gate. Inevitably, the campaign ended in violence when, on the evening of Sunday 8 November 1964, between sixty and seventy demonstrators went into the Admiral Nelson to protest. The police were called and a large fight broke out, resulting in several arrests, and a policeman being knocked to the ground and kicked. It became apparent to those involved in the licensed trade that the situation and the adverse publicity could not continue. With lame excuses from the landlord of the Admiral Nelson that he did not operate a colour bar but only sought to refuse entry to disorderly elements, the practice of discrimination in public houses in the city effectively ceased.

A watershed was reached in 1967 when national figures, published in April, attempted to put things into some sort of perspective. During 1966 51,000 Commonwealth immigrants took up residence in the UK. The largest ethnic group was 18,200 from India (4,500 males; 5,400 females; 8,300 children), followed by a further 8,000 from Pakistan. These figures easily eclipsed the number from the Caribbean (perceived to be the next high-profile immigration area), which for the twelve-month period was 4,700.

In May 1968 it was estimated that there were between 14,000 and 16,000 immigrants living in Leicester, most of them settling in the Highfields and Belgrave areas and of whom more than 500 were children. Six months earlier, in November 1967, the Leicester Education Committee had begun to express concerns over the large groups of newly arrived children in these districts, who were flooding into the limited number of schools available. The committee reported to the Council that 'for some time children have been arriving to take school places at the rate of about 40 per month. This has doubled to 80 since mid-July. A problem is that schools in Highfields are now receiving large numbers of children who do not speak any English. . . .' At the same time, complicating the situation further, the Chairman of the Leicester Health Committee, Neville Hangar, announced that the city's health care provisions were being overloaded by the volume of people arriving from overseas.

To deal with the logistical problem, the Education Committee decided to implement an experimental dispersal of pupils, with buses taking children from Highfields out to Beaumont Leys and Thurnby, and a campaign was launched to recruit extra teaching staff. It was not only in Leicester that this solution to education difficulties was tried. In January 1969 the practice was discontinued when the Minister of Education, Edward Short, issued a directive to the effect that the dispersal of immigrant children to schools in areas other than where they lived was only recommended where the proportion of immigrant pupils exceeded one-third of the school's intake, otherwise such dispersal diluted the school's effectiveness as an integral part of the local community.

The migration of people and cultures across the globe has, since the earliest civilisations, been an unchanging fact of life. The challenges encountered in the 1960s, and culminating in the early 1970s with the expulsion of Asians from East Africa, were problems not so much of migration itself, but of the greatly increased volume of people involved in a migration that occurred within a very short timescale. Over the years following these two decades, those who were children when they arrived in Leicester became adults with families of their own; by the turn of the century another new generation had been born, creating an integrated social structure within the city.

CHAPTER TWELVE

The Swinging Sixties: The Later Years

While the Planning Department under Konrad Smigielski was busy with slum clearances and schemes to solve the city's traffic congestion problems, other independent but equally important organisations were also contributing to the changing skyline, none more than the General Post Office with its two major new telephone buildings, in the Wharf Street area and a tower block in Charles Street.

Post Office Telephones, as part of the General Post Office (GPO), was the name used until October 1969, when the Post Office ceased to be a government department and the telephones division of the organisation became Post Office Telecommunications. The telephone service continued under this name until taking the name British Telecom twelve years later in October 1981.

The Council's slum clearance programme provided an opportunity for the GPO to build a new main exchange in Wharf Street, at the back of Lee Circle, which was opened on Saturday 10 December 1960 by the Lord Mayor, Councillor Mrs Dorothy Russell. The subsequent completion of an additional £80,000 exchange at Birstall, which became operational in July 1963, brought all Leicester numbers onto the STD system. By October 1969, work on the construction of an international exchange in Erskine Street was also on schedule for completion in 1970.

In Charles Street, near to the police station, on the site that had once been earmarked for Leicester's first £1 million Europa Hotel, between 1968 and 1971 a nineteen-storey office block was built by the GPO at a cost of £2 million. This was to be the home of a mechanised sorting system that could not be accommodated at the head Post Office in Bishop Street, with an adjacent three-storey building to house the motor transport section of sixty vans. Once completed, the tower block also became home to the Telephone Manager's Department.

In July 1960 the Sheffield Regional Hospital Board, responsible for the development of Leicester's hospitals, decided, in addition to building a new complex on the site of the Leicester Isolation and Chest Unit at Groby Road, to spend money on the Royal Infirmary and the City General hospitals. The Infirmary was to have a new casualty department and a dedicated burns unit, along with a maternity wing that was intended to take over from the maternity hospitals at Westcotes and Bond Street. The City General was to be provided with three new wards and new operating theatres, along with a nurses' home with accommodation for 200 staff. (At that time the nurses were using a small hostel and some single-storey wooden buildings).

Two other healthcare projects were begun in the middle and late 1960s. In the private sector the Nuffield Trust decided to build a hospital, to be known as the Leicester Clinic, at Scraptoft. Containing forty beds, a children's ward, two operating theatres, an X-ray department and laboratory facilities, it was costed at £360,000

When the Leicester City Transport Depot in Humberstone Gate was pulled down to make way for the Haymarket Centre project, the City Transport Operating Centre moved to new purpose-built premises in Rutland Street. The 'topping out' ceremony was conducted on 2 October 1968 by the Chairman of the Transport Committee, Alderman T.A. Harris. *(Courtesy: Urban Design Group, Leicester City Council)*

and work commenced in October 1968. The Nuffield Trust put up £100,000 and the remaining £260,000 was raised from subscriptions.

The second major undertaking was the decision in February 1966 that a new maternity unit should be sited at the Leicester Royal Infirmary. Concerns had been growing for some time about the lack of facilities – and the Dickensian nature – at the Bond Street Maternity Hospital which, along with Westcotes on Fosse Road, was the main maternity hospital for the city. With sixty-six lying-in and six first-stage beds, one delivery room and one operating theatre, the facilities were inadequate and outdated for the 3,000 patients that the hospital received each year. The building was made up of four cottages, originally knocked together to create the Faire Hospital, and among other things lacked washing and toilet facilities, with patients (who were either pregnant or had recently given birth) being required to climb the stairs from the ground floor to first floor to use a toilet.

The new LRI maternity unit was estimated at £1.2 million, and on Thursday 17 October 1968 the foundation stone was laid by the senior gynaecologist at the Infirmary, Mr T.E. Elliott, and Miss Gertrude Taub, who until her retirement in August that year had been Matron at Bond Street.

This was the first phase of a two-phase £16.7 million development at the Leicester Royal Infirmary involving the building of ten operating theatres and new outpatients and accident and emergency departments, which were designed to make the LRI a 1,300-bed general hospital.

After two and a half years of work the completed five-storey maternity unit opened on Monday 1 February 1971. Some £100,000 was spent on equipment. The 120 staff at Bond Street transferred to the new site and a further 80 were recruited to make up the full strength of 200 needed to service the unit's six wards. Bond Street was closed down immediately, followed in early April 1974 by the closure of Westcotes Maternity Hospital.

Among the projects envisaged by John Beckett in his plans for postwar Leicester was a swimming pool in the area created by his ring roads network near to the

Southgates Underpass. Completed at a cost of £480,000 at the beginning of 1966, the St Margaret's Baths was opened on Friday 12 February by the Minister of Sport, Denis Howell. The pool complex was designed and created by the City Architect's and Engineer's Departments and great things were planned for it. It had a seating for 600 spectators and two swimming pools, one of which had diving stages up to a height of 16ft and measured 110ft by 49ft. The larger of the two pools was intended to be a major regional sports centre, while the smaller one was to be used for teaching purposes and by swimming clubs. After the building was opened it was discovered that, owing to a construction fault, the larger six-lane pool did not comply with Amateur Swimming Association National Standards and could not be used as a competition venue. Thereafter the facility reverted to use as a public pool.

While theatres and cinemas in the city were closing down in favour of the entertainment provided by television, another institution was about to be created – Leicester was to have the first local radio station in mainland Britain.

Starting in January 1967, the government agreed to set up eight experimental local radio stations across the country. One of the prerequisites of the experiment was that local authorities should contribute towards the cost of equipping and running the stations. Leicester City Council would have to find £50,000 a year for two years, a condition that was not universally well received. Four months later, on 27 May, after some deliberation on the matter, Councillor Bernard Toft, the leader of the Council's Conservative group, came up with a different suggestion. An alternative favoured by the Conservative members, this was to support the establishment of a commercial radio station that would be self-funding. Leicester City Council was not alone in its reticence over the government's funding plan, which was also rejected by Manchester City Council.

After further discussions Leicester City Council eventually agreed to participate in the scheme and on Wednesday 8 November 1967, under the direction of its first manager, Maurice Ennals, BBC Radio Leicester went live, broadcasting from the eighth floor of Epic House in Charles Street. It opened to the strains of the 'Post Horn Gallop' and a short broadcast made by the Postmaster General, Edward Short, who said, 'this is the first home town radio station in Britain – it opens a new and exciting chapter in the story of British radio . . .'. The event was not

The Leicester Clinic
Part of tomorrow's Leicester

...constructed by J.H.Hallam & Sons Ltd., a builder of quality with work extending to many fields, including Industrial building, Hospitals, Universities, Colleges, Residential building, and Municipal Authority building.

We have our own Design Service, and facilities for Open Tendering and Package Deals, and would stress that contact at Director level is a company policy.

J.H.HALLAM & SON LTD.

Builders and Contractors

306 LEICESTER RD., WIGSTON FIELDS, LEICESTER. Tel: 88554

Begun in late 1968, the Leicester Clinic on Scraptoft Lane was the first of the Nuffield Trust hospitals to be built in Leicester. *(Courtesy: Urban Design Group, Leicester City Council)*

Opposed to local authority funding of Radio Leicester, Councillor Bernard Toft was in favour of an option to open a commercial station that would be virtually self-funding. *(Courtesy: Urban Design Group, Leicester City Council)*

without incident. Outside, in Lower Hill Street, a group of protestors, members of the Free Radio Association who did not want local radio to be controlled by the BBC, marched up and down with placards, and shortly before Edward Short's broadcast a hoax message was received that there was a bomb in the building.

Radio Leicester was the first local station to begin broadcasting, followed in the next few weeks by the opening of Radios Sheffield and Merseyside. Just under a year and a half later, with the experimental period approaching its end, the members of Leicester City Council's General Purposes Committee were once again exercising their minds over the pros and cons of the BBC's initiative, and decided that

Leicester City Council will tell the Post Master General that it cannot agree to finance Radio Leicester to any considerable extent and that the greater part of the funding should be met by the BBC. . . . [Leicester] City Council would be prepared to make a contribution on a far more modest scale than during the experimental period. Funding would have to take into account how much was to be subscribed by other Authorities within the reception area. [At this stage the County Council was steadfastly declining to make any sort of contribution.] . . . If it was decided that the BBC should continue to operate local radio

Radio Leicester quickly established itself as an integral part of the Leicester scene, with outside broadcasts such as this early one from the Clock Tower by Greg Ainger (originator of the *Six o'clock* Asian show) and Dan Chisholm. *(Courtesy: Radio Leicester)*

One of Radio Leicester's earliest presenters, Morgan Cross. (Courtesy: Radio Leicester)

stations after the experimental period, financing should be varied so that the burden carried by local authorities was materially reduced. The Council were willing to participate in the experiment . . . as it was apparent [during the experimental stage] that the financing of operations of any local radio would have to be underwritten to a considerable degree by local government they agreed to undertake this commitment to the extent of £1,000 a week for the two years period of the experiment and in the knowledge that the station would also serve an area extending far beyond the boundary of the city of Leicester. Offers from the County Council or any other authority or organisation to share in meeting the cost would be welcomed . . . there have been no offers or contributions and it is clear that no [such] reliance can be made.

August 1969 saw the government giving the BBC the go-ahead to set up forty local radio stations at a cost of £5.2 million – the cost to be borne entirely by the licence fee. (At this time the annual fee for a combined radio–television licence was £6.) The national network grew by 1978 to twenty-two stations, and by the 1980s thirty-eight stations were transmitting to 90 per cent of the population. Radio Leicester started in 1967 with a 50-watt valve VHF transmitter located on Anstey Lane, and after five years added a medium wave frequency when a 160ft transmitter was commissioned on Freemen's Common. In time the transmitters were replaced by the present FM transmitter at Copt Oak. The station remained in its tower-block home at Epic House until moving to a new centre in St Nicholas Place in 2005.

Local radio was not the only entertainment medium to appear in the 1960s. For some years there had been a feeling among many people in Leicester that the city needed a civic theatre. With the closure of the Theatre Royal and the Opera House, the only remaining playhouse was the Little Theatre in Dover Street. The Leicester Drama Society, formed in 1922, had bought the old Baptist chapel in Dover Street

Martin Lane, Radio Leicester's Engineer in Charge, leaving the Anstey Lane transmitter site for the last time. *(Courtesy: Radio Leicester)*

in 1929 and converted it into a theatre, opening in 1929 with *The Florentine Tragedy*. Productions ceased during the war, when the theatre was used for army entertainment. In 1955 fire destroyed the stage area and the theatre was closed for three years before reopening in 1958.

Plans were put in hand and a new theatre and bus station were built during 1963 in Newarke Street. The building cost £20,000 and an appeal was launched to raise £10,000 to equip the Phoenix Theatre, which opened on 8 October 1963 with Thornton Wilder's play *The Matchmaker*. Donations were slow to come in, not least of all from the County Council which, as a perceived beneficiary of the new theatre, was asked under the Local Government Act 1948 to contribute towards its upkeep. Not unexpectedly, the request was turned down. In the early days the Phoenix, funded by the City Council and the Arts Council, encountered difficulties. In June 1964, with running costs standing at £600 a week, there were considerable difficulties in meeting expenses, even with full houses (it only had 275 seats). The problem was exacerbated by the fact that the theatre was heavily patronised by schools and students, who were entitled to reduced entry fees. Matters were not helped when the Council decided in 1966 to include a much larger theatre in the Haymarket project, and in September 1967 the General Purposes Committee, supported by the Arts Council and the Leicester Theatre Trust, endorsed the proposals for a 710-seat theatre, the Haymarket, to be included in the design of the complex. Not everyone was in favour of this latest venture, and with the Phoenix already running at a loss (in 1968 the deficit was £5,565) Councillor Tomlinson presented an objection to the Council that it was being asked to accept a similar situation in respect of the Haymarket, which was expected to lose up to £67,000 annually. Despite the financial implications, the Haymarket Theatre was opened in November 1973.

The 160ft-high Radio Leicester transmitter at Freemen's Common. *(Courtesy: Radio Leicester)*

Opened by the Duchess of Gloucester in May 1967, the Saffron Lane Sports Stadium provided Leicester with a major venue for regional sporting activities. *(Courtesy: Urban Design Group, Leicester City Council)*

In July 1964 the Parks Committee, chaired by Alderman Frederick Jackson, decided to go ahead with the construction of a major sports stadium with cycle and athletics tracks on Saffron Lane. (This again had been envisioned in Beckett's postwar reconstruction strategy.) The plans, to be completed in three phases, were approved at the end of March 1965. The first phase, costing £148,855, was a contract for the building of a 333m cycle track, the only one of its kind in the country; an all-weather athletics track, and the first stage of the terracing. Phase two, the least costly at £55,000, was for the construction of changing rooms, toilets and refreshment facilities. Phase three, at £203,000, was for the building of a sports hall and covered spectator accommodation. Completed in May 1967, the stadium was opened by the Duchess of Gloucester.

Saffron Lane featured again in the news in July 1968, when the area was flooded by heavy rainfall. On Wednesday and Thursday 10–11 July torrential rain caused flooding to a depth of 4ft in the Saffron Lane area. Houses had to be evacuated and the Leicester Welfare Department set up a feeding centre in Cavendish Road and brought in drying equipment borrowed from the RAF. A similar flood two years earlier, caused by a burst water main in the district around West Bridge, had prompted the Council to appoint the City Director of Welfare Services, K.J. Powell, as Emergency Co-ordinator for the city.

Areas on the south side, such as Lothair Road running between Saffron Lane and Aylestone Road, were also affected by the flooding and angry residents demanded an inquiry into the cause. There were strong suggestions that the channelling of rain water away from the Freemen's Common Wholesale Market and the newly built sports stadium, into the old Washbrook, had overloaded the drainage system. A week after the incident the Lord Mayor, Alderman Kenneth Bowder, launched a flood relief appeal to aid the 500 householders who had sustained losses in the deluge. In September a report submitted to the Committee of Inquiry set up by the Leicester City Council indicated that a major increase in the amount of flood water

Following the flooding of properties on Saffron Lane, as a result of the building of the Freemen's Common Wholesale Market and the sports stadium, in February 1969 the Leicester Flooding Committee set up by the City Council had new drainage systems installed between Saffron Lane and Aylestone Road.

emptying into the Washbrook and the Saffron Brook meant a risk of repeated flooding. It recommended new and enlarged culverts and additional water courses to divert the water away from the two existing water courses.

In February 1969 the Leicester Flooding Committee, chaired by Councillor Bernard Toft, agreed to spend £3.75 million over the next eleven years on the provision of drainage in the areas of the Washbrook, Saffron Lane, Bushby and Evington.

Leicester during the 1960s was famous for the fact that, in comparison to many other cities, it provided its citizens with full employment and good wages. In 1961–2 a bottle of Haig's Whisky cost 37s 6d. Trade Wind Jamaica Rum was 41s 6d a bottle. At the Leicester Co-op a tin of red salmon (a delicacy at the time) was 3s 4d, large eggs were 1s 7d a dozen, and tinned peaches, depending on the brand, varied between 1s 7d and 2s 6d. Gammon was 4s a pound and cooked ham 1s 7d a quarter. In 1966 a man's suit from C&A cost 16 guineas. A *Leicester Mercury* cost 4d. Bread cost 1s 3d a loaf, and a baker earned £15 for a forty-hour week.

A snapshot of 1968 shows that while a GPO telephonist could earn up to £14 15s a week (traditionally a female occupation; at a time when there was still a pay differential, this was a good wage for a girl or woman), in contrast an apprentice telephone engineer received £5 12s 6d; a senior sales representative for a company could expect to earn around £1,000 a year (£20 a week). A warehouseman at Sainsbury's worked for £16 a week, and the rival store Safeway paid £18 for butchery staff. Highlighting the difference between a man's and a woman's pay, the manageress of a city centre shop would earn around £15.

For those among the growing numbers who could now afford to run a motorcar, in February 1968 Cox's Motors in Conduit Street offered the new Morris Mini at £509, or the larger Morris 1800 for £923. At Leman's the Austin Mini 1000 Super was priced at £579. Aware of the growing number of motorists, many of whom were running old and non-roadworthy vehicles, the government introduced a piece of legislation that would affect 1.5 million of the country's car owners. As from 15 February 1961 all motor vehicles over ten years old had to be issued with a Ministry of Transport Test Certificate. With testing beginning in September 1960, the earliest vehicles – those registered before January 1937 – had to be certificated by February 1961; the latest date for certificating all other cars was May 1961.

Prospective house buyers could expect to pay around £5,900 for a three-bedroom detached house with full gas central heating. Mortgages were particularly difficult to come by at this time, and building societies such as the Leicester Temperance in Charles Street would not take into account a wife's earnings as they considered a young married woman to have a short-term earning capacity.

Anyone wanting to watch a film would pay 6s 6d for a seat at the Odeon in Queen Street (the chain of cinemas, owned by the Birmingham-born son of Hungarian immigrants, Oscar Deutsch (1893–1941) took their name from the slogan 'Oscar Deutsch Entertains Our Nation'); and the price of admission to the city's latest night spot, the Top Rank Suite, was 7s Monday to Saturday. The Top Rank's rival attraction, the ten-pin bowling alley in Lee Circle, charged 3s a game.

Another new phenomenon, eating out, was now introduced into the local lifestyle. An abundance of eateries such as one of the city's first Chinese restaurants, the Oriental on the Clock Tower (soon to be followed by the Lotus

House in Charles Street), where a couple could enjoy an evening meal and pay around £3 for the privilege, began to spring up towards the middle of the decade. At a time when children were strictly prohibited anywhere on licensed premises, and when the days of public houses serving food were still a long way in the future, Berni Steak Bars appeared, their attraction being that a young couple with a family could go out and eat together. Restaurants such as the Italian Roma Bar, on Charles Street offered a three-course lunch for 5s 6d. This trend, which extended over the next thirty years to include the vast majority of pubs throughout the county, brought the area a wide reputation for gastronomic excellence.

There were two catalysts to this development in the local food industry. First, the introduction of the breathalyser test in the late 1960s portended the ruin of country pubs that relied solely on the sale of alcohol and the majority quickly directed their attention towards clients who spent money on good food. Second, with a rapidly growing Asian community, many of whom were experienced restaurateurs at home, a natural development was to combine their culinary skills with a high degree of business acumen (especially after 1972 when the traditionally commercially minded East African Asians began to arrive in the city) and set up Indian restaurants in the city centre and environs. The indigenous community of Leicester was quick to espouse the new cuisine, and by the 1990s Leicester was renowned as the top Indian food centre in the provinces, easily rivalling its nearest competitor, Birmingham.

Shown below is a typical shopping list with the prices that a housewife could expect to pay in February 1968. It is based on a range of stores across the city, including Tesco, which at this time was offering the ubiquitous and short-lived Green Shield Stamps; given against sales, these were redeemable for free gifts.

Kellogg's Cornflakes 1 lb packet	2s 3d	Tin spaghetti	8½d
Maxwell House Instant Coffe ¾lb tin	4s 8d	1lb packet frozen peas	2s 6d
Brooke Bond Dividend Tea ¼lb packet	1s 4½d	1 dozen large eggs	5s 1d
Stork margarine ½lb packet	10½d	12oz tin corned beef	3s 3d
1lb lard	1s 8d	Large Vim scouring powder	9½d
1lb packet Cow and Gate butter	3s 6d	Large Harpic cleaning fluid	1s 11d
1lb packet chocolate digestive biscuits	1s 9d	Twin pack toilet rolls	1s 4½d
Bottle Robinson's orange juice	3s	Bar toilet soap	10½d
Loaf Mother's Pride bread	1s 5½d	Head of lettuce	1s
Dutch Edam cheese ½lb	1s 6d	5lb King Edward potatoes	1s 11d
1lb unsmoked bacon	4s 8d	1lb onions	7d
2lb bag sugar	2s 9d	1lb tomatoes	1s 10d
1lb jar Hartley's strawberry jam	1s 9d	Cabbage	1s 6d
1lb jar Golden Shred marmalade	1s 6d	1lb fresh haddock	4s 8d
Tin pineapple pieces	1s 2d	1lb pork sausages	3s 6d
Tin peaches	2s 6d	1lb rump steak	10s 4d
Tin Heinz Scotch Broth	1s 2d	1lb minced beef	4s
Tin Batchelor's processed peas	10½d	1lb stewing beef (shin)	5s 2d
Tin baked beans	1s 1d	Total:	£4 10s 6d

Begun towards the end of 1962 and developed as a private housing estate by Jelson Ltd, the new village of East Goscote on the outskirts of Leicester was created on the 138-acre site of the old War Department Ordnance Depot between Queniborough and Rearsby. Originally intended in 1942 as a munitions store, the land had never been used for the purpose. The development, with 880 houses, was scheduled to take three years to build at a cost of £3 million, and catered for a large percentage of the population overspill from the city.

A short time later, in October 1966, the City Council decided to go ahead within the next five years with an ambitious plan to develop 2,000 acres of land at Beaumont Leys. Originally a sewage farm and already owned by the Corporation, it was seen by the planners as a prime site on which to build houses for 40,000 of Leicester's ever-expanding population. In view of the land's prior usage there was much preparatory work to be done before building work could be commenced. Over 170 acres of the area had been covered to a depth of 6ft in liquid sewage, which would have to be left for four years to dry out before it could be cleared away. On some sections of the site there was an underground piping system, used for pumping, and work began here by 1969, the pipes being retained as part of the estate's drainage system.

Plans for the completed project were ambitious, and aimed to create a satellite town on the outskirts of the city. At 310ft above sea level, the estate would be 110ft higher than the Clock Tower, so the planners decided to site the housing on the flat levels and use the sloping areas for community purposes. The overall design was for 13,650 dwellings in blocks divided by pedestrian ways and cycle tracks. Some 740 acres were allocated to residential building; for schools 194 acres were set aside; 490 acres were devoted to open spaces, and a further 196 acres to playing fields. The remaining land was to be given over to community facilities, roads and agriculture, and – still built into the Chief Planning Officer's overall strategy – a monorail terminus.

The creation of the new suburb went ahead as planned and it was completed within the timescales envisaged. Some small parcels of land were sold off in 1971 to private developers such as Tom Wheatcroft, the Leicester Housing Society, and Bruce Fletcher Ltd; plans for the monorail terminus were shelved in favour of the creation of a major shopping centre.

One other major housing project on the outskirts of Leicester city was conceived in the mid-1960s. In January 1965 it was announced that a new suburb would be created on the Belgrave side of the town, in the area bounded by Melton Road, Rushey Fields, the Midland Railway line and the northern boundary of the city. Work would be split into two phases, divided by the line of the new ring road, the first being the southern sector. This was scheduled to be a combined public and private sector estate, and as part of the first phase the Council would make a start on the Clarke's allotments site (acquired some years previously by compulsory purchase) to build amenities such as schools, accommodation for the elderly, shops etc. At the same time groundwork would be started on services such as sewers and roads. Once this was done disposal of land to private developers could begin. The southern sector comprised an area of 168 acres, of which 71 were reserved for 800 houses. Of the remainder, much was set aside for schools, a church and a community centre. The northern sector, covering 98½ acres, two-thirds of which was for private housing and amenities similar to those in the southern sector, would be developed later. In a separate move at this time, the Town Planning Committee also decided to allow 43 acres of land in the Western Park area, near to Liberty Road, to be developed for housing.

As with Beaumont Leys, work went ahead as planned with the Rushey Mead estate and by March 1975 Wimpey was offering its first completed houses for sale. A two-bedroom semi-detached house was offered at £7,695; a three-bedroom chalet-type house for £8,125; and a detached residence for £10,195.

Probably the last major development of the 1960s was the introduction into the city and county of the North Sea Gas programme. It was announced at the beginning of 1968 that work on converting gas appliances in the district would begin in the spring of the following year, at Hinckley. Working at a rate of 1,000 homes per month, the project took until 1973 to complete.

The 1960s were seen by most in Leicester who lived through them as a golden era. Full employment for both men and women brought to the city a reputation as one of the wealthiest in Europe. More families than ever before were buying their own homes – it was estimated that between 1965 and 1995, based on the replacement of substandard properties, the relief of the current housing shortages, and accommodation for population increases, 30,000 homes would need to be built. The number of motorcar owners rocketed after the end of the 1950s, to the extent that an application from a new buyer for a mortgage on property that did not have a garage was likely to be turned down. The development of housing projects was going ahead smoothly, and pay packets were keeping up with the cost of living.

Sadly, during the following few years there were to be changes in the city's economy that would alter this situation for many.

CHAPTER THIRTEEN

The Early 1970s

In 1970 Harold Wilson, who had been Prime Minister since 1964, lost the general election and power passed back into the hands of the Conservative Party under Edward Heath – where it remained until Heath in turn was beaten in the 1974 elections and Labour returned to power. During the period in which he was Leader of the Opposition Edward Heath had proposed a programme of trade-union reforms, spending restraints and tax cuts. Once in office, the Conservatives found that, due to escalating prices (including crucially, the price of oil), their manifesto pledge could not be implemented, and instead Heath found himself in the unpopular position of having to adopt stringent prices and incomes policies. Disastrously, in 1973 Heath entered into a head-on collision with the trade unions during the miners' strike, resulting in the return to power of Labour in the 1974 general election.

A national census taken in 1971 provides a snapshot of the situation in Leicester at the opening of the decade, and places the city in a national context.

During the decade 1961 to 1971 the combined population of the city and the county rose from 682,649 to 772,102 – of which Leicester city accounted for 284,208. This increase was a little over the national average, and meant that there were now more people than ever in the district requiring housing and employment. A hundred years earlier, in 1861, when the old town became established as an industrial centre, the population stood at just over 68,000; forty years later, in 1901, the number had increased to 211,579; and in 1948, after the Second World War, it stood at 281,400. In the 110 years since 1861 the population had more than quadrupled.

Nationally, in the same ten years there was an average annual increase of 77 people in every 10,000, with a further yearly increase of 51 in every 10,000 through immigration. The combined numbers for immigration and emigration confirmed an overall gain through immigration. Leicester had received a higher number of immigrants than the national average, yet the figures for the city indicated that the population had actually fallen by about 1 per cent. The reason for the apparent anomaly lies in the long-standing conflict between the city and county authorities over population expansion. While immigrants were arriving in the city, as a result of housing projects and natural population drift, existing occupants were moving out into the surrounding county. This is clearly shown in the population increases in districts on the immediate city boundaries: Oadby's population rose by 61 per cent; Wigston's by 41 per cent; and Blaby's by 47 per cent.

The census showed that, across the whole of Leicestershire, 49,500 residents were born outside the UK. Of these two-thirds (34,760) lived in the city and constituted around 12 per cent of its population. (The national immigrant average for England and Wales was at this time 5.5 per cent.) This snapshot appears to confirm that in the decade to 1970 the overall movement of population *into*

Leicester city was marginally lower than the national average, but the mini-migration of people *out* of the city into the county masks the fact that, combined with a higher immigration figure, there was actually an increase in the demand for employment. Those who moved a few miles away to new homes in the county usually remained in their original place of work within the city.

One inescapable fact of life in the city during the 1970s was economic depression. This was not something peculiar to Leicester; things were hard for everyone throughout the country. The decade opened with a Tory government coming into power which was then succeeded by two Labour administrations, each one dogged by financial crises.

The Heath administration was particularly beset by industrial dissent, and in an effort to win an ongoing battle with the mining unions, in 1973 Heath introduced a three-day working week that almost crippled the country's industry. In 1974 and 1976 the Labour Party, first under Harold Wilson and then under James Callaghan, inherited such a weakened economy that by 1976 the government was forced to seek a loan from the International Monetary Fund, and a year later unemployment levels reached the 1.6 million level. In these circumstances many Leicester firms, already suffering from a situation in which competitive trading was hampered by there being more jobs than workers, found themselves in deep trouble.

A frequent indication that things might not be as they seem is the merging of a smaller, locally based company or group of companies with a larger, amorphous group. Such a takeover came in early 1970 when the Coats Paton Group bought up the Leicester hosiery manufacturing firm of Byford's for £2 million. Byford's had subsidiaries at Maltby in Yorkshire and Immingham in Lincolnshire, making the firm attractive to Coats which, with a worldwide base, employed between 70,000 and 80,000 people. The bid came on the heels of Coats's acquisition of H.L. Driver at Barrow upon Soar, which gave it control of a further fourteen companies employing a total of around 1,300 people. Significantly, during the year before the takeover Byford's trading profit fell by over one-third, from £240,342 to £174,503.

At the beginning of the following year the National Union of Hosiery and Knitwear Workers was in agreement with the employers that things were not going well (there was great opposition at this time from the trade unions to the government's attempts to bring in an Industrial Relations Bill, designed to restrict their freedom to strike), and while the idea was unpalatable, short-time working was one of the solutions that had to be accepted.

Although the boot and shoe trade at this point was just about holding its own, in March 1970 the Leicester Footwear Manufacturers' Association gave a gloomy assessment of the industry's prospects: 'during the early part of 1969 order books began to shorten, in general manufacture of children's shoes was the only area of improvement, women's were particularly down . . . a difficulty is being experienced where factories have upgraded their technology and speeded up production, only to find that suppliers cannot keep up with their needs . . .'.

That there was a decline in the trade was clearly shown when, just over three months afterwards, GUS Footwear closed its Melton Road factory, putting 240 out of work. The board issued a statement that this was due to a downsizing and the transference of work to the company's more modern premises at Worcester. However, the company's closing room on Fosse Road, with 100 workers, remained in operation.

In July that year an unexpected turn of events came when the printing firm of Lonsdale & Bartholomew Ltd announced that it would be closing its Leicester operation in September with the loss of 100 jobs. Printing had traditionally been viewed in Leicester as one of the more lucrative trades, and Lonsdale & Bartholomew had other plants in Nottingham, Manchester, Rochdale, Bath, Wellingborough and Bristol. Originally trading as the old-established firm of George Gibbons, it had been taken over by its present owners in 1963, and the Leicester closure, as the result of yet another merger, gave cause for concern. H. Downing for Lonsdale & Bartholomew made the bland statement that 'there is need for specialisation in the printing industry – at all of our other factories there is specialisation – but at Leicester work is of a more general nature and we have had to rationalise . . .'.

Another hosiery firm to be sacrificed in the opening weeks of 1971 was that of Robinson & Pickford, which had been manufacturing in the city since 1928. The company had recently been taken over by Hirst & Mallinson of Huddersfield, in yet another 'rationalisation', and 200 of the firm's 230 shop-floor workers in the making-up departments were made redundant when the new owners decided to re-equip with new machines and expand their profitable jersey knitting operation. Once more, trading losses incurred since the company had been bought out (on this occasion £104,000 in the preceding year) were given as the reason for the reorganisation and subsequent job losses.

Already a pattern was emerging of local companies being bought out by larger groups, ostensibly for investment purposes, and then, their trading potential having been absorbed, closed down.

The Industrial Relations Bill being pushed through Parliament by the Conservatives despite fierce opposition from the trade unions now became the cause of one of the main battles between Edward Heath and the country's organised labour groups. Across the country during the first week of March 1971, car plants, shipyards and engineering workforces went on strike in protest against the restrictive practices proposed in the legislation.

Firms in the Midlands were badly hit by the industrial action, with over 500,000 workers on strike throughout the region. Operations at factories in Leicester, such as Bentley Engineering, were severely affected, with all of the Amalgamated Union of Engineering and Foundry Workers members refusing to work. The British United Shoe Machinery Co. was in a similar position, with only apprentices and technical staff turning up for work. Other companies, including Goodwin & Barsby, were more fortunate, with only 30 per cent of their shop-floor workers out (unions such as the Transport and General Workers Union and the General and Municipal Workers Union continued to work); at Frederick Parker's the workforce was split about half and half.

This action coincided with a postal workers' strike which ran for just over six weeks and was estimated to have cost the Post Office £23 million. With the promise of a public inquiry on the table, the 1,100 Leicester members of the Union of Post Office Workers held a meeting at Granby Halls on Saturday 6 March, at which two-thirds of those present agreed to return to work the following Monday.

Vulnerable through the parlous state of British industry, in April 1971 another old-established local company was absorbed by a large multinational group. For some years the Leicester firm of Adcock & Shipley (founded in 1914) had been making vertical milling machines under licence for Bridgeport Machines, which in turn belonged to Textron Ltd, a subsidiary of Textron Incorporated of Providence, Rhode Island, USA. It was announced that Adcock & Shipley, which employed 750 people in their factories at Leicester and Bridlington, was to be taken over by Textron in order to provide it with backing for expansion.

Nationally unemployment stood at 904,117 (3.7 per cent) by August 1971, the worst figure since 1940. By March 1972 the national figure was, for the third month in succession, over 1 million, and in Leicester there were 5,248 unemployed. Things eased a little, both nationally and locally, over the next twelve months and figures for March 1973 show that unemployment in Leicester had dropped to 3,873, which, at 2 per cent of the available workforce, was 1 per cent less than the national average.

The situation did not hold for long and by November 1974 the numbers out of work in the city had climbed to 4,696, rising three months later to 6,092 before hitting 8,199 (3.6 per cent), in March 1975, inflated by the massive numbers thrown onto the dole by the closure of the Imperial Typewriter Co.. Unemployment was now spinning out of control and it was not until February 1976 that the Leicester figure dropped, for the first time in twelve months, to below the national average, when it stood at 12,305 (5.5 per cent).

During this period closures in the manufacturing sector came thick and fast. Dunlop in April 1971 closed its St Mary's Mills factory with a loss of 670 jobs. At the end of June A.J. Portch in St Margaret Street was closed down and production moved to the holding group's Scottish-based facility; Wolsey in Bruin Street also laid off workers. Companies all over the city and county were either closing down, working short time, or making redundancies, on a weekly basis.

In January 1972 the National Union of Miners, for the first time since 1926, went on strike in pursuit of better conditions and pay. It was winter, and with coal stocks rapidly dwindling, a decision was taken on Thursday 25 January that fourteen of the city's infant, junior and secondary schools would close immediately, with a further twenty-five to follow suit in the next week as their heating systems shut down. By the end of the month the city was experiencing severe power cuts as

Imperial Typewriter factory, viewed from St Saviours Road, was the scene of a major industrial dispute during the 1970s, resulting in the American owners, Litton Industries, deciding that the company was no longer viable and the subsequent closure of the site. (Courtesy: E. Welford)

The progress of the Imperial Typewriter dispute was closely followed locally by the media. Seen here is a crew from Radio Leicester conducting an interview inside the factory with a member of the shop-floor staff. *(Courtesy: Radio Leicester)*

electricity supplies were cut back. At the beginning of the second week in February the Home Secretary, Reginald Maudling, was granted the powers to implement a state of emergency, with a view to the government imposing restrictions on the use of electricity and releasing generating companies from the responsibility to provide uninterrupted supplies – giving them flexibility to implement power cuts.

Coming on top of their other problems, the miners' strike was a serious blow to many Leicester manufacturers. A ban was imposed on heating offices, shops, catering establishments and places of entertainment and a three-day working week was introduced. Across Great Britain power stations began to fail, and in the middle of February it was estimated that 750,000 men and women were unable to work. Leicester Social Services (both the city and the county) made plans to open feeding centres where people could go to obtain meals and keep warm.

A pay deal of sorts was eventually brokered at the beginning of 1973 and, with the strike over for the time being, supplies of coal began to arrive in the city during the third week of February. Unable to continue under these conditions, Brevitt Shoes closed its Leicester site in October 1972 and regrouped at its factory in Northampton, with 200 redundancies in Leicester. In February 1973 Stead & Simpson, who had been shoe manufacturers in the town since 1856, closed their two factories with a further loss of 400 jobs. Airborne Shoes at Anstey, employing 200 people, had already gone into receivership the previous year.

These were joined in the summer of 1973 by Litton Textile Holdings (not to be confused with the American Litton Group who owned the Imperial Typewriter Co.) of Alexandra House in Rutland Street, along with its three subsidiary textile and dyeing plants in the city.

A period of respite now ensued in the form of an uneasy truce between the government and the miners (albeit in the interim the Tories were forced to deal with a major dockers' strike) until, in November 1973, when relations broke down, a further strike was called. The government's immediate response was to once more declare a state of emergency, and with another winter fuel crisis looming, it hinted broadly that petrol rationing was soon to be brought in. This move, irrespective of the reality of a coming oil crisis, was designed to alienate the general public from the miners' cause.

For hosiery manufacturers this was the beginning of another damaging episode. On behalf of the Hosiery Manufacturers Association, Peter Bailey, the Head of H.T.H. Peck, explained the industry's predicament:

> manufacturers in the Leicester district are being forced by shortages to eat into their stocks of man made fibres, this will result in lay-offs and redundancies in the trade . . . because of price restrictions in this country and escalating prices abroad, large quantities of fibres are being sold to European countries and then bought back by British manufacturers at up to 70 and 80 per cent above UK prices . . .

The employers' problems were compounded in December 1973 when the National Union of Hosiery Workers in Leicester negotiated a wages and conditions deal that gave workers an increase of £2.25 a week (the average wage in the city at this time for a married man was £28) and a guaranteed fifty-two weeks a year of paid work, with improved holiday and sickness benefits.

Life in the city became difficult during 1973. Petrol coupons were printed and held in readiness in post offices, power cuts once more became commonplace across the county, and firms unable to feed their boilers ceased production, with subsequent losses in revenue (they could not circumvent this situation by providing ancillary power, due to a ban on the use of independent generators in factories). Shops and restaurants in the city, bereft of any form of heating, were forced to close down or operate in untenable conditions.

There were indications early in the decade that the retail trade in the city centre was also suffering when some of the town's oldest-established retailers closed their doors. R. Pochin & Son Ltd, one of Leicester's long-standing ironmongery stores closed down in November 1970 with thirty redundancies. Pochin's who had traded in Granby Street since 1861, had decided that the retail side of the business was no longer viable and it would concentrate on its builders' merchant's depot in Queen Street.

The second establishment was the grocery store belonging to Simpkin & James. Seen as the 'Fortnum and Mason' of Leicester, Simpkin & James had traded at their Horsefair Street/Market Place shop for 160 years, and were a part of old Leicester. Citing parking problems, excessive taxes and the customers' preference for supermarket shopping, the firm ceased trading in early 1971. Not far from Simpkin & James's city-centre shop, Lipton's in the Market Place closed its provisions store at the end of July 1973.

As 1974 dawned, industrial relations were at an all-time low. ASLEF, the rail workers' union, had its members out on strike, disrupting rail services; the mining and engineering unions were locked in dispute with the government; and a three-day working week was in force. At midnight on Saturday 9 February the National Union of Miners called yet another strike. In a desperate 'who governs?' move, Edward Heath called a general election – and lost. With Heath, the miners' arch-enemy, removed and Harold Wilson back in the Prime Minister's seat, the new Labour government resolved the mining dispute quickly, and the latest strike lasted only four weeks.

However, by now the country's economic position was almost beyond recovery and the resulting depression persisted for several more years. Closures in Leicester continued at an alarming rate throughout 1974–5. At the end of 1975 the Knitting Industries Federation estimated that in the hosiery trade alone 11,000 jobs had been lost in the United Kingdom during the year. In January 1976 unemployment in Leicester stood at 14,366, 6.4 per cent of the available workforce. The national unemployment figure was 6 per cent.

Aside from the collapse of several local industries, there was now a major national industrial crisis which had an impact on Leicester's engineering factories. In the 1960s the American company of Lockheed began work on its wide-bodied L-1011 Tri-Star airliner, and the engines to power it were to be produced by the Derby-based British manufacturer, Rolls-Royce. The RB 211 engine proved enormously expensive to turn out and Rolls-Royce quickly got into serious financial difficulties. The extent of these difficulties became apparent when, in November 1969, the directors approached the government for a cash injection of £60 million to help fund work on the jet engine project. By the beginning of the next year, with no offer of assistance on the table, the company was unable to go ahead with production, a factor which severely compromised Lockheed's own prospects.

Rolls-Royce was in dire straits, and in February 1971 it was announced by the Board that the company was to go into receivership. Deeply involved in government defence contracts, the Board hoped that the company's losses would be underwritten. However, this was not a view shared by the government, which had its own problems. Locally, with many engineering firms subcontracting to Rolls-Royce, the calling in of the receivers was a potential disaster. If work on the RB 211 engine was scrapped it would lead to 400 job losses at the company's Mountsorrel plant alone.

The crisis was a doubly unfortunate circumstance for the district, as the Beagle Aircraft Co. at Rearsby (formerly Auster Aircraft) was also in deep financial trouble. Immediately after Christmas 1967 the company had suffered a major setback when, following on the heels of the loss of a £1 million South African order, a £½ million Argentinian contract for eighteen Beagle 206 aircraft was cancelled. The circumstances were made even more unfortunate by the fact that Beagle was not responsible for the losses – the South African order had been cancelled as a result of American political pressure, and the Argentinian one as a reprisal against Britain cancelling meat sales from the country during an epidemic of foot and mouth disease. At the beginning of 1970 Beagle called in the receivers and 300 staff were made redundant. Despite the best efforts to save the company, it went into liquidation in December 1971 with a loss of around 500 jobs.

Among the Leicester firms affected by the Rolls-Royce crisis was Cannon & Stokes Ltd of Orson Street at Aylestone and its associated company J.P. Engineering. Employing between 600 and 700 workers, they were heavily committed to Rolls-Royce's Derby plant. Other local companies involved were Slack & Parr, employing 650 people on aero-engine work at their Kegworth factory; Saunders Engineering at Sileby; G.T.G. Engineering at Loughborough; and North Bridge Engineering at Wigston. It was estimated that if Rolls-Royce were to collapse a possible 2,000 firms in the Midlands, including Leicester, would be affected.

The factor that eventually saved the situation was that if Rolls-Royce were declared bankrupt, its failure to produce the massive RB 211 turbo-fan engine (which was critical to the production of the L-1011 Tri-Star) would result in the collapse of the

Lockheed Co., something that the US Administration could not afford to allow. When Rolls-Royce Aero Engines was put into receivership in 1971 the production of Tri-Stars was halted immediately. Dan Haughton, the Chairman and Chief Executive Officer of Lockheed, brought pressure to bear on the US Congress, which in turn exerted influence on Edward Heath's already beleaguered government.

A deal was arrived at whereby the US Administration guaranteed a loan of $250 million to Lockheed, and the British government made a similar gesture by nationalising the Aero Engines Division of Rolls-Royce, thus securing the future of both firms. (The cars division of Rolls-Royce was the subject of a flotation in 1973 as a separate entity, and the aero-engine side of the company returned to the private sector in 1987.)

May 1974 saw one of Leicester's most famous industrial disputes played out – the strike at the Imperial Typewriter Co. on East Park Road. Leicester had a history going back to before the First World War of producing typewriters. At the turn of the century there were four manufacturers in the town, the Monarch Typewriter Co. at 6 Pocklington's Walk; Arthur Moore & Co., 53 London Road; the Oliver Typewriter Co., 34 London Road; and the Imperial Typewriter Co. in Wharf Street.

Imperial was established in 1908 when two Leicester businessmen, J.W. Goddard and W. Evans, put money into the Moya Typewriter Co. which, since 1902, had been producing machines designed by a Spanish-American, Hidalgo Moya; the newly formed company was called the Imperial Typewriter Co. The success of the enterprise was such that in 1911 the firm moved to new premises on East Park Road, where it remained until it ceased trading in 1975.

May 1966 signalled for Imperial a sea-change in its organisation, when the California-based Litton Industries Group made a £2.5 million bid for the company with the intention of creating an amalgamation with its own Royal Typewriter Co.. From the beginning, the bid caused waves of consternation to sweep through the establishment, and ten months later shareholders were attempting to block the move amid allegations that its existence had been concealed at the previous annual general meeting. The opposition was unsuccessful and the deal went through, with Imperial becoming a subsidiary of the American-based Litton Industries.

Initially things appeared to be going well when, in January 1972, the group's Royal Typewriter Co., based in Hartford, Connecticut, reduced its workforce by 1,500 and transferred a large part of its production to the British plant. The move created over 300 jobs at the Leicester site, and from Imperial producing around 2,000 manual and electric typewriters a week, combined production went up to 5,000 a week. (At the time, Imperial was employing around 2,000 people at the East Park Road site.) At its site in Hull, which was making parts and components to ship to America for assembly, the company employed a further 2,000. Royal controlled interests in Europe and the Far East and had a factory in Holland (Amsterdam), the Adler company in Germany, and other sites in Japan. Leicester, Hull and Amsterdam operated as a single integrated unit and now included business machines, photocopiers and calculators in their range of products. The transfer of production from the United States was accompanied by plans to expand the Leicester operation. Marketing and administration offices were opened in St

Nicholas Circle, the East Park Road factory was expanded, and a distribution centre was planned for Glenfield.

By 1974, however, many of those at management level were aware that despite outward appearances Imperial was in financial difficulties, and what began as a grievance over pay eventually sealed the company's fate. On Wednesday 1 May 1974, following a dispute over bonus rates, a group of Asian workers at Imperial began an unofficial strike. Two days later, on Friday, following a mid-morning meeting attended by about 400 of the company's Asian employees on nearby Spinney Hill Park, around 300 of those present, led by Hasmukh Khatani, a 22-year-old Ugandan Asian, joined them. The strike was not recognised by the Transport and General Workers Union (T&GWU), to which most of the strikers belonged, on the grounds that the claim by the disaffected members for a pay increase of 60 per cent was unreasonable; also the works convener, Reg Weaver, was, even at this early stage, worried about a disruptive element which had high-jacked the proceedings and was resorting to the intimidation of members who were standing aside from the action.

Production at Imperial's nearby Copdale Road site was quickly affected. By Tuesday of the following week about 500 of the company's Asian workers were on strike and the thirty-nine workers who had initiated the dispute were sent their cards and told that they were deemed by the company to have terminated their employment. At this point the strikers were rallied together and addressed by an outside political activist named Bennie Bunsee, who had a history of organising industrial disputes in the Midlands area. With the strike extending into the following week and the management of Imperial refusing to negotiate with either Hasmukh Khatani or N.C. Patel, another of the strike leaders, whom they held to have constructively dismissed themselves, the situation deteriorated rapidly.

Michael Stamper, Director of the East Midlands Engineering Employers' Association, on Monday of the following week, warned that 'the strike at Imperial may result in cut-backs, and even Imperial closing down'. To the strikers this appeared to be a deliberately alarmist warning, but to those in the know it was not an unrealistic supposition. There were feelings, certainly among some of the senior staff at Imperial, that, with the company's financial position less than stable, an unofficial strike without union backing could be the perfect excuse for Litton's to close down its UK operation and regroup elsewhere in the United States and Europe.

Meanwhile, the strikers continued to press on with their grievances, which now included allegations that the organisation of the company and the structure of the union were inherently racist (this latter assertion in relation to the T&GWU was based primarily on a rule in the constitution that a worker had to have been a member of the union for a minimum of two years before being eligible to become a shop steward). The district representative of the T&GWU, George Bromley (who was also a magistrate sitting on the Leicester city bench), tried in vain to persuade the dissidents that they should be negotiating through the approved union channels, and endorsed the fact that through their actions they were running the grave danger of the plant being shut down.

On Wednesday 15 May notices were served on 320 of the strikers to the effect that they must return to work by 8 a.m. the next day or face dismissal. After they were told by Bunsee to ignore the notices, only thirty returned to their jobs on the factory floor.

A strike meeting was then held at the Highfields Community Centre, followed on Friday (the day after the expiry of the notices) by a march to the T&GWU offices in Eldon Street, where a letter was handed in demanding that George Bromley, as District Secretary, recognise the validity of the strike. In an attempt to obtain some sort of a deal that would resolve matters, Bromley agreed to enter into talks with the management. His attitude was that, realistically, the other workers at Imperial would not support the dispute, and the best that he might be able to do was broker a deal whereby those on strike would be reinstated. Imperial, for its part, extended the deadline for a return to work until 8 a.m. on Tuesday 21 May.

As part of the attempt to damp down the situation, it was arranged for the Race Relations Board to carry out an inquiry into the strike leaders' allegations of racism. Both the union and the company welcomed this move, but it did not suit Bennie Bunsee at all, and he advised the strikers to boycott the inquiry.

Matters came to a climax at lunchtime on Thursday 30 May when 150 of the dismissed pickets came face to face with half a dozen policemen who were manning the gates to the factory on East Park Road. Fighting broke out between the police and the pickets, who successfully forced an entry through the gates and into the yard, and it was only with the arrival of police reinforcements under the command of Chief Superintendent Clement Adkin that order was restored. The fact that BBC television cameras were present when the episode occurred cannot realistically be dismissed as a coincidence, and it is likely that the clash was carefully orchestrated by the strike organisers. Bennie Bunsee, who had, interestingly, not been present when the fighting took place, denied any prior knowledge, asserting that the strikers had been sold out by the union and that other people were making it into a racial issue.

Following the incident at the factory yard, 200 of the strikers went to London to the headquarters of the T&GWU, intending to put their case to the General Secretary, Jack Jones, in an attempt to gain union support. While 150 strikers held a demonstration outside Transport House, three of the delegates spent an hour and a half in a meeting with Moss Evans, the national organiser for the union and the District Secretary, George Bromley. Bunsee was refused admission to the meeting as he was not an employee of Imperial Typewriter.

At this point, Litton's decided to draw a line by stating that so far as they were concerned there were no strikers at their factory – the 380 Asian workers who had participated in the unofficial industrial action were now dismissed. If management considered the matter closed, those dismissed did not. On Friday 31 May a meeting was arranged between management and the 1,200 people who were continuing to work normally at the East Park Road site because of their fears of violence from the constant picketing of the premises. In the meantime, the Race Relations Board began its inquiry at Nottingham into the allegations of racism (an inquiry with which, although they had instigated it, the strikers refused to cooperate) and Litton's blithely announced that it was confident in the continuing stability of the Leicester plant – and that it would in the near future be engaging more staff.

Talks reached a stalemate. The dismissed workers, realising that they were not going to achieve their original objectives, now based their demands on what they considered to be a reasonable offer, namely that they would return to work provided there was no victimisation and they received an assurance of continued employment and improved union representation. Management, with its own agenda, was not interested, and an offer of re-employment was not something that it was prepared to consider.

Litton Industries chose now to bide its time for some months until, at 3 p.m. on Friday 17 January 1975, without any prior warning, the trade union representatives were told that the Leicester plant was to be closed down and the entire workforce made redundant in five weeks' time – the employees were told thirty minutes later.

Claiming that the production of Imperial typewriters was no longer a viable option, the American parent group stated that in the last eight years the Leicester operation had lost £9 million, £5 million of this in the two previous years, and that continued trading would create a further £3 million loss in the next year. With recent closures of factories in the United States and Holland the trade union immediately accused Litton of asset-stripping. Whether or not this was true, it had no effect on the outcome. The offer was that if the workforce cooperated, the close-down would take place on 21 February; if the workers or the union attempted to stage any form of sit-in or other delaying tactics, the closure would be immediate. Inevitably, the firm's factory at Hull also closed, resulting in a total loss of 3,200 jobs.

After the closure, the assets of the Imperial Typewriter Co. were sold to Office and Electronic Machines Ltd (OEM), which employed 300 people and was based in St Nicholas Circle. OEM was to assume responsibility for the distribution of Imperial products throughout the United Kingdom and Eire, through a new and separate subsidiary. Imperial Sales and Service was to be retained and typewriters manufactured abroad (Triumph-Adler, the German-based manufacturer, carried on producing the Imperial Model 90) would be sold through OEM.

To the very end, the Litton Group maintained that when it bought the Imperial Typewriter Co. in 1966 it had been for less than the market value because the organisation was losing money and that it had continued to do so – and that the closure had nothing to do with industrial relations.

So far as the citizens of Leicester were concerned, two things happened during the 1970s that affected their everyday life. In 1971, on 15 February, the familiar pounds, shillings and pence in their pockets were replaced by a brand new coinage with the introduction of decimalisation, and later that same year, in October, Edward Heath successfully secured the UK's entry into the European Economic Community. Decimalisation resulted in a 'rounding up' (rather than a 'rounding down') of prices, which created an immediate and widely decried increase in the cost of living, and entry into the Common Market resulted in an escalation of the process, accompanied by a virtual severing of trading ties with Commonwealth countries such as Australia and New Zealand.

Physical local changes included the pedestrianisation of Gallowtree Gate in October 1971 (although City Transport buses continued to thread their way through throngs of shoppers); the opening of the refurbished Retail Market Place, also in 1971; and in 1976 the City Council moving into its new – if controversial – home at the top of Welford Place. In April 1973 the old-fashioned system of adding purchase tax to the sale of goods, calculated at various levels depending upon the merchandise involved, was scrapped in favour of a new universal Value Added Tax

Looking along the line of Charles Street, many of the postwar city-centre developments are visible. On the left is Lee Circle car park, and the Epic House tower block built on the site of the old horse repository, opposite is the Haymarket Centre, with the frontage of Lewiss's department store still dominating Humberstone Gate. In the background, at the far end of Charles Street, are the GPO tower block, and a view of the rear of the police station, showing the addition made in the early 1970s, on the right-hand side of the complex, of an extra wing. The fact that the old buildings at the back of the police station are still in existence dates the picture to just before 1974. *(Courtesy: Urban Design Group, Leicester City Council)*

(VAT), seen at first as a simplification of the system for manufacturers and retailers, but later to become the bane of many businessmen's lives.

A final blow to Leicester's civic pride was the loss of one of its oldest institutions, the Royal Leicestershire Regiment. The roots of the regiment (universally known from its cap badge and collar dogs as the 'Tigers') went back to the seventeenth century when it was first formed. Then, however, fundamental changes within the structure of the British Army were to lead to its eventual dissolution.

Postwar revisions of the army affected many county regiments, including the Tigers. The first cold winds of change were felt as far back as October 1956 when it was decided that the 9th Independent Armoured Brigade, based at Brentwood Road, would change from an armoured to an infantry division. This directly affected the Leicestershire Yeomanry, which was part of the 9th, inasmuch as it lost two of its four tank squadrons and amalgamated with the Derbyshire Yeomanry. In July 1957, with the formation of a Midland Brigade comprised of the Royal Leicestershire Regiment, the Royal Warwickshires, and the Sherwood Foresters, the famous 'Tiger' cap badge was replaced by a dedicated brigade badge (although the old Tigers battalion continued for the time being to wear its dedicated collar badge). Later, in August 1960, this in turn became the Forester Brigade, based at Glen Parva Depot. The slum property and road development programme in the city counted the historic Magazine Barracks buildings among its casualties. Consequently, in April 1961 the 5th Battalion (TA) of the regiment moved into new quarters in the Territorial Army Centre at Ulverscroft Road. (The occupants of the houses at the barracks were moved out by the Council in April 1964 before demolition.)

A further restructuring in 1964 saw the 1st Battalion Royal Leicestershire Regiment become the 4th (Leicestershire) Battalion, Royal Anglian Regiment and it moved out of its barracks at Glen Parva to a new headquarters at Bury St Edmunds.

Local officials and dignitaries did their best to preserve what remained of the identity of the regiment. Alderman Monica Trotter, at the time Lord Mayor of Leicester, paid a visit to the 4th Battalion of the regiment in Malta during 1966, when she conferred upon it the Freedom of the City, giving its men the right to 'march through the city streets with fixed bayonets, colours flying, and band playing', a concession which it exercised in a 'Freedom of the City' march on Saturday 12 October 1968 when the battalion was reviewed by the then Lord Mayor, Alderman Kenneth Bowder.

The efforts were of little avail. In mid-January 1970 it was announced that the Tigers Battalion of the Royal Anglians was to be disbanded. Given one final reprieve in August 1970, Major General Michael Forrester, Colonel Commandant of the Queen's Division, announced that rather than be disbanded completely, the Tigers of the 4th Battalion Royal Anglians could continue in the reduced role of a company formation made up of 120 officers and men. To be known as the Tigers Co. under the command of a major, it would be used as a training and reinforcement unit. Split into two platoons, 'A' Platoon under Major John Heggs took up barracks at the Royal Military Academy, Sandhurst, as a battle demonstration squad, and 'B' Platoon went to the Mons Officer Cadet School on similar duties. In March 1974, with Tiger Co. now the only independent Rifle Co. in the British Army, it was returned to duties with the Royal Anglians, and finally disbanded in July 1975.

The 1970s were without doubt disastrous years for Leicester. Dominated by economic decline, the city, which in previous decades had been blessed with the reputation of being one of the wealthiest in Europe, saw its position slip away rapidly when the fortunes of the country changed. To offset this, much work was done on the physical structure of the town – new roads were laid out and old slum properties disappeared to be replaced with bright new housing. The balance was, however, that the golden years had now passed and much work and effort would be required if the city was to be restored to its former position.

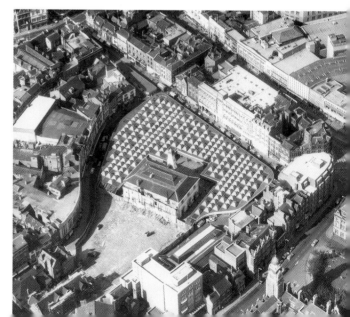

Seen from the air, sometime between October 1971 and November 1974, the newly refurbished Market Place. The area at the rear of the Corn Exchange (site of the indoor market) has not as yet been built upon, and the High Cross has not been repositioned in Cheapside. *(Courtesy: Urban Design Group, Leicester City Council)*

Postscript

In 1975 Margaret Thatcher successfully challenged Edward Heath for leadership of the Conservative Party and, following the disastrous 'Winter of Discontent' under Labour, won the general election four years later with ease, to become Britain's first woman Prime Minister – a position she held until November 1990 when she was replaced by John Major. As in earlier years, the country, and along with it Leicester, was beset throughout the period by continuing labour disputes and inflation problems.

The precarious state of many industries continued into the 1980s and '90s, punctuated by the collapse of such companies as the Bentley Group, Stibbe's, the Ex-Cell-O Corporation, and one of the last casualties, Pex, at the end of the 1990s. Pex factory – West Bridge Mills – built in the early Victorian era for Whitmore & Sons (worsted spinners) survived both the demise of its owners and the developers' hammer, to remain in its prime position overlooking West Bridge as the district's Land Registry Office.

A scheme involving a 26-acre site in the West Bridge, Eastern/Western Boulevard district produced the Bede Island development. In the same area, Leicester City Football Club moved from its home ground at Filbert Street to the new purpose-built Walker's Stadium on the site of the old Leicester power station in August 2002.

In the city centre two new shopping areas have been created. One, in Silver Street, is the St Martin's shopping precinct, the other and more ambitious is the Shires, stretching from Eastgates back along the line of Churchgate to St Peter's Lane.

John Beckett's vision of a massive outer ring road encircling the city was completed by 2000, and this in turn is home to new shopping developments at the Fosse Park and Grove Farm Park sites, near to junction 21 of the M1 motorway.

Leicester Royal Infirmary, with 1,100 beds and employing 5,300 staff, has become the county's prime medical facility and one of the largest teaching hospitals in Europe.

By the turn of the century, according to the 2001 census, the population of Leicester had grown to 279,921, and the creation of De Montfort University in 1992, from the original Leicester Polytechnic College, has given the city the final accolade of having a second university.

Work continued until well into the twenty-first century on the development of new road schemes to alleviate traffic flow in and through the city. Seen here under construction in 1988 is St George's Way link between Charles Street, Northampton Street junction and Humberstone Road. *(Courtesy: E.R. Welford)*

Hosting his prime-time morning radio show, John Florance interviewed Prime Minister John Major on Tuesday 8 February 1994. Unfortunately for the PM it was the day after the body of Stephen Milligan, the Conservative member for Eastleigh, had been found in suspicious circumstances, and John Major was faced with answering difficult questions from the host regarding the validity of his newly introduced 'back to basics' morality programme. *(Courtesy: Radio Leicester)*

In 1985 a heavy fall of snow caught the city unawares. With traffic brought to a standstill, Radio Leicester journalist Matthew Hill has taken the opportunity to ski down London Road on his way to work at Epic House in Charles Street, beating the congestion. *(Courtesy: Radio Leicester)*

Evocative more of a Victorian or Edwardian scene, Rupert's Gateway in the Newarkes. Taken during a snowstorm in the winter of 1990, this picture records one of the last occasions that heavy snow hit the city before the turn of the century. *(Courtesy: G. Wilson)*

Hard winters became less frequent towards the end of the twentieth century, although as these pictures show, heavy – if short-lived – falls of snow continued to blanket the city from time to time.

Events 1945–75

1946 – January	Work begins on building New Parks estate.
1946 – March	Private enterprise allowed to resume building houses.
1946 – September	New housing schemes proposed at Evington Valley and Braunstone.
1948 – June	Provisions of the Beveridge Report implemented to create the Welfare State.
1948 – November	Last of the German POWs in the city and county repatriated.
1949 – April	Several Leicester men involved in the Yangtse incident.
1949 – November	The last tramcar run in the city.
1949 – December	Leicester Boundaries Extension Bill proposed.
1949 – December	First television transmissions received in the city.
1950 – February	Cold War escalation with the Klaus Fuchs spy trial.
1950 – February	First Civil Defence recruiting campaign begun in the city and county.
1950 – February	End of petrol rationing.
1950 – June	Beginning of the Korean War.
1950 – July–September	Tramlines removed from the city centre and suburbs.
1950 – September	Soap taken off ration.
1951 – June	First proposals for 'no-waiting regulations' to be introduced in the city centre.
1951 – October	1st Battalion Royal Leicestershire Regiment sent to Korea.
1952 – July	Tigers battalion returns from Korea
1952 – October	New ambulance station opened on Welford Road.
1953 – January	Major building work begun on Eyres Monsell estate.
1953 – February	Leicester Emergency Services (police, fire, civil defence) sent to assist at the east coast flood emergency.
1953 – March	Inquiry into the Leicester Development Plan.
1953 – April	Charles Clore becomes a Director of Bentley Engineering Group.
1953 – June	Coronation of HM Queen Elizabeth II.
1954 – January	Leicester City Council applies to Parliament for powers to introduce compulsory smokeless zones.
1954 – March	Slum clearance in the Wharf Street district begins.
1954 – July	Meat rationing ends.
1954 – September	City Council accepts the initial tenders for building work on Netherhall estate.
1954 – October	Work begins on the Percy Gee Building at Leicester University.
1955 – October	1st Battalion Royal Leicestershire Regiment posted to Cyprus
1955 – November	State of emergency declared in Cyprus.
1956 – January	Leicester City and County Police officers seconded to Cyprus.
1956 – February	First broadcast in the Leicester area of Independent Television.

1956 – October	Closure of the Theatre Royal.
1956 – October	Russia occupies Hungary – small number of Hungarians arrive in Leicester.
1956 – October	New casualty and X-ray Departments opened at Leicester Royal Infirmary.
1956 – October	Petrol rationing imposed as a result of the Suez Crisis.
1957 – March	Leicester becomes a university city.
1975 – May	Petrol rationing ends.
1957 – May	Theatre Royal site sold to Leicester Permanent Building Society.
1957 – September	USAAF move in at Bruntingthorpe air base.
1959 – February	Palace Theatre closed down.
1959 – March	Martin's Bank opens first 'drive-through' bank in Charles Street.
1961 – February	New MOT regulations affect Leicester motor vehicle owners.
1963 – March	Publication of the Beeching Report leads to rail cuts in Leicester.
1963 – July	All Leicester telephone numbers become STD.
1963 – October	Phoenix Theatre opens in Newarke Street.
1963 – October	Initial proposals for the building of Rowlatt's Hill estate.
1965 – September	Leicester City Transport sets up CCTV camera to assist bus management.
1966 – January	First tenants move into Rowlatts Hill estate.
1966 – July	*Leicester Mercury* moves from Albion Street to new purpose-built premises in St George Street.
1966 – August	Work begins on Southgates underpass.
1966 – October	Outline plans submitted for Beaumont Leys estate.
1966 – December	Highfields redevelopment plan begins.
1967 – May	Saffron Lane Sports Stadium opened.
1967 – June	Work begins on the new Wholesale Market at Freemen's Common.
1967 – November	Radio Leicester begins broadcasting.
1968 – May	Southgates underpass opened.
1968 – July	Saffron Lane flooded.
1969 – September	All work stopped on St Peter's housing estate owing to financial problems.
1970 – July	Work recommenced on building St Peter's estate by private contractors.
1971 – February	Decimalisation comes into force.
1971 – October	Retail Market development opened.
1971 – November	Gallowtree Gate pedestrianised.
1973 – April	Value Added Tax (VAT) replaces Purchase Tax.
1974 – May	Industrial action at Imperial Typewriters.
1975 – February	Imperial Typewriter Co. closed down by Litton Industries.
1975 – March	First private houses on the Rushey Mead development offered for sale.
1976 – August	City Council takes up occupation of New Walk Centre.

Unemployment during the early 1970s

Date	Great Britain and Northern Ireland	Leicester	
August 1971	904,117 (3.7%)		Worst national figure since 1940
September 1971	929,121 (3.9%)		
March 1972	1.01 million	5,248	
February 1973	753,293	4,263	Lowest figure in Leicester for eight months
March 1973	717,669	3,873 (2%)	National average 3%
June 1973	576,286 (2.5%)	3,201	
July 1973	435,037	3,310	
June 1974	515,730	3,604	
September 1974	682,685	4,410	
October 1974	643,442	4,049	
February 1975	792,892 (3.4%)	6,092 (3.1%)	Does not include redundancies at Imperial Typewriter Co.
March 1975	802,630	8,199 (3.6%)	National average 3.4%
April 1975	939,767	9,345 (4.3%)	
June 1975	869,822 (3.7%)	8,618 (3.9%)	
August 1975	1.25 million (5.2%)	13,031 (5.8%)	Highest since 1948
October 1975	1.6 million	11,628	
November 1975	1.17 million	11,569	
December 1975		12,066	
January 1976		14,366 (6.4%)	National average 6%
February 1976		12,305 (5.5%)	Leicester below national average for first time in a year
March 1976	1.28 million (5.5%)	12,222 (5.4%)	

Members of the Royal Leicestershire Regiment who died while serving in the Cyprus conflict 1955–8

Argyle	J.T.	Pte	23192032	1 June	1956
Attenborough	J.T.	Pte	23192033	30 May	1956
Bott	G.A.	Pte	23247315	31 August	1956
Bowman	R.N.	Pte	23148225	27 March	1956
Crisell	R.A.	WO2	14762327	17 May	1956
Hebb	K.M.	Pte	22978337	30 May	1956
Hill	H.G.	L/Cpl	23137483	30 May	1956
Holden	W.R.	Cpl	23019741	13 June	1956
Morris	D.A.	Pte	23201814	13 October	1956
Pegg	J.	Pte	23163892	19 April	1957
Philips	T.	Sgt	19043364	24 October	1957
Pinner	A.F.	Sgt	14475648	11 April	1956
Poultney	R.K.	Pte	23424962	19 April	1958
Rowley	M.	Pte	23121764	9 March	1965
Sheffield	G.W.	Pte	23148259	27 February	1956
Shilton	R.	Pte	22969484	19 February	1956
Walker	S.J.G.	Lt	433260	27 March	1956

(National Memorial Arboretum and Cyprus Veterans Association)

Bibliography

Boynton, Helen, *History of Victoria Park* (no date)

Boynton, Helen and Seaton, Derek, *From Tollgate to Tramshed*, 1999

Brown, Cynthia, *Wharf Street Revisited*, Living History Unit, Leicester City Council, no date

de Groot, J., *Blighty, British Society in the Era of the Great War*, Longman, 1996

Elliott, Malcolm, *Leicester a Pictorial History*, Phillimore, 1983

England, Steve, *Magnificent Mercury*, Kairos Press, 1999

Forty, George, *Called Up*, Ian Allen, 1980

Goodlad, Douglas and Syvret, Anita, *Leicester in the Fifties*, Steve England, Leicester Mercury, 1989

Hollins, Peter, *Transport Memories of Leicestershire*, Leicester Mercury, 1990

Leicestershire County Council, *County Hall, Glenfield, Leicestershire* (pamphlet) (no date)

Marett, Valerie, *Immigrants Settling in Leicester*, Leicester University Press, 1989

Mark, Robert, Sir, *In the Office of Constable*, no date

Nash, D. and Reeder, D., *Leicester in the Twentieth Century*, Sutton, 1993

Newman, Aubrey and Lidiker, Patricia, *Portrait of a Community: A History of the Leicester Hebrew Congregation*, 1998

Richardson, Matthew, *Fighting Tigers*, Leo Cooper, 2002

Royal Army Pay Corps Journal (various issues)

Sawday, Deborah, *Peep-Hole to the Past: The Shires Excavations*, Leicestershire Museums, 1989

Simmons, Jack, *Leicester Past and Present*, vols 1 and 2, Eyre Methuen, London, 1974

Smigielski, W.K., *Leicester Today and Tomorrow*, Pyramid Press Ltd, 1971

Wheal, E-A. and Pope, S., *Macmillan Dictionary of the Second World War*, Macmillan, 1989

Willbond, Bill, *A Home of Our Own*, Leicester City Council, 1991

Williams, David R., *Cinema in Leicester 1896–1931*, Heart of Albion Press, 1993

Index